Powerful Devices

Powerful Devices

· ·

Prayer and the Political Praxis of Spiritual Warfare

ABIMBOLA A. ADELAKUN

Rutgers University Press

New Brunswick, Camden, and Newark, New Jersey, and London

Library of Congress Cataloging-in-Publication Data

Names: Adelakun, Abimbola Adunni, author.
Title: Powerful devices : prayer and the political praxis of spiritual
    warfare / Abimbola A. Adelakun.
Description: New Brunswick : Rutgers University Press, [2023] | Includes
    bibliographical references and index.
Identifiers: LCCN 2021058216 | ISBN 9781978831513 (paperback) | ISBN
    9781978831520 (hardcover) | ISBN 9781978831537 (epub) | ISBN
    9781978831544 (mobi) | ISBN 9781978831551 (pdf)
Subjects: LCSH: Pentecostal churches—Nigeria—Customs and practices. |
    Prayer—Christianity. | Christianity—Influence. | Christianity and
    politics. | Spiritual warfare. | Evangelicalism—United States.
Classification: LCC BX8762.A45 N622 2023 | DDC
    269/.409669—dc23/eng/20220615
LC record available at https://lccn.loc.gov/2021058216

A British Cataloging-in-Publication record for this book is available from the British Library.

♾ The paper used in this publication meets the requirements of the American National Standard for Information Sciences—Permanence of Paper for Printed Library Materials, ANSI Z39.48-1992.

www.rutgersuniversitypress.org

Manufactured in the United States of America

For my dear friend, Prof. Adetokunbo Lucas (1931–2020)

Contents

Preface

Three different instances that seemingly had no correlation culminated in this book. One was the study I carried out on social media among Nigerian supporters of the forty-fifth president of the United States of America, Donald Trump, to understand the passion that underlies their patriotic support for his presidency. I noted that some of the most ardent support for Trump came not from among Black people in his own country, but from Nigerians who live in Nigeria, most of whom had never visited the United States. So ardent was their passion that some staged a rally for him on the eve of the 2020 presidential election. As will be evident in the coming chapters of this book, an intriguing relationship exists between Pentecostal Christians in Nigeria and their evangelical counterparts in the United States. While much of this interaction is owing to the history of evangelism and soul winning that have taken place transnationally over the decades, the present phase is being driven by the nature of sociality that social media makes possible. The difference between what exists now and what used to be in earlier times is that these interactions are far more organic; they tend to bypass the institutional authority that mediated missionizing between the countries.

The ability of Christians in several cultures to converge at certain sites in the digital sphere—which can range from polemical exchanges in the comments section of well-known news media organizations (CNN, for instance) to other cyber activities like blogging—allowed the transnational formation of ideological divides. Even when the issues at stake for the respective countries seem too localized to matter elsewhere, they still polarize. It is not uncommon for a Nigerian living in Nigeria to support the political cause of evangelical Christianity in the United States or to have an American living in the United States "following" the social media accounts of a Nigerian Christian social media influencer to stay abreast with the politics of faith in

Nigeria. In this book, I have tried to capture how the phenomenology of these connections manifests in the praxis of spiritual warfare. As a research study that moves back and forth between the activities of Christians in the two countries can lead to some confusion, I have tried to alleviate that prospect by adding some notes to differentiate them where necessary.

The second instance that propelled this work happened when I was stuck at an airport in Nigeria for what seemed like endless hours. To pass the time, I strolled into a bookshop run by a church renowned for spiritual warfare activities—the Mountain of Fire and Miracles Church, founded by a scientist, Dr. Daniel K. Olukoya. Having grown up in Nigeria, the prayers and practices of the MFM church were already quite familiar to me. However, on that day in that airport shop, their materials spoke to me differently. I was intrigued by their colorful invocations of the supernatural, and I thought it was worth pursuing their social understanding of prayer more closely. I bought some materials that day. The more I studied them, the more fascinated I grew with the phenomenality of the spiritual warfare that the MFM practices—their goals, militant modes, and a polemical approach that brooks no middle ground in antagonizing a secular social order they insist is chock full of demons. The polarizing nature of spiritual warfare praxis resonated with me as a performance scholar, and I came to recognize how much of the activist performance I was used to witnessing from leftists and ideologues was part of the tactics of spiritual warfare. Thus, as will be seen in chapter 1, much of the primary data on prayer literature came from the MFM. They are not the only church that practices spiritual warfare, but they are about the most famous in Nigeria and abroad. I should also note that although the repertoire of spiritual warfare practice is quite diverse, I deliberately limited most of my analysis of prayer production in chapter 1 to the MFM church and the works of Olukoya. Since I had privileged private interviews with Olukoya in which he told me about how his trajectory impacted his ministry on spiritual warfare, I restricted aspects of the analyses to him and his church so as to not overstretch the lessons of his biography to others. Some of the data that make up chapter 2 involved being on their church campuses during large gatherings.

Also, because I was interested in the literature of prayer and how it might be connected to the combative convictions of the spiritual warriors whose activities I frequently witnessed online, I also sourced materials from churches' online stores, blogs, websites, social media pages, and so on. Though the brick and mortar spaces of churches like the MFM carry a vast amount of materials, their digital spheres are an equally rich and growing archive. Spiritual warriors themselves now vigorously use social media to organize prayer assemblies against the kingdom of darkness. Fieldwork for this book involved following as many warfare prayer sessions held on social media as possible. Through my regular participation in their continuous prayer sessions, I could see how prayer warriors are moving with the reality of the times. They factor in the increasingly busy lifestyles of prayer warriors and their dispersal to different parts of the world to organize round-the-clock prayer activities on social media, where people congregate for all kinds of businesses. I am, of course, aware of the limitations of this method of data gathering on social media. I know those materials can be ephemeral and the data sets likely to change, factors that can affect their dependability. However, I also found them a valuable complementary source for ethnographic data collection because they feature spontaneous outpourings of subjectivity. Unlike the one-on-one interactions during fieldwork that usually offer relatively measured responses, individuals online feel shielded by the anonymity of the internet and express themselves relatively freely. I also used internet sources frequently because, in some of my interactions with spiritual leaders, they respond to certain questions by asking me to check out their past sermons already posted online. I take this referral to their online archive as meaning either that these leaders do not want to repeat what was available in the public domain, or that they want me to view their videos or read their books—or perhaps they simply want me to cite them accurately. Whatever their motive for referring me online, the reader will find several instances of sermons archived online cited in the coming chapters.

The COVID-19 pandemic was, of course, a setback for the field research. Like millions of others, I was stuck behind a computer where—thankfully, though—I could still keep up with developments in the social sites where spiritual warfare is enacted. Not being able to leave home to work on this project, I made judicious use of the time by collecting a data set that would prove invaluable for chapters 3 and 4. My field assistant, Kalu Daniel Chibuike, also helped me with gathering these materials. Many of the discussions and news reports that pervade the social space from people equally stuck at home during the early days of the pandemic were quite revealing of their fears and anxieties about the spectral forces of modernity that threaten collective survival. Those declarations helped put a lot of ideas they poured out in the broader context of the politics of disestablishment of political authorities. The famous church leaders who waded into the matters that arose as a consequence of the historical event of the pandemic also provided a lens through which one can view and understand the responses of church members who joined them in the discourses of warfare, raised the stakes of the COVID-19 controversies, and helped circulate the issues as sensationally as possible. Much of chapters 3 and 4 was written during this period because they illustrated—and attested to—many dimensions of my inferences regarding the politics of spiritual warfare.

The third instance that led to this book came from a rather mundane conversation with a senior scholar and Nigerian professor of Pentecostalism, Prof. Nimi Wariboko. The discussion took place at a period when I faced several overwhelming challenges and had shared some of them with him. He listened for a while and then said, "You know, you must have faith like a Nigerian Pentecostal." He went on to remind me of the radical ways that Nigerian Pentecostals perform their faith. He mentioned how they take their stand against difficult life situations in prayers, believing that every mountain that faces them must give way for them as God's children. His profound insight into what these rather dramatic and militant prayers seek to achieve struck me most intensely and inspired me to study spiritual warfare by focusing on various aspects of the performances of these practices. By taking a performative approach to studying spiritual warriors, I explored their instinct to move the mountains of oppressive forces in social and political life. Throughout this book, I show that the impulse of the spiritual warrior is to disestablish all forces that threaten their potential for social flourishing, whether they be personal or institutional. Performance as means of studying these developments shows how the social and spiritual epistemes for these battles are generated, how norms are created, how the spiritual warrior identity is reiterated through certain consistent behaviors, and also how social practices structure the underlying ideas behind how spiritual warriors see and act. The actions through which spiritual warriors purport to disestablish reigning authorities are thus construable as performance activism, demonstrating their moral convictions about how the world should be and the radical changes necessary to achieve this goal.

Through their various performances, I have tracked the processes by which the radical project of disestablishment becomes naturalized and calcifies into the very nature of spiritual warriors. In the coming chapters, I show how prayer is the apocalyptic device through which spiritual warriors discern the times and seek to disestablish the forces of habit that encode into the everyday and ultimately oppress. Their instinct to disestablish also necessitates self-rewiring, a process of formatting the self into an enhanced being whose destructive abilities link to God's character and are therefore only "natural" to them. The sensational nature of the COVID-19 global pandemic turned out to be another chance for spiritual warriors to enact their impulse to disestablish on a grand global scale by tackling science-based and global political institutions. The book captures the politics of the COVID-19 pandemic as well, while also showing the pragmatism of church leaders—those who saw the pandemic as an opportunity for spiritual warfare on a global scale and those who explored other creative means of churching. By looking at spiritual warfare through the lens of performance, as I do in this book, I shed light on spiritual warriors' performances of prayers as radical means to facilitate social change.

Powerful Devices

Introduction

• •

Spiritual Warriors:
Powerful Devices and the
Devices of Power

Pastor Joshua Talena, towering above the rest of the church from an elevated and godlike height, prayed evocatively before his congregation. Senior pastor of the Shepherd's House International, Pastor Talena is a northern Nigerian youth leader of the Pentecostal Fellowship of Nigeria and one of the pioneer members of the Northern Youth Christian Association of Nigeria. At this service, he sat in a plastic chair suspended by six men who moved him around on the altar so that he could face different parts of the church as he released a declaration of prayer in their direction. The men who carried him, their lips moving in prayer, would pause now and then (probably to rest from their labor) before resuming their task of carrying the pastor around the altar space. Pastor Talena's voice booming into the cordless microphone in his hand was accompanied by the resonant sound of drums and music wafting from a piano in a corner of the altar. Mostly on their feet, the congregation members were equally engaged in performing their prayers as their pastor prayed. The camera panned from one person to another. Some of them had their hands fully stretched out to the heavens, and some had their hands rolled into taut fists, pushing up the air above their heads. Some threw invisible stones in the direction of their enemies. Their eyes were closed, their heads were moving from side to side, and their lips were gushing out a torrent of words to the divine as their bodies enacted fervent prayers. He prayed,

1

Anybody flying in the night, because of you. Anybody hanging between the heaven and the earth . . . I prophesy, they shall die! They shall die! Any wizard flying in the night, I Joshua Talena, I fly. I jam them. I jam them. In your village! In your compound! In your father's house! Wherever they are, they shall surely gather, but not by me. For your sake, they shall scatter . . . they shall die. Die! Die! Die! Die! Die! Die! Die! Die! Die! Die! Die! Whoever is not sleeping because of you, whoever is flying like a bird. . . . Today, I fly on your behalf. . . . They shall die. . . . Any choir member that Satan said will not marry, I prophesy, today, your husband is released.[1]

The congregation shouted thunderous amens, jamming the amplified voice of their pastor with their collective voices. They prayed. They jumped. They shouted. They cried. They marched like soldiers. They even danced as they shouted their prayers and intoned "Amen" to the prayers rendered by the Talena, a well-known megachurch pastor.

Warfare prayers, consisting of what are popularly called "deliverance prayers" or "violent prayers" in Nigeria, are typically colorful displays such as this one, and there is no single staging that exhausts its multidimensional scope. Spiritual warfare prayers are human confrontations with unseen forces and presences, and their spectacular dramatization impresses the psyche. The dramatic touch that underwrites the performance of spiritual warfare is typically reflected in phantasms of a cosmic plot and the role of the spiritual warrior who is, of course, strategically placed by providence to be the protagonist of this showdown between good and evil. By thus aggregating temporalities and sequencing them into a dramatic narrative of good vs. evil, protagonist vs. antagonist, provocateur vs. complacent or "un-woke" public, spiritual warfare prayers gain much of their character as adversarial and toward righteous ends. The prayer modes discursively battle against the devil and his human agents embedded in social and spiritual spaces, and whose activities impinge on social flourishing.

Featuring insurrectional speech, imprecations and declamations, these prayers seek to performatively overthrow the enemy that actively works against social flourishing, to disestablish these forces from the places they have been founded. Rather than a prayer form that somberly solicits God or prays for one's enemies, the animated prayers of spiritual warfare employ the language of militarism to simulate a battle arena wherein litigants conduct prayer strikes against perceived enemies. Spiritual warriors' imagination generates the context through which they can unabashedly appropriate the rhetoric of war to produce the rituals of warfare and violently vanquish the enemy.[2] Through these prayers they dramatize their self-redemption from negating life forces, and many of them typically reference the Bible verse that says "the men of violence taketh it by force" to accentuate the necessity of their excessiveness.[3] Mostly irruptive, spiritual warfare prayers perform conquests by often inventing spirit characters whose phantom nature makes them mold-able into virtually any kind of enemy, and conjuring fantasies of defeating them. The ultimate goal of these aggressive prayer modes is to disestablish a prevailing power or authority believed to be either a threat to one's flourishing or responsible for one's diminishing, and to restore less opaque (or relatively manageable) truths in its stead.

The depreciation of life and its enriching resources which practitioners of spiritual warfare work to override through their warfare prayers can be carried out either for personal matters—such as Talena praying against forces that hin-der his congregation members' chances of getting married or achieving mate-rial success—or it could be staged as a battle against larger ideological conditions. Prayer as a political praxis is about generating the necessary instinctive knowl-edge to apprehend the threats that coexist within a polity and developing a transcendental form of muscularity to overcome them. Spiritual warriors within a social imaginary conducive for understanding that the factors that contend against their social flourishing are powered by unseen malevolent forces that work through human agents, and the fact of their invisibility accentuates their capacity to do evil even more. Defeating these active forces that are ever-present in social life requires reaching deep into the spiritual imaginary where the ultimate power of God exists to strip these evil forces of their opacity, battle them until they are defeated, and establish the righ-teousness of God in their stead. "Righteousness" here is a moral conviction about how the society and its various resources could be reorganized in ways that preponderantly favor the spiritual warrior.

An instance of confronting forces that structure life on a larger scale can be illustrated by the actions of the evangelicals who stormed the U.S. Capitol on January 6, 2021. Some of them were captured in photographs and videos clutch-ing Bibles to their chests, weeping and praying, convinced that the end of Western civilization had come, just as people like American evangelical preacher Franklin Graham had warned them weeks earlier.[4] Some others held up the cross as they prayed ardently for God to dislodge the political opponents of the incumbent president, Donald J. Trump, who stood to gain if he were to leave the office. After that fateful day, "spiritual warfare" was serially intoned in popular commentary as people blamed the actions of the insurrectionists who stormed the seat of the legislature in the nation's capital—one of the most symbolic sites of American democratic power—on evangelical leaders who pushed the stakes of the election to the point of sedition. Quite a bit of ink was spilled in media commentary describing their revolt against democratic pro-cesses as a physical enactment of a war that started in the spiritual realm. Truly, the nature of spiritual warfare boils down to removing something in order for some-thing else to take its stead. Although the goals of the Nigerians praying in Tale-na's church might seem different from those of the Americans, spiritual warfare for both groups entailed disestablishing a force of authority reigning within the commons that one inhabits and reimplanting an auspicious moral order.

Looking back to the days before the fateful January 6 event, several events had heightened the political stakes and the sense of mutiny in those who stormed the Capitol. On November 5, 2020, a day after the U.S. presidential elections were conducted and it was becoming certain that incumbent Donald Trump would lose, Pentecostal preacher and special adviser to the White House Faith and Opportunity Initiative Paula White went viral, praying against the "demonic confederacies" that were attempting to "steal" the election.[5] In Nevada, while ballots were being counted, a couple of women wearing the iconic red Make America Great Again caps fell on their knees in front of a polling center to pray for the president's electoral victory.[6] In Nigeria, a group of congregants met in a decrepit church building to also pray for victory for the incumbent U.S. president in the election.[7] Their prayers summoned angels to cancel the ballots in favor of the Democratic contender and then thumbprint the ballot papers—which is the style of voting in Nigeria—in favor of Trump. All of these added to instances of the praxis of spiritual warfare as a means of the disestablishment of powers, rulership, authority, processes, and orders. As a discourse of disestablishing reigning authorities, spiritual warfare enables a contest with hegemony by striking at the unseen forces that are believed to uphold them. The underlying belief is that all such authorities are supported by immaterial forces that supply the aura and an ineffable authority to their human agents, accounting for their efficaciousness in doing evil. Thus, the debilitation of such powers can only be orchestrated through the destruction of the spectral architecture of support that upholds them.

This book thus takes a performance studies approach to the study of the spiritual warriors and their preoccupation with disestablishing the confederacies they hold responsible for how the world is shaped, and how its ideological structures impact them as believers. Their actions and counteractions in the public sphere, where they seek to impose the imagination of a restructured world which they have fashioned through spiritual means, provide an analytical lens to understand the politics and poetics of spiritual warfare. By exploring how they engage in spiritual warfare as heuristic devices that enable an understanding of the structures of power that rule in a time and a place, I demonstrate their imperatives of mounting a spiritual campaign to transform such arrangements. The various chapters of this book will critically explore how they apprehend the social relations of power, develop their confrontational and ideological self in their bid to bring down established rule and authority, and affirm their identity as God's warrior subjects in the process. The radicality of the spiritual warrior, this book will demonstrate, is to control the wild march of history, to disestablish the reigning authorities of secular truth, and inaugurate—or restore—a world in which their sacred values and desires would be dominant, and also to define the social order. The staging of acts of spiritual warfare generates meanings that shape an understanding of the world—as it is and as it is becoming—and what activist work they might need to undertake to reform it. Such reformation entails translating the justice people conceive through spiritual means into political realities. Prayers against "demonic confederacies" thus do cultural work that shapes a sense of self-recognition within a time and place they occupy.

Religious Activism, Performance Activism, and Spiritual Warfare Politics

Studying spiritual warfare as disestablishment of existing power and hegemonies implies the progressivism of the warriors who engage in such prayer activity. However, positing American evangelicals and their counterparts elsewhere as political progressives—rather than reactionaries—especially after citing how they deployed the weapons of their fervent prayers to support the occupant of one of the most powerful offices in the world definitely runs against the grain of destabilizing hegemonic power as it is typically understood. In performance studies where scholars like Soyini Madison, Jill Dolan, and Diana Taylor have, each in their own way, explored how performances facilitate social change, subversive acts are typically associated with radicals and leftists, not generally with conservative groups like evangelical/Pentecostal Christians.[8] Yet, the ethical and cognitive structures of performance and its features of political resistance that have always been ascribed to one ideological wing has also become a part of the repertoire of public engagement of the other. In his study of evangelical performances of proselytizing and social change, John Fletcher also grappled with how the social activism typically associated with progressive leftists applies to studying conservative evangelical Christians in the United States. Fletcher notes that "evangelicals usually aren't part of the performance activist conversation in the United States except as the Bad Guys, the forces of oppression, bigotry, or narrow-mindedness that activist performers have to work against."[9] His observation about how Christian/Pentecostal spiritual warriors are perceived is spot on, and also shows a paradox in their self-perception as social progressives. While non-Christian observers see the ideologies underwriting Christians' performance activism as reinforcement of their already dominant power—hardly ever about the reformist logic of their impulses to take down the hegemonic orders against the inauguration of their truth convictions—Christians (evangelicals, Pentecostals, and spiritual warriors generally), on the other hand, tend to see themselves as the marginal and oppressed. They conceive their activities as oriented toward a radical reformation of a social ethos they deem violently anti-Christian. Construing evangelical activities as projects of performance activism thus raises methodological questions. How does one properly speak of activism and social change when investigating the evangelizing efforts of those whose values have long defined the social ethos—even if they argue otherwise—and yet consider their preaching to convert the public as performance activism and acts of social change?

In this book, I explore the activities of spiritual warriors as an overlapping of religious and performance forms of activism. Studies of religious activism generally investigate how the subject based on faith conviction mobilizes causes and the sociopolitical conditions under which it happens. On the other hand, performance activism looks beyond the moral convictions of the social actors to encapsulate how such radical actions are aestheticized, as inventive means of responding to various problems by seeking social change. Both forms of activism feature in this work, although by analyzing the actions of spiritual warriors as performance, it is obvious that the preponderance of the analysis is performance activism and the ways it highlights the dynamic ways humans demonstrate their ability to comprehend their social circumstances and initiate radical change through their actions.

Fletcher is not the only one who has noted how the performance artistry and its ascribed features of instruction, conviction, mobilization, disturbance, and destabilization might disrupt an existing order when carried out by people who do not subscribe to leftist ideologies. Christopher Grobe also critically explored how the same performance techniques, having been seized upon by President Trump, as well as by cyber trolls and alt-right cliques, expose the limitations of performance studies' persistent valorization of the transgressions of social norms. Trump's populist performance, transgressive of the norms of governance due to its over-the-top nature, did not dislodge his fervent support among his partisan followers but, in fact, contributed to his presidential power. Grobe observes that performance studies' persistent evocation of liminality as an emergent site of possibilities "focused primarily on acts of resistance and critique from the margins—ignoring, by and large, how our tools could explain acts of commitment and construction at the center, the sorts of acts that sustain establishment politics."[10]

The concerns about how the provocative performances of alt-right protesters and trolls generate theories of political performances and efficacies is critical to the continued relevance of the propositions of the field and provokes a conversation on how to engage the performances of those who put on the MAGA cap and pray against the "demonic confederacies" about to steal an election. Performance studies will have to continuously reckon with an increase of impropriety from politicians and leaders who appropriate the radicality and disruption of norms—a form of power performance and self-assertion associated with minorities—to ground and intensify their ruling power. These leaders' partisan followers, having long settled to the idea that power is always performed, and its ability to make things happen—that is, to successfully dislodge established bureaucracies and its self-justifying traditions—relies on theatrical excess, will mostly remain unmoved by the "double-dealing" of dominant political power assuming the pose of a subaltern and deploying radical methods to expand the scope of their authority and legitimacy. Thus, regardless of whether their intent falls under the rubric of progressive politics or not, these spiritual warriors perform a politics of disestablishing hegemonic powers similar to the radicals and liberals who tout an agenda of social reformation when willfully breaching the bounds of social propriety. What both sides reveal, ultimately, is the neutrality of the tools and techniques of activist performance—its efficacies have less to with the noble ideals or the purity of purpose of the performer. It works because it is performed well for its audience.

This ideological paradox of the praxis of spiritual warfare as a resistance mechanism brings me to another observation about its construal in various contexts. Scholars of spiritual warfare like Nimi Wariboko who explore the practice in Nigeria and Africa more generally tend to focus on its activities as a means toward social redemption and social flourishing by Pentecostals who live in social conditions of antagonism. Spiritual warfare prayers in developing societies are not taken as the performances of the dominant, but as a redemptive politics of the subaltern. The politics of spiritual warfare lies in how it is undertaken to bridge the abyss between present circumstances and desired conditions.[11] Wariboko observes in his study of the political force of spiritual warfare that it is "a way of discerning and critically reflecting, contesting, and resisting the play of powers in the ontological conditioning of being, the forces weighing down on current life, and the agonistic tensions dragging bodies to increased vulnerability of death by exclusion from centers of life-enhancing supports."[12] For those minoritized by race or gender, as one sees in the instances of communities and cultures of Latinx and Black people, spiritual warfare and its combative methods are similar instrumental means of holding a confrontational dialogue with the creator of one's existential conditions to carry out a project of a re-creation of the terms of one's existence.[13] The intent of achieving self-realization within socially strangulating conditions notwithstanding, spiritual warfare also manifests in the moral obligations that justify the domination of an identified other.

Spiritual Warfare: Beyond Nations and Nationalism

Sean McCloud's take on spiritual warfare, *American Possessions*, explores Americans' obsession with possessive demonic forces. Characterized by possessions—both by demons that occupy bodies and spaces, and by material accumulation—the study looks into the themes of consumerism, haunting, and the therapeutic, and how these ideas are interwoven with various cultural activities from economic to political and cultural. His analysis, though it revolves around the United States, still helps raise the questions of the overriding motive of spiritual warfare, considering it is a faith formation that transcends national borders. How do these ideas of "possession" feature among spiritual warriors outside the capitalist and context-specific haunting of the United States? What, for instance, ties spiritual warfare and its modes of performance among Pentecostals in Nigeria with Christian evangelicals in the USA? Probing a transnational dimension to spiritual warfare is crucial because the radical militarist ethic spiritual warriors generate through their activities is also directed outside their countries and tends toward expanding God's kingdom throughout the earth. This attitude even spurs imperialist impulses in spiritual warriors, who then see a moral duty to deliver the world from demonic influences. When, however, spiritual warfare is an intramural national dialogue with the spiritual, historical, and ethical forces that rule the nation-state, as Jonathon O'Donnell and Virginia Garrard note of the contexts of the United States and Latin American countries, respectively, it ends up facilitating modes of political and social organizing that also structure social hierarchies of power.[14] For O'Donnell especially in *Passing Orders*, this shaping of relations of power expressed in the vocabulary and acts of spiritual warfare is soon revealed to be underwritten by the project of white nationalism.[15] Demonic discourses expose the tensions and the tensile strengths of sovereign power, an order whose force is passing because its norms are also being bypassed.

Nationalism in spiritual warfare does not limit itself to politics within provincial borders but also carries an ambition of world domination—to go beyond individual countries and capture the world for Christ. Ruth Marshall's exploration of spiritual warfare techniques of prayer across the United States and Nigeria highlights its radical praxis as it seeks to expand the kingdom of God on earth.[16] Her study of the expansionist agenda of spiritual warriors focuses primarily on linguistic components such as prayers, prophecies, praise, and testimonies in the construction of a reality that makes such a mission possible. The polemical nature of the language elements and the disputatious disposition of those who deploy them, she shows, is part of the efficacy of spiritual warfare. The contrarian performances of activism by spiritual warriors are—as Fletcher also notes—thus an investment in a world transformation agenda based on a moral conviction of personal faith.[17] Spiritual warfare, Simon Coleman argues, is the tactic of the Christian ambition of world occupation. Not simply galvanizing warriors to reform the social order through the force of religious mysticism, spiritual warfare also helps in the constitution of the identity of the believer.[18] Elizabeth McAlister's study of spiritual warfare among Native Americans, who include in their techniques actual boot camps where people are trained in combat techniques along with prayer, also shows how the rites and understanding of how past history affects the present shape the identity complex of spiritual warriors.[19] The growing scholarship on spiritual warfare provides various dimensions to the subject, and one way to understand the connection between the disparate contexts and themes these writers have focused on is to explore the performances that constitute the activities.

Devices: Making the Unseen Visible

As stated earlier, my approach to spiritual warfare focuses on the spiritual warriors to understand their mission to disestablish various forms of authority. This task of disestablishment is the factor that ties spiritual warriors together regardless of their nationality, culture, or disparate histories, especially in contemporary times when spiritual warriors—through the affordances of global communication technologies—are more connected than ever before. Pentecostalism and its practice of conversion, as Ruth Marshall described in her study of Nigerian Pentecostalism, has long taught an ethic of kinship and belonging that extends beyond the identity matrices of ethnicity.[20] Over the years, they have forged several practices of expressing Pentecostal identity kinship that transcends the provinciality of both ethnicity and nationality, and instead takes its common denominator from rootedness in Christ. Consequently, Pentecostals everywhere see themselves as part of the global community of people who belong to Christ and whose spiritual destinies are impacted by the politics that promotes or undermines Christianity everywhere else.[21] Thus, whether they practice spiritual warfare as a hermeneutics of self-transformation or as the expression of conservative ideologies that fan nationalist sensibilities in its bid to precipitate the kingdom of God through a contingent rearrangement of this worldly politics, what spiritual warriors everywhere seek is to dislodge reigning political powers and to establish themselves (and their faith practices) in their stead. Throughout this book, I will demonstrate the congruence in how Pentecostals in Nigeria and evangelicals in the United States tap into the sacred realms to pursue the radical politics that purports to establish righteousness within their respective social orders.

Spiritual warriors work toward achieving this mission to overcome all opposing forces that threaten the flourishing of Christians as an activist project of moral reformation and social renewal. They employ various devices through which they diligently carry out these practices as a project of social responsibility and a matter of their duty to the world. In their study of social practices, scholars like John Searle, Theodore Schatzki, and Nimi Wariboko have variously explored how human relations and their interactional patterns generate a range of activities that not only define social norms, but also become regenerative. Schatzki's generation of a social order entails patterning, stabilizing, and interdependence—a string of concepts that describe the rules, systemic practices, beliefs, and institutional ideologies that weave together into a tapestry of social reality. When a recognizable order is formed and stabilized, it becomes definitive over time. This order comes to be the domain of activities that constitute social reality. Searle's formula of social practices features objects, how humans impose functions on certain entities, and how relating to those items makes them surpass certain limits of their physical structure. For instance, the dollar is otherwise a piece of paper with magnetic traces, but the social context of the economy makes it "money." This configuration of social practices and things, of course, leaves open the question of relating to money in electronic forms or its other nonphysical variants. When Wariboko took on Searle, he argued that social interactions define objects such as money, and not the other way around. According to him, money—or objects—are not only part of social relations; social relations give money its very nature. Premising human interaction and making it the locus of social practices, as Wariboko does, helps account for an approach to objects without physical entities such as "liquid money" and others that this book examines at length—performance arts and aesthetic practices. Altogether, these scholars present social practices as expressions of humans and things as they interact and mutually constitute each other. For spiritual warfare, social practices are also about the configuration and stylization of performative actions, and the various tools spiritual warriors creatively deploy to achieve their mission. This alchemy of humans, social relations, and tools makes spiritual warriors a most significant device in the overall praxis of spiritual warfare.

With the term "devices," I will therefore be looking at a range of tools and techniques—spiritual, artistic, social, ideological, and even technological—that enlighten the operations of spiritual presences for the observer, formats the knowledge into curated content, and mass circulates them. Unlike social practices' entitative objects such as physical money, I am also interested in aesthetic contraptions—such as devised or staged performances that encircles the ritual performances of prayer—and the technological objects of the new media. This range of devices comes together for spiritual warriors to battle radical evil and its human agents. Devices are necessary instruments of counter-surveilling the institutional and corporatized entities that monitor people. Through devices, spiritual warriors materialize the unseen and render it apprehensible for meaningful engagement. Devices make the unseen seeable, and Pentecostals have always manifested their fixation with making things seeable in various ways. For instance, René Holvast's study of spiritual mapping—that is, the application of cartographic and anthropologic knowledge to a territory to discern and surveil the spirits inhabiting it, and subsequently control them through the power of prayers—shows one use of a device.[22] Birgit Meyer's work on video in Ghana's Pentecostal culture also highlights how the supernatural is represented through technological devices, a visualizing means that captures the tensions that roil the society and that are expressed through demonic encounters.[23] This study looks beyond how seeability functions as a missionizing tool to capture how it features as part of the ontologies of political contests, and the organized social activities through which these battles are publicly enacted.

Devices make all presences—spectral, material, and human—ultimately see-able, and spiritual warriors' seemingly endless creativity in apprehending and moving to disestablish the order of the society through their activities make them powerful artificers. Spiritual warriors believe that disestablishing reign-ing authorities in the world demands that the forces that prop up their rule in the material world need, first of all, to be seen. The ability to map it for the pub-lic attests to an inner power or spiritual virtuosity. The spectral forces that support those authorities and that will eventually be taken down must first take a discernible social shape and defined metaphysical attributes so that both their threatening otherness and possibilities of conquest are made visible. Since what is unknown easily assumes the dimensions of monstrosity, fantastic imagi-nation and aspirations to stand outside the everyday reality illuminate social consciousness. Devices reveal the unseen, and spiritual warriors—by deploy-ing their agency, creativity, knowledge, and even inner eyes to frame the opera-tions of spectral forces in society—make them seeable for eventual defeat.

In her study of spiritual warfare, Naomi Richman draws attention to the spiritual warriors' bodies as a site where the divine and the demonic meet, and how such intertwining results in the prayer of violent enactments as a means through which the body tries to deliver itself.[24] However, my emphasis on the warriors and the actions they take through their bodies is on how they project themselves, their morality—or moralized self—into the public's line of vision to influence collective consciousness through both persuasion and combat so that witnesses can interrogate the version of reality they present. This phe-nomenological self-projection is as much a part of spiritual warfare as other elements of its praxis that scholarship has engaged, because it compels the imagination of witnesses who, viewing the agency of the specters from the per-spective of the powerful devices of spiritual warriors, generate the multiplier effects that give it so much potency. In the age of ubiquitous technological devices, the making of the unseen seeable is, of course, also hypermediatized. In times where one can "go viral," spiritual warfare actively employs techno-logical tools in its art and artifices of enacting the goals of militant prayers. Already, the intensity of the prayers makes spiritual warfare an invigorating activity. The physicality of the prayers produces a degree of vitalizing energy in which everything around us is commanded to urgently respond to our author-ity to affirm and disestablish forces, and the various media contrivances deployed in these tasks help to both propagate and hasten achieving these aims.

In considering how spiritual warriors process unseen reality, Wariboko explores their knowledge production through the "spell of the invisible." He argues that the Pentecostal epistemology is sought from the unseen—the spir-itual realms where the multitude of possibilities harbored in the unknown realms ignites an alternative imagination of what constitutes reality, truth, and self-governance. Supernatural possibilities are thus translated into the technology of existence and everyday concrete actions.[25] This compulsion to pierce the phenomenal veil over reality and access another order of reality is not exclusive to Pentecostalism; it is a subject of study across disciplines, revealing a persistent pattern of human fascination with the invisible. Harry West's survey of the people of the Mueda plateau in northern Mozambique also finds that the invisible realms, where the mythical possibilities of transformation happen and are monitored by the power of sight enhanced through supernatural means, form a repertoire of power through knowledge. The beneficial dimension of this power emerges when someone gains entrance into the otherworldly realm to reverse or un/remake a previous exercise of power that had had an impact on a person, thwart evil, or increase one's possibilities for human flourishing. In aesthetic practices, unseen presences equally stretch the imaginative human capabilities, as Andrew Sofer demonstrates in *Dark Matter*. His exploration of "dark matter"—an invisible dimension that has consequential effects even though it cannot be observed—in theatrical performances shows how what is not materially represented on the stage can still carry a mysterious force that drives onstage actions.[26] In all these instances of tussling with the unseen, the specter highlights *what is* and also heightens possibilities of *what can be* in the perception of the audience. In social practices, such power of perception of the invisible drives human creativity and fashions an innate conviction in the spiritual warrior that can be quite animating.

Going from these perspectives on the interaction of the mutual permeability of the seen and the unseen, and how it grounds, complements, and vivifies spiritual warriors' ability and identity, I employ the interpretive lens of devices in this work to stimulate fresh thinking about the mutability, form-shifting nature, and evolutionary dynamics of the age-old relation between human agency and forces of the supernatural. Spiritual warriors' performative actions—whether through prayer or through political engagement—brings their disestablishment politics into relief. Driven by motives of an ethical revolution and/or a restoration of collective moral sensibility based on Christian values, they devise performances through which they seek to disestablish reigning authorities. As a theoretical tool, *devices* spotlight the resourceful ways spiritual warriors draw from existing knowledge of history, social culture, political and civic relations, aesthetics, rituals, technology, science, and faith/theology to create the performances through which they aspire to achieve their vision of a world morally reformed and that conforms to their Christian values. In their pursuit of this ideal, spiritual warriors relate to both intangible knowledge and tangible materials and creatively devise the various performances that make the unseen currents of history and social sensibilities seeable. Their various roles in making cultural consciousness apprehensible make them the *powerful devices*.

This work emphasizes how Pentecostal bodies *perform* spiritual warfare to defeat the devil as an imperative of spiritual activists who have a divine mission to disestablish prevailing orders and index their status as God's warriors, the "good guys" reforming a debilitated moral order by bypassing its orders and authorities. They take this task as an act of war because they are certain that the demonic forces they contend with are quite powerful, institutionalized, and have become established sociopolitical traditions that are reified in the performance of daily affairs. These forces, lodged as habits and dispositions that happen every day, are both habitual and habituated. Since these contending powers are also embodied by humans who will not yield without a struggle, spiritual warriors spend every day enhancing themselves to effectively war with them. Daily life is thus a combination of war and the anticipation of an apocalyptic war, *the War*. Even the most private devotion of a spiritual warrior is about preparing for an impending public showdown against the architecture of power structuring the world order, a public fight that might come—and will come—at any moment.

Do Your Research! Disestablishing Science

One of the main sociopolitical authorities and the architecture of power that spiritual warriors invest in disestablishing is the enterprise of science. Studies of spirituality in Africa hardly account for this tendency because they preponderantly look at the forces that spiritual warriors antagonize in terms of occultism, witchcraft, and the spirit world. Exceptions would, of course, be Katrien Pype's study of Congo Pentecostals who variously interpret technological devices through the social relations they mediate and the potential consequences for their ways of life, and Damaris Parsitau's no-holds-barred criticism of Kenyan Pentecostal churches in the early phase of the pandemic.[27] Pype's analysis of Congolese suspicion of modern technological gadgets and their ability to restructure social relationality does not quite delineate between "science" (both as a body of knowledge and as a formalized means of inquiry that generates new knowledge) and its follow-on, "technology" (tools and machines resulting from scientific discovery), and so does not broadly capture the scope of the Pentecostal attitude to science.[28] Parsitau, on the other hand, argues that the responses of Pentecostal pastors to the COVID-19 pandemic showed that their faith healing and miracle industries are shambolic. The true path for Africa, she argues, lies in pursuing scientific knowledge.

Both Pype and Parsitau capture important dimensions of the tensions between faith and the enterprise of science, especially in Africa's developing context, but they do not go far enough in demonstrating the nuances of how science and its knowledge system have allowed Pentecostal spiritual warriors to also perform power. Pentecostals (at least in Nigeria) have passed the age of suspicion about devices of modern technology and embraced their potential fully, something that will be evident in the coming chapters. Even the churches that practice spiritual warfare have taken a judicious advantage of the knowledge systems of science and employed technology in their confrontations with the demonic. Such "objectivity" has helped them to interpret and control reality as well as to predict it. For instance, through the empirical knowledge of a physical territory, spiritual warriors have sought clarity in the histories and cultures of the inhabitants to understand factors that might facilitate their conversion. Joel Robbins points out that the evangelizing mission of spiritual warfare that arose in the 1980s challenged the demonic barriers that impede Christian conversion in some localities by bringing scientific modes of research to the missionizing projects.[29] As Robbins recognized, and as is quite true for Nigerians, this accommodating attitude was partly a result of the advanced education of their leaders, and even of their congregation.

Science, as a body of knowledge, has been invaluable for Pentecostals' spiritual quests and their performances of power because its ability to provide the lens to see the reality that underlies human–nature interactions is not only analogous to the methods of spiritual warfare, but is the strongest means of establishing authority through rational knowledge. Both the scientific enterprise and spiritual warfare derive their social power from the putative ability to denude natural reality, a second sight through which one sees—and therefore knows things—beyond the pale. Within a cultural context where physical manifestations are thought to be metonymic of the ongoing contests within the domains of the spiritual, and obvious reality pregnant with other possibilities, the one savvy enough to conjectures interpretations beyond the obvious demonstrates distinguishing epistemological prowess. The heightened intuition that enables access to the realms where the things that are invisible to others become seeable, sets one apart from the confines of banal reality. Since such distinction elevates one beyond the status quo, spiritual warriors have included the tools of science in their repertoire to enable superhuman sight and consolidate their power. As hermeneutics of suspicion and the control of reality, both science and spirituality empower the one who can simultaneously claim both domains. In chapters 1 and 3, I will touch on the specific ways advanced education and professional profile features into spiritual warfare praxis.

Over time, seeing through the lens of scientific rationality has moved beyond the conversion of souls within territories to stabilizing the victories of their missionizing. Spiritual warriors have generated a "synthetic ideal" of forms of authority by mixing science with spirituality, a tactic that preempted a dismissal of their religious truth by synthesizing it with the epistemic authority of empiricism.[30] Through this combination, they have achieved remarkable social success. Some of the churches, especially the richer and more dominant ones, built schools to educate people up to the university level, with pastors superintending.

They regularly emphasize the essence of acquiring scientific knowledge and technological competence, even while exorcizing demons. Thus, their use of the symbols of rational learning has brought a degree of legitimacy to these religious leaders. The plausibility structures within religion blended into those of rational learning, and the synced lenses of interpreting reality became mutually corroborating. Science thus enlightened the limits of spiritual sight and helped pastors establish themselves as spiritual authorities. On the surface, the nature of science as a body of knowledge that premises both objectivism and empiricism would seem to be antithetical to spirituality, whose modes of knowing are mostly intuitive. At a closer glance, one sees differently, though. Their worldviews might be different, their modes of perceiving reality and interpreting truths might be incommensurable, but spiritual warriors are flexible enough not to be prevented from appropriating the knowledge propositions of science to further their missionary goals and the task of disestablishing orders.

However, science has a stronger objective basis for its assertions, enough to alleviate the intuitive truth claims of faith; this relationship sometimes results in agonisms. In the coming chapters, I will explore where and why spiritual warriors both affirm and antagonize science in their quest to disestablish—and supplant—the authority of scientists. Chapters 3 and 4 are a study of spiritual warfare and political contests during the COVID-19 pandemic. The politics of the pandemic and the role of religious leaders revealed the inherent instability in this science–spirit arrangement, because the uniqueness of the historical moment in current history demanded a meaning religious leaders could not immediately provide without a knowledge of science. Scientists understood the arithmetic of the disease, a role that could also allow them to claim a moral space at the expense of faith leaders. Spiritual warriors who had always asserted the ability to see beyond the limits of collective perception and the (in)sight to situate things in relation to other things in a vast world full of interminable realities thus had an epistemic crisis to resolve. The religious leaders tasked with finding an interpretation of how the pandemic could have occurred on their spiritual watch had nothing to offer that could stand up to the body of knowledge that scientists authoritatively deployed to confront the pandemic. The resulting discomfort, with their epistemic limitations in tackling a confounding social experience, made them both antagonize global organizations whose authorities are science-based and allege malevolence on the part of those who wield controlling knowledge, leading to anti-science and anti-expertise outbursts. Such an adversarial approach both provided an opportunity for them to disestablish the authority that scientists were gaining at the expense of religious authorities, and also to establish the spiritual knowledge they embody as commensurate with that of experts. Demonization of specialized scientific knowledge by linking the traits of radical evil and suspicions of scientists' ethical corruption, became the means of forcing the impenetrability of the epistemes of scientific rationality to account itself and do so on the terms set by spiritual warriors.

For instance, around March 2020, one of the pastors who prayed against the disease and in support of scientific and spiritual solutions was Chris Oyakhilome of Christ Embassy Church, a preacher and a miracle healer further discussed in chapter 4. His church is one of the largest in Nigeria, with branches throughout the country and even in North America, Europe, and other places. Pastor Oyakhilome prayed against "the deadly virus orchestrated by the devil" and invoked the power of God to break the influence of the disease. He also prayed for countries to find solutions to both the disease and their national economies, which were beginning to crumble as a result. He prayed to dispatch angels to go forth and "make vaccines to be made available, come into operation," for "solutions to come to men in their various nations," and for "care to be available and cheap by the wisdom of God." He further prayed for this wisdom to be "released unto the nations." Months later, he had flipped from this position that ceded the authority of the moment to science and had become the face of the Nigerian story of global conspiracy theories about COVID-19 and 5G technology—the conspiracy of a confederacy of demonic forces, powerful countries and their evil elites who wanted to unleash an agenda of control of human behavior into the world. His influence in peddling these stories spread to different parts of Africa as his videos were shared and recirculated by a band of conspiracy theorists who did not disaggregate his status as a preacher and miracle healer from his ability to propound scientific truths.

In a sermon around January 2021, by which time he had gone neck-deep into conspiracy theories, Pastor Oyakhilome claimed he had sent people to hospitals in different parts of the world to investigate the claims of the causes of death, and those people had found "very few or no sick people." He added that he had video evidence to prove that "a lot of the hospitals were empty" and COVID-19 was not a killer disease as the world had been told, but a "fraud." He also said there was no scientific evidence that either masks or lockdowns ever worked, and all around us were "findings of pseudoscience" that were all untrue. He said,

> These are simple truths. If you cannot ask the right questions, then you open yourself up to destruction. Ask yourself what is the [scientific] evidence that a mask [or lockdown] works? They told you so! I have done an enormous research on it. Question: Have you? Don't just listen because somebody said so, or the WHO said so. I disagree with the WHO and for clear reasons. They have made too many mistakes and they don't apologize. They just change their minds and expect us to follow. Remember, they didn't drop from heaven in the WHO. We can ask them questions. They are not God. Even God accepts questions, and he

answers. Why not these ones? ... Already, many of the virologists have shown
that more than 90 percent of people who get it recover without any problems.
So, why the destruction of nations? Why the research? People have done a
research without this it was an intelligent and proper research. But because it
is a fraudulent research by men and women of corrupt minds. This is why
this is happening.[31]

He did not stop trying to disestablish the scientists' authority as they made pronouncements about the pandemic; he also claimed their truth-finding methods
of fieldwork and data gathering in his interpretation of the pandemic were a conspiracy against humankind. His claim of having done "enormous research" and
his position on asking questions (as scientists do) demonstrate a desire for the
power that knowledge experts wield, a voyeuristic projection of how an agenda of
social control can be conjured through knowing *more than others,* and possessing
the institutionalized means to turn this resource into a naturalized field of power
relations. For, where else could active evil be resident than institutions staffed
with people who access and control a level of knowledge others do not have? For
people who regularly use the phantasmagoric to map the operations of unseen
beings, the ability of experts to see beyond the conventional appearances of reality unsettles and even stimulates desire to usurp technocrats' power.

The covetousness of the power of science experts, in some ways, explains why
one popular mantra among conspiracy theorists, the promoters of pseudoscience such as anti-vaxxers, and spiritual warriors (who may also be conspiracy
theorists and promoters of pseudoscience) when challenged on their claims is
to "do your research!" Or they might say, just like Pastor Chris, "I have done
my research, you do *your* research!" Despite several assertions by cultural commentators that those (e.g., anti-vaxxers, flat-earthers, climate change deniers,
etc.) who ask their interlocutors to research a topic want to escape the burden
of substantiating their various claims or repatriate such a task onto their inter-
locutor, asking someone else to do research is not about sheer laziness on their
part. Again, despite the popular label of "anti-science" slapped on these people,
they take great pride in using the methods of science—a culture of reasoned
argumentation toward a revision of an earlier position—to challenge scientists.
Bringing up "research" in their supposed debates with scientists is self-validation
because what such moments express is the covetousness of the knowledge of
what scientists do and how they do it. Saying "I have done my research, you do
yours!" tucks subjective opinions on science-based issues within an established
universal framework of reasoned knowledge—and the techniques of its acquisition such as observation, inquiries, study, critique, and generation of new
forms of thought.

In these times of instant search engines, Wikipedia pages, endless numbers
of blogs purporting to demystify arcane knowledge, and digital library shelves

laden with tomes of materials, people have access to specialist knowledge more than at any time in history. The heady feeling of omniscience—produced from accessing what used to be remote—fuels a desire to perform that empowerment through contention—and a publicly staged one too—with renowned expert authorities. Most people would readily agree that we live in the Age of Information, but that over-surplus of information itself has not translated into knowledge.[32] What is called "research" could boil down to merely creaming off pared-down information or dissensions among experts to find what supports spiritual warriors' and conspiracy theorists' initial gut instincts on a subject. However, the point of the conspiracy theorists or the spiritual warriors who claim to have researched their assertions is not so much to build a repertoire of knowledge at the same level as actual scientists. Instead, it is to make known their contention, and this is achievable by using a lens similar to the one through which the scientists themselves see another order of reality. Researching as scientists do, or even merely claiming to have done so, adds a perlocutionary force to their contention with the experts. Beyond mere mimicry or an appropriation of scientific methods too, the "do your research-ers" demonstrate that standing up to the social power of the scientific enterprise demands discernment that they too possess, both intuitively and through the rigorous work of learning. *Do your research, I have done mine* expressed a leveling up with expertise, a desire to shape a world where anyone who demonstrates enough diligence to inquire beyond the official account of reality can enrobe themselves into the priesthood of specialized knowledge and technocratic dominance.

What Pastor Oyakhilome, as well as other spiritual warriors who forefront their contest against powerful global and local science-based authorities strive to achieve with claims of having done their "research" demonstrate is their inscription of their "affective politics of truth and revelation" within the institutional frames of modern rational-legal learning.[33] Thus, their judgment becomes tenable because it is "reasoned," and therefore can be considered "reasonable." As activists whose social performance is to see the world changed, spiritual warriors covet the authority—that is, "a measure of the capacity to instill belief; to engender not only understanding, but also assent; to move those affected toward changed attitudes; and to encourage actions"[34]—scientists enjoy because of the power of their knowledge. Scientific knowledge entails the production of rational authority commutable to moral authority. This moral authority, "a measure of the capacity to speak convincingly about what *ought to* be, as opposed to what is," derives from rational-legal authority and its objective verification procedures and universally institutionalized methods.[35]

The authority of science lies not in the body of facts that forms the knowledge base, but in the actual embodied human who personifies the intellect, the person who makes all those facts around the nature of the physical seeable. With training that has enabled spiritual warriors to develop a second sight through which they see the microscopic details that converge to operate our world—the terrible evil that can be and will be unleashed if not bridled—they also grant themselves, through intense spiritual rites, the power to issue corrections against both physical and spiritual realities as they manifest in the social. Scientists' prowess, says Glen Scott Allen, is communicated in a language—and perhaps processes—that strikes noninitiates as magical. Because the knowledge they display is mostly esoteric, scientists become suspect as the "Wicked Wizard," a trope of the scientist who functions "through incantations, summons powers dark and esoteric, powers that seem to operate outside the boundaries of 'natural' material laws." Thus, such scientists are "also perceived as someone who stands outside the social laws of everyday communities."[36] By combining intuitive religious revelations with scientific insights, spiritual warriors encrust their task of disestablishing hegemonic orders with the objectivity of science and the universality of its methods of truth assertion. More importantly, they draw on the perception of the autonomy of the wizard—or of the wizardry of knowledge—to also portray themselves as able to operate outside natural laws.[37] By claiming the ability to similarly denude reality as scientists do while also policing their intentions for humanity, the spiritual warrior establishes their identity. This contention between science and the spirit in a bid to see beyond the pale will feature throughout the chapters of this book.

Chapter Breakdown

In chapter 1, "Aborting Satanic Pregnancies: Prayer as Apocalyptic Devices," where I explore the milieu in which spiritual warfare thrives, I closely study a scientist turned demonologist, Dr. Daniel K. Olukoya of the Mountain of Fire and Miracles Ministries, to underscore how the apprehension of both domains of knowledge has helped him to devise apocalypticism as a means of interpreting reality and confronting evil omens through the profusion of prayers rained by spiritual warriors every day.[38] Much of the feature in his works—which I shall call the literature of prayer—through which he trains people to daily instigate the apocalypse in order to disestablish the oppressive social order and inaugurate an auspicious reality. By opening up congregants to another reality where spectral presences seep into the natural world from a proximate one, they devise the means to apprehend and vanquish these forces and are thus empowered to transform extant reality.

As I will demonstrate in chapter 2, "Rehearsing Authority: Spiritual Warriors as God's Human Weapons," people whose eyes are open to the truth surrounding their immediate reality—which is not obvious to all—also are radicalized enough to claim the power of knowledge that regulates the metaphorical light and darkness that guide the world. However, their motive in spiritual warfare is not merely to master the natural laws of physics—as scientists do—but also to break them through supernatural power. This chapter demonstrates the self-reconstituting force of prayer performances by elaborating how spiritual warriors dis-member bodies—a process that culminates in their becoming organic ciphers of God's power. By engaging in the practices of self-authorization facilitated through techniques of prayer and other religious rituals, they develop not only the knowledge of what else exists out there but also the orientation of being privileged possessors of truth. I critically explore how the human agent becomes an embodiment of the truth of God, and how the resultant psychological complex fashions a subjectivity that authorizes them to claim to be—and act as—the human weapon of the divine agenda.

In chapter 3, I explore how spiritual warfare's politics of disestablishment could go global and latch onto local (dis)contents. This chapter, "The Noisome Pestilence: COVID-19 and the Conspirituality of 'Fake Science,'" shows how the condition of a global pandemic spurred the disestablishing impulses of spiritual warriors cutting across national divides. The case study is around Dr. Stella Immanuel of Firepower Ministries International in Texas, a physician who combined spiritual warfare with conspiracy theories against scientists and science-based organizations. Through her, I also explore conspirituality—the convergence of conspiracy theories and New Age spirituality as they come together in achieving the noble objective of overturning the reign of certain established authorities. Immanuel's contention through the power of supernatural sight was an enactment of public defection from the elite cult of science to undercut the power and authority conferred upon notable scientists. She thus became the hero of the spiritual warriors who want to take down an ascendant regime of technocrats.

The pandemic threw up the existing world order. In chapter 4, "Churches Going Virtual: Empty Auditoriums and the Essential Services of Prayer," I demonstrate how the disruption made room for a redefinition of secular and religious political structures. In the lockdown phase of the pandemic, Christian religious leaders used the liminality of the period to try to extricate themselves and their churches from the hold of secular authorities. Using the examples of Nigeria and the United States, I further highlight how discourses of spiritual warfare and rational cum moral authority latched onto nativist and nationalist sentiments during the COVID-19 pandemic. In the concluding chapter, "Jesus Has Won," I discuss how the vastness of the possibilities of the spiritual world means that there is no foreseeable end to these affective politics mediated by the spiritual warriors' spiritual economy of seeing beyond the pale.

1

Aborting Satanic Pregnancies

• •

Prayer as Apocalyptic Devices

> *We declare any strange winds—any*
> *strange winds that have been sent to hurt*
> *the church, sent to hurt this nation, sent*
> *against the president, sent against myself,*
> *sent against others—we break it by the*
> *superior blood of Jesus right now. . . . In*
> *the name of Jesus, we command all satanic*
> *pregnancies to miscarry right now. We*
> *declare that anything that has been*
> *conceived in satanic wombs will miscarry,*
> *it will not be able to carry forth any plan*
> *of destruction, any plan of harm.*
> —Paula White, White House Spiritual
> Adviser

While waging spiritual warfare prayers at a Florida church at the start of 2020, Paula White, a televangelist and religious adviser to the forty-fifth president of the United States, Donald Trump, made the remarks cited in the epigraph. The prayer, a curious combination of Judeo-Christian ideas of evil and horror film genre grotesquery, generated some backlash from the denizens of Twitter, who took the content of the prayers about the intentional miscarriage of pregnancy literally. White responded that she was only using a metaphor, and that her critics mischievously took her words out of context.[1] A Twitter discussion that would have passed as just another day in Trump's America took on a new perspective when a professor of religious studies at Concordia University in Montreal, Quebec, André Gagné, intervened. He linked White's prayers to books by Nigerian pastor, deliverance minister, and the general overseer of the Mountain of Fire and Miracles (MFM) Church, Dr. Daniel K. Olukoya. According to Gagné, who posted excerpts from the book *The Mysteries of Life* in which Olukoya had discussed satanic pregnancies, the logic of Paul White's prayer was clear: "What is the command for all 'satanic pregnancies' to miscarry? Nigerian evangelist D. K. Olukoya simply says that these represent the plans that Satan has against a person's life (see his reference to the story of Job). White is commanding that Satan's plans be aborted."[2] Several Nigerian newspapers and blogs picked up the story, gleefully sharing how the modes of "dangerous" and "violent" prayers that Olukoya was (in)famous for in the country transcended cultural barriers to emerge in North America.[3] Although there is no way of truly knowing if White had read Olukoya's books or whether it was a mere coincidence that her words echoed his, the use of the metaphor of "satanic pregnancy" by a preacher whose ecclesiastical niche of demonic encounter and rituals of exorcism provides a significant means of understanding how spiritual warriors use prayers as apocalyptic devices to disestablish both social orders and the norms that institute them.[4]

This chapter studies spiritual warriors' ideas of aborting of satanic pregnancies through the lens of MFM prayer literature and the work of Olukoya as a form of time control. In a broad sense, time is the subjective experience of the unfolding of history through the social actions and events that organize reality. Alice Rayner, for instance, describes time as a "modality that dismantles fixed subjects and objects and turns past, present and future into ways of manners of attention."[5] In his childhood memoir narrating the experience of growing up in Nigeria and observing the people caught in a phase of social transition, Toyin Falola also describes the attitude of the older people in his community who have to mediate between tradition and modernity's radically different ideas of time. To them, "time can be an idea, a concept. Time can be measured by comparing people, relating one event to another. Like logs of wood placed on top of another, time can be delineated by the placement of one log in relation to another."[6] Apprehending time as relative to a major event differs from modernity's objective modes of keeping time due to factors such as technology and industrialization. Steve Dixon's study of theater, technology, and time noted contemporary technology culture's modes of disrupting the rationality and linearity of chronometric time and pointed out that this development might be redirecting us back to "earlier notions of time as static, mythic, cyclical or sacred."[7] The Pentecostal conception of time is equally inflected by the cosmological worldview that relates time to events, and modernity's chronometric ideas of time. Thus, Pentecostal time measures distances— between the social stage people aspire to occupy and where they are at currently. Even though prayers are devised as a consequence of their apprehension of time as a measure of the distance between two realities and the subsequent means of bridging them, spiritual warriors also know that the time between "here and there" is not merely vacant. In the stretch of time that an individual experiences their own life, they confront the conventions that fill up the time by establishing new social orders and redetermining the experience of everyday reality.

The spiritual warrior's temporal experience equally composes the discernment of spiritual operations—the ability to see the unseen and sense that somewhere in the spiritual realms there are evil forces conceiving a diabolical agenda that will thwart one's potential for social flourishing—and correlate it with habituations and dispositions in the material world. The nefarious work of these demonic agents gestates over time, creating satanic pregnancies—that is, individual and institutional practices become habits that are gradually woven into the social fabric to eventually become normative and definitive, bringing such pregnancies to fruition. These practices, and the demonic forces behind them that turn them to oppressive monstrosities, must be discerned at the early stages of conception so they can be effectively terminated. The vacuum suction that aborts them is the "violent" or "dangerous" prayer, or as I will call them, "apocalyptic devices," a form of spiritual supplication pungent enough to end satanic malice right at its inception. Thus, abortion of satanic pregnancies is how spiritual warriors approximate the auguries of the time in which they live, divine the negativities, and dissolve the threats through the apocalyptic devices of prayer. These practices become their investment in a "deeper structure of religious feeling that can tie together disparate, even contradictory, experiences, bodily sensations, feelings and thoughts."[8]

As confrontational means of averting the vicissitudes of life and human malevolence, these prayer forms break down historical formations and recalibrate the calculus that defines temporal experience so that the spiritual warrior can enter a reordered future. For instance, Paula White's prayers about the abortion of satanic pregnancies conceptualize the formation of a partisan political agenda contending against her and those who belong to her side of ideological truth and attempt to forestall their eventual realization. This chapter will examine these violent prayers as apocalyptic devices and identify their goals as a daily activity of triggering an end to the established social orders that militate against spiritual warriors. By construing these prayer forms as apocalyptic devices, I divine the ways spiritual warriors control time's portents through the apprehension of the diabolic forces that undermine their human potential, the location of the sites and modes of these satanic operations, and the transcendence of material reality to disestablish these reigns of terror. Prayers are a habitual ritual practice for the Christian, and spiritual warriors' deployment of them as apocalyptic devices creatively destroys established orders of the social imagination, aborts satanic pregnancies, and elides the amount of time it takes to move from the oppressive phase of the present to a radically reformed future.

Prayer as an apocalyptic device draws on both biblical literature and the literary genre that treats apocalypse as an end to an existing order. A necessary caveat: through popular cultural representations, there has been a tendency to immediately think of the apocalypse as a disaster, "the end of the world as we know it." Such aesthetic treatment has evoked imaginations of how the end might eventually happen: natural and man-made disasters, technology gone awry, alien invasion, extinction of species, nuclear war, environmental devastation, zombies, and any similar horror that collapses social order. The spectacle of the death of species and the familiar way of life notwithstanding, what underpins the apocalypse is not the disaster itself—not the violence of nuclear bombs exploding while bodies and human civilizations crumble into rubble, or even the subsequent feeling of terror that is experienced. The apocalypse is the revelation of true reality, that epiphanous moment when the cataclysmic event starkly reveals the vulnerability of reality and things subsequently change.[9] Such revelation brings about a radical understanding of experiences, the comprehension of the paradoxes quartering the full realization of one's destiny. In the revelatory moments where the extent of what is possible is revealed, banal details of social life gain cosmic significance.

By referring to these regularly performed spiritual warfare prayers as apocalyptic devices, I appropriate the metaphor of various doomsday devices—the nuclear bomb, for instance—that have facilitated world-ending events in social and literary imaginations and apply it to the ritual devotions of spiritual warfare prayers. Thus, apocalyptic devices discern how the fantasies of the disestablishment of reigning power within society have become built into the organizing structures of everyday life for spiritual warriors, such that their performance of the social and spiritual self, labor forms, subversive activities, consumerist practices, and even leisure are oriented toward this purpose. Conceiving prayer as an apocalyptic device draws on both biblical literature and popular literary genres that treat the apocalypse as an end. As a worldview of ancient Israelites plagued by oppression and dispersal, the apocalyptic accounted for their brutal suffering and oppression and also tried to end it without delegitimizing God's place in their history.[10] In literary genres, the apocalypse is typically about a looming end to an existing order, and that is why the overriding themes typically include cosmic dualism, abrupt finality to a seemingly interminable social order, and redemption and renewal. In works where the apocalypse is taken as a future event, they have variously marked the time between when the world exits an imperfect present, and when a newer one begins.[11] By framing prayer as apocalyptic devices, I thus show how these prayers serve the radical ends of revelation and the overturning of an existing social order to give way to one underwritten by the ethos of Christianity. They are also boundary-marking practices that define the status of the spiritual warriors who will be saved at the end, as against those who will perish.

The apocalypticism in popular literature and the Bible speaks of the future as expectations of a time—sometimes—ahead, where present circumstances are escaped. The forms of prayer I characterize as apocalyptic devices do not treat the future as an unspecified length of time, though. They are tropes of revelation and insight that critique the existing social hierarchies. Their cycles of social breakdown and expectations of renewal are daily reformations through the activities of spiritual warriors who rain down prayers to disestablish organized social systems they perceive as evil because of their oppressiveness. These prayers are a form of historical practice because they provide a heuristic structure to the chaos of normative life and its inherent moral decadence that creates adversarial conditions. As moral weapons, apocalyptic devices reflect the hopes of a restructured or renewed future that spiritual warriors hope comes quickly. James Cascio observes that construing an apocalypse as a cataclysmic end, either as an expression of pessimism or a means to motivate people to action, can be counterproductive.[12] He reframes the apocalypse as an "ongoing traumatic shock" to foster an appreciation of present circumstances that is already apocalyptic. Another consequence of applying the apocalyptic trope as an ongoing action—rather than a one-time spectacular event—is how its urgency sediments into banal performances. Rather than a long spell of time when something expectedly happens, the daily expectations of an imminent end to an existing order conditions social behavior.

The adversarial circumstances that deform social life muddle the experience of time, and spiritual warriors control their temporal disorientation through apocalyptic devices that reformat time. In difficult social situations where life seems to be permanently at war, and one faces an imminent death—both a social and an untimely physical one—in everyday affairs, the distinction between the past, the future, and the present blurs and contracts "into one intense moment of precariousness."[13] Living in such conditions, spiritual warriors' experience of time changes, and "time no longer governs the rhythm of development; it is a pure manifest and acts as an incubus. Time as having severed the nexus between human activities and transformation of society becomes only the tormenting pure noise of clocks, chronometers, tower bells, and aches, all sounds of the echo chamber of gigantic torture apparatus. In this perverse state, the present deepens anomie, ensures futility, and resists redemption. Time itself is an anomic figure."[14] Given that nothing definitive ever really happens between the tick and tock of time, the reality of being locked in an ouroboros cycle of sterile social systems disorients.[15] The inertia of living in a fast-paced world without being fully engaged with it or benefiting from the rewards, yet all the while being impacted by its vagaries, creates a perplexing feeling of being caught in this time warp. Time typified by an extended phase of nothingness turns malicious, and its passage drives people to earnestly use the apocalyptic devices of fervent prayers to discern and abort the satanic pregnancies inhibiting regenerative life forms.

Through a narration of the contributions of Olukoya to spiritual discernment, the next section will explore aspects of spiritual warfare prayer as apocalyptic devices. He is a significant figure in a Nigerian study of spiritual warfare because he has not only created a genre of prayer literature that features apocalyptic devices by borrowing the corpus of oral narratives of myths, metaphors, and metonyms; he astutely balances narratives of demonic encounters in modern society with perceptions of scientific rationality. He also deepens his moral authority as a man of God with the moral authority of a trained scientific expert. His works promise the power of enhanced sight to see what lies beyond familiar reality and help spiritual warriors take individual charge against militating forces. The idea of the demonic imaginary across Nigerian and several other African churches is partly owing to his church's discursive—and relentless—approach to diabolism.[16] His prodigiousness in seeing the demons that haunt the social imaginary molded spiritual warfare ideas across the social landscape and informed spiritual warriors' perceptions, social practices, and responses to worldly affairs.[17]

Olukoya's influence in shaping the spiritual economy includes the ways Pentecostals frequently enter a future timescape where the satanic pregnancies that will imperil them can be preemptively aborted. Through their various prayer speeches that deploy graphic violence and appropriate the vocabulary of militarism, they established a genre of public communication now popularly known as "MFM prayers." In the Nigerian parlance, these aggressive prayer modes unabashedly use corporeal performances of violence and imprecations. For example, their signature commands of "Die!," "Die by fire!," and "Fall down and die in the name of Jesus!" are performative utterances meant to enact change in the present world.[18] While "MFM prayers" references his church, the style has been taken up in many churches, especially those that make spectacular demonic encounters their mission focus. I focus on the angle of these prayers as apocalyptic devices—the portal through which the doors of the imagination open to let in a transcendent reality and allow spiritual warriors to control how time functions in their lives by disestablishing present social and political formations that threaten their social progress.

This chapter also notes that prayers as apocalyptic devices are now absorbed into the models of capitalist production surplus and are produced by spiritual warriors as "prayer rains," examined in the third section.[19] That is, prayers are endless profusions sent into the spiritual atmosphere every minute of the day to trigger the apocalypse, not as a decisive final event but to identify the forces— indwelling and external—that harbor satanic seeds and to suck them out (abort them) so that spiritual warriors can thrive. Although the apocalyptic event of ending an existing order is diffused into the everyday, it does not register as any less urgent to spiritual warriors. For instance, some warfare prayers urge spiritual warriors to command forces to respond to their spiritual litigations, *Now! Right now! Today today!* Both the urgency of the command and the repetition underscore the haste that drives spiritual warriors seeking to shorten their path toward future transformation. The command responds to their sense of urgency and their desire for a compression time; a wish to *fast-forward* to the future when a glorious destiny would be realized.[20] The riotous nature of these *Now now! Right now! Today today!* prayers when being performed reflects the exigencies of hastening the end of time. Afe Adogame noted that these prayers are "the rendition of extemporaneousness prayers with prodigious enthusiasm and avidity, sometimes with such verbosity as if the supersensory entities are being forced to grant their petitions and request."[21]

There is always the fear of a future filled with anomic content, and spiritual warriors preempt satanic malevolence through an abortion of what evil the time ahead will bring, and this is examined in the fourth section. To confront the social chaos and the futility of meaning within an endless stretch of the present, the apocalyptic devices of prayer generate the protocols of regeneration that will inaugurate a better world order. Apocalyptic devices raining down every single day is a formula for harnessing God's promise of rest and peace for his children, not to be attained in an otherworldly plane of the New Jerusalem or the heavenly City of God, but right here *now now*, *right now*, and *today today* on this material plane where their right to *being* is being assaulted. They hypothesize the problems at stake in the language of militancy and warfare, and then turn to prayers—an unquenchable source of everlasting power— for a showdown. Their forceful prayers apprehend the destabilizations of their reality, like marking an X on the vertiginous grounds of daily existence. Collectively generated from the felt experiences of daily life, the prayers' contents induce a harmonious and God-willed order by hastening the time and the promises of social regeneration that *that* life after the end of *this* time holds.

Spiritual warriors' obsession with seeing where satanic pregnancies are growing so they can thwart negative futurity at an embryonic stage opens them up to the forces of capitalism and neoliberalism, the subject of the fifth section. Discourses on neoliberalism in Pentecostalism tend to focus on the prosperity gospel and the spiritual strivings of the Pentecostal subjects as they struggle with social inequalities and the attendant indignities, as well as the futility of such attempts.[22] Nimi Wariboko's study on this subject concludes that they follow the routines and promises of prayer only to find their souls "reformatted by late capitalism for its profit."[23] Annelin Eriksen, Ruy Llera Blanes, and Michelle MacCarthy read such spiritual efforts of the Pentecostals they studied as means of intensifying life at the expense of death or what is decaying. Not only for economic empowerment, spiritual warriors also sow seeds and live piously as daily enactments of life over death. Pentecostal neoliberalism shows how the life-affirming practices that seal their triumph over death mesh with their cosmological cycles of life and death, which they reorient to extend the time of living over when death comes.[24]

These observations about the connections between the neoliberal economy and desires for social progress are germane to understanding how spiritual warriors' constant bombardment with prayer rains prepackaged to confront the demons of modernity exposes the self—the part of a subject that privately connects to divine transforming power through prayer rituals—to the barrage of mercantilism. The cycles of decay and renewal that the apocalyptic devices instigate not only expand the realms of spiritual imagination where demonic operations are apprehended, they also necessitate 24/7 prayers, which are bounteously supplied through organized channels of capitalist consumerism. The inscriptive rituals of prayers expose the spiritual aspects of one's subjectivity that, ideally, should be outside the domains of practices of economic control. Such (over)exposure to the mercantilist practices that supply the resources for these prayer rituals causes even more vulnerability to the demons of modernity. Adam Kostko's study of the political theology of late capitalism shows how the economic philosophy of neoliberalism and its promises of individual freedom in a competitive marketplace structure a sociopolitical construct that cedes the responsibility for survival to individuals; those who fail to be saved by the configurations neoliberalism inaugurates are demonized.[25] Indeed, the political economy of demonization mass produces specters so that the more the apocalyptic devices of prayer are triggered, the more they need to procure these prayer resources to counter even more demons that consequently emerge. Sean McCloud rightly asserts that we cannot account for neoliberalism in modern times without also considering how it reverberates on religious imaginations.[26] I note this connection through some of the ways that the apocalyptic devices of prayer travel are the same networked media routes of online marketplaces, such as Amazon.com, that have allowed global capitalism to penetrate homesteads.

The persistent motif in this form of prayer is the event of revelation, which is further explored in the final section of this chapter.[27] Prayer lets spiritual warriors achieve a transcendent position and see into another spatial realm where possibilities abound and where interactions with phantasmagoric beings maximize the scope of possibilities. From this perch of enlightenment, they see *what is* and how their perceptions are structured against other incarnate realities, and

they instigate an end to an existing social order. The economy of seeing deon-
tologizes the self-reiterating construct of existing meanings and demands an
assertion of fresher possibilities. Fantasies of the apocalypse offer a glimpse of
a better reality beyond the present one, and the visions induct even the socially
unprivileged into the concealed glories of the future possibilities of a different
existence mode. The conscious processes that produce social flourishing within
a society that have long been sublimated within the pacifying norms, and which
have kept people from exploring what else there is to existence, thus yield to a
lucid dream of what else could be. The apocalypse not only breaks down the
order of reality, but even the vested interests that want to sustain normative life have their moral and legal authority challenged. This apocalyptic
juncture is "the place where the future pushes into the present. It's the breaking in of another dimension, a new wine for which our old wineskins are
unprepared. That which apocalyptic proclaims cannot fit into existing ways
of thinking."[28] Because the period also includes a breakdown of meaning,
the crisis brings a liminality, the in-between moments where transformation
becomes possible.

Dr. Daniel K. Olukoya: Man of God and Man of Science

In the auditorium, Dr. Daniel Olukoya stood on a dais with his back turned to
a crowd of seated scholars, all of them berobed in academic regalia. The occasion
was an honorary doctorate from the University of Lagos, his alma mater. The
crowd in the hall, composed of the academic community and members of
the MFM church, cheered exultantly as a voice over the speaker read out Olukoya's academic and professional/pastoral achievements. The speaker noted that
he had excelled as a microbiology student, obtaining the first first-class degree
the department ever granted in 1979. After a brief stint as a researcher in Nigeria, he received a scholarship to study molecular genetics at the University of
Reading in the United Kingdom, where he obtained a Ph.D. in 1984. They
noted his scientific publications, that he was the "first Nigerian scientist to
establish an indigenous laboratory of molecular biology and biotechnology in
Nigeria . . . [and also] the first to clone genes in the country."[29] They also noted
that he had graciously donated the Dr. D. K. Olukoya Central Research Laboratory to the university.[30] The introduction over, the university chancellor rose
from his seat to read the pronouncement that Olukoya was being conferred an
honorary doctorate. As the vice chancellor proceeded to present Olukoya with
the paraphernalia of the honor and then enrobe him in matching regalia, a
standing choir rose up on the dais and broke into the "Hallelujah Chorus."[31]

This publicly staged performance reconciled the realms of science and
rationality with that of religion—specifically, the fantastical world of demonic
encounter Olukoya specializes in—and is one of the reasons Olukoya is a

fascinating figure. Paul Gifford describes his church as one that is "totally, exclusively, and relentlessly concerned with spiritual forces. The church exists to identify and drive out the evil forces blocking one's destiny. That is why people attend."[32] This is not exactly hyperbole; Olukoya's world is truly permeated by demons and demonic encounters. A visitor to any of his hundreds of churches all over Nigeria and in several countries worldwide would get a similar impression of people obsessed with demonic specters. Yet Olukoya judiciously balances his public representation as a demonologist with the wizardry of intellectualism and scientific learning, as the event at the University of Lagos shows. Simultaneously striving to be seen as a wizard whose power over natural laws is rooted in both science and faith, Olukoya moves on a spectrum between narrating the character of specters and navigating the rarefied world of scientific learning and rationality. Thus, the politics of disestablishment that he propounds takes its efficacy from both scientific and spiritual authorities.

Perhaps more than any other preacher on spiritual warfare, Olukoya has significantly contributed to creating the modern African enchanted imagination through his teachings on spiritual encounters. He helps people see the ancestral forces and demonic specters that reside in the cultural atmosphere, define them, and then expel them. This ability, in some ways, mimics the scientist's insight in piercing the depths of a reality that is not immediately obvious to discern how disparate causes converge to shape extant reality. One of the places that Olukoya, incidentally, has displayed this savviness happened to be a university, the same one that later gave him an honorary doctorate. Years before, the vice chancellor of the University of Lagos—who, at the time, also happened to be the president of the Nigerian National Academy of Science—had invited Olukoya to the campus to perform a ritual of deliverance (or exorcism) for them from the evil forces causing violence and mayhem in the institution. Olukoya held a prayer meeting on the campus. During the session he named seven or eight demons and said he had expelled them from the grounds of the university.[33] In the same period he exorcised demons from the campus, he also offered to donate a laboratory to the university, although that would not be officially inaugurated until five years later.[34]

According to Olukoya in a personal interview, he was moved to donate a laboratory so he could supply sorely needed advanced equipment and facilities that the university could not otherwise afford, and their upcoming researchers in their science programs would never have been able to access otherwise.[35] Like his fellow pastors and leaders of Pentecostal denominations who run megachurches, Olukoya too runs a chain of schools, from primary to secondary levels, and also a university called Mountain Top. He is the chancellor of Mountain Top University, and he also teaches courses in biotechnology, creativity, and even entrepreneurship. He says he supervises students' theses and trains them in scientific research techniques. In some of his sermons, he sometimes alerts his listeners to the credibility of his assertions because he is a scientist and should know what he is talking about. He is about the most famous demonologist in Nigeria, yet he is also a scientist who takes great pride in his ability to discern through secular and rational techniques.

Anyone encountering Olukoya cannot but note how his elite education and scientific training stand in stark contrast to the fantastical world of demons that he frequently pictures and for which he develops books and manuals for people to pray against them. These materials—I will call them prayer literature—are wholly devoted to training spiritual warriors' inner eyes or spiritual binoculars to apprehend the various forces behind quirks and to control them through prayer. This prayer literature consists of discourses on demonology, and their blurbs never fail to carry the legitimating stamp of his expert authority as a scientist. The ones he personally wrote number in the hundreds, although many of them are pamphlets and some were transcribed from his sermons. His many cultural productions that locate sites of demonic activity and teach spiritual warriors to fight them through spiritual warfare prayers—or "deliverance prayers" as they are more popularly called in Nigeria—contributed to making the apocalypse a banal event, osmotically absorbed and enacted through the performance of daily life.

Thus, through his various investments in secular and scientific enterprises such as his generous financial contributions to the academy and by projecting his own image as a man of science, he puts a base of scientific rationality under the magical world that he exposes through his sermons and his vast corpus of prayer literature. His works glorify the magical elements in African conceptualization of the world, and his simultaneous appeal to rational learning and the authority of embodying the knowledge of modern science validates them further. Scientific investigations and the knowledge of its methods have given certain people the power of the establishment. Because their various findings "display themselves in the open and uncertain field of everyday life, whether embedded in social policies with which we must all come to terms or embodied in new technologies with which we must all grapple," scientists are figures of epistemic envy for those outside the domains of power they manifest through elite knowledge.

As indicated in the introduction, spiritual warriors who contend with them to supplant their reach of authority do so by mimicking their methods of inquiry. Olukoya, however, goes beyond merely posturing omniscience. As both a scientist and a spiritualist, he sees himself as a master of both the rational and intuitive domains of knowledge.[36] By demonstrating an ability to extrapolate the metaphysical, whether in the spiritual, social, or scientific realms, he is seen as a privileged possessor of the truth hidden from everyday sight—the truth of nature's wonders and the truth of human nature. By grandly investing in concrete sites of methodological processes of inquiry—building schools and laboratories, and teaching in the classroom—he distorts the view of those who would see him as proclaiming certain truths out of mere intuitive knowledge. His ostentatious appearances in spaces of secular rationality force a reckoning of his spiritual methods as systematized, and therefore have objective substance.

The modern Nigerian spiritual sensibility that the likes of Olukoya have shaped did not happen simply because Africans have what is akin to a natural tendency to believe in the supernatural, but because those who are in the vanguard of promoting supernaturalism partially embody the credibility of being trained in rational modes of knowledge *before* they took up pastoring. Their trajectory as credentialed scholars turned men of God—especially Olukoya, who was trained as a microbiologist with a Ph.D. from a UK university, a geographical region in the so-called bastion of modern Enlightenment—makes for a compelling story of a professional in the field of science who has seen the futility of possessing knowledge of the natural world without spiritual empowerment. By stringing together both the spiritual and scientific domains of knowledge simultaneously, these men of God sync the authority accruable to them as charismatic religious leaders with the respect that society offers to the men of science. As Olukoya himself said about how he manages to reconcile his métier as a deliverance minister with being a scientist, "When I come to science, I switch on my scientific head. When I leave the laboratory, I go into my spiritual realm. The two are different and to me, they don't contrast each other. I see them as complements. It is only foolish scientists that will say there is no God. When you are with God, you forget everything about science and concentrate on everything about prayers and faith. It does not mean science is not working."[37]

Olukoya's biography bears out his journey into the mechanics of supernatural reality. His apprehension of the occult started while he was growing up in Ondo state in southwestern Nigeria. He told me that his father, Amos Yusuf, was a policeman, a Muslim who was born again at a church crusade by the famous Aladura church preacher, Prophet Timothy O. Obadare.[38] Since Amos Yusuf did not want his children to grow up bearing Muslim names and remain tied to a past life he wanted to shake off permanently, he changed his name from Yusuf to Olukoya. Thus, the son was raised in an Aladura church, Christ Apostolic Church (CAC), a denomination of Christianity noted for Africanist ritual practices that include fierce and unceasing prayers.[39] As a child of a devout convert and an evangelist, Olukoya was quite active in church activities, many of which, he noted, were composed of "many many many many hours of prayers."[40] His father later became an evangelical director for Prophet Obadare. When his father left the police force, he took up pastoring in the CAC and later died in the mission field. Olukoya recollected from his years growing up how his father would drive him away from the playground and force him into the church. The church and what they did there became a fixture in his young mind.[41]

Growing up in a pastoral town in the 1960s, where the picturesque background of the many surrounding hills surging toward the sky triggered the fanciful imagination about how agents from the spectral realms—ghosts, gnomes, and other fantastical characters—regularly infiltrate material reality, he was socialized into ideas of a proximate and penetrable otherworldly realm.[42] Concurrently raised in an Aladura church system, whose ideological foundation was "a reaction to various aspects of colonialism: the monopoly of power in the church; the strangeness of the polity, ethics, and doctrine; the dullness of liturgy and the modes of expressing the spirituality; and as a quest for a place of belonging in the midst of political oppression and marginalization,"[43] Olukoya also grew into an instinctive understanding of the force of primal ritual practices and how they could be reimagined to confront the new demons that modernity had vomited up. Like several famous pastors of his generation, the Aladura churches Olukoya attended while younger turned into a Pentecostal breeding ground for young people, some of whom would later go to tertiary institutions, become part of the Scripture Union, and eventually become pastors of Pentecostal churches.[44] These Pentecostal leaders and their fixation on sacking the demonic forces that interfere with human destinies were partly owing to this historical background.

Though he grew up in an Aladura church in a rural town where he absorbed the ideas of diabolic forces hovering around, he traces his understanding of the world filled with evil to a specific incident in his childhood.[45] At the time, he narrated, he was in a phase of life where he faced the school certificate examinations. Given how brilliant he was and how he had aced past examinations, he was quite confident of his success and had no reason to think the world was not at his feet. One day, as he passed by a house, a young woman inside called out for help. She was screaming that the palm oil she was bleaching in a pan had caught fire, and she needed help to put it out. He turned right to the house. When he got there, though still at the door, he said he saw the fire rise from the pan and form into a ball, move in a perpendicular line, come toward where he stood, and land on his legs. His leg burned. For a while after the incident, he was incapacitated and lived with agonizing pain. While still dealing with the painful leg, he suffered physical abuse from an overzealous schoolteacher who broke his arm. He said while he was lying on his sickbed wracked with the pain and agony of both a broken arm and a leg covered with burn sores, he suddenly heard a voice. The voice asked him how come he was facing all those issues when he had an important examination coming. Had it not occurred to him yet that someone or occult forces somewhere did not want him to take the examination and was putting those accidents in his path to dispirit him? That, he said, was his moment of epiphany. The revelation from the voice gave him insight into how seemingly disparate incidents were part of a demonic agenda that wanted to prevent him from realizing his destiny. His eyes now opened, he saw how his life was being controlled by malicious forces that kept throwing a series of misfortunes in his way to truncate his destiny. That moment of dawning was also when he took control and began to terminate the seeds that these forces were planting in his path, aborting a future satanic pregnancy. He said, "It was on that bed that I started praying the kind of prayers that you are hearing now."[46]

That moment, his eyes opened to see how the world he inhabited was full of vindictive evil forces that, though he could not see them, could see him. They also saw his future potential and wanted to kill him preemptively. This death was not necessarily going to be physical, but both social and metaphysical. If the series of accidents he was having could crush his spirits, he would fail or miss the career-defining examination before him.[47] The distance between him and his glorious destiny as a gifted young scholar would have been interminably lengthened if he did not keep to the path of secular education offered for upward mobility. Fortunately, while on that hospital bed, time and space collapsed, and the transcendent realms opened to him when he heard a disembodied voice showing him the pattern in his misfortunes. He could suddenly see how the time of his life was being seeded with occult malevolence, and he also learned that he could control the evil gestations that wanted to thwart his destiny. His moment of strength and supernatural power came through his ability to begin to see beyond the ordinariness of the events. He moved from the first order of thinking where the happenings were mere incidentals, to a second order of thinking where spiritual causality was established between the events. He not only saw the forces surveilling his social progress and controlling his social mobility by weaving malevolent details into his life, but he also began to see them back. By being able to weaponize his inspired sight against these unseen forces, he could control their activities in his life. He could end their reign by foiling the means by which they were already growing satanic pregnancies in the trajectory of his still-unfolding life. By disestablishing their agenda in its rudimentary stages, he could progress from the juvenile phase of life to full maturation and self-realization. In short, he could move through time, which had become stilled. But it was not until he saw what was at stake that he could pray more targeted prayers to do so.

When he left that hospital bed, he went on to take the examination. He passed, and his life journey proceeded onward from university in Nigeria to the UK, where he earned his Ph.D. with the support of a commonwealth scholarship. Olukoya returned to Nigeria and worked as a geneticist with the Nigerian Institute of Medical Research. God's call for him to start a church had, by now, become strong in his life. More importantly, the prayers of warfare that got him through that traumatic period in his formative years remained with him and sustained him through his academic journey. His recollection of the fire incident where his leg was burned, the pain of a broken limb, and the anxiety of facing a life-defining examination had all converged at a vulnerable stage of his life. They helped him control the time of his life by mapping his present circumstances and pointing a future path for him. Amid the physical and mental anguish in the hospital, he had had a dawning moment where the source of his problems was clarified for him through a revelation of what he stood to lose. The prayers he prayed about the situation not only bolstered his resolve to rise from his sickbed and defy the forces that had planted satanic seeds in his path; the efficacy of those prayers in helping him get through one defining phase to another also impressed upon him intensely. His biography and personal testimony of overcoming through launching apocalyptic devices against satanic gestations form the basis of the church he would later establish. An intensely prayer-focused ministry, the MFM church is a monument to this second-order thinking.

The MFM Church and (Neoliberal) Production of Prayer

Today, the MFM church is best known for discerning the operations of malignant supernatural forces and spectacularly praying for their violent annihilation in the name of Jesus, exercises in the apocalyptic cycles of destruction and renewal that have become a daily affair. Prayers are hauled around in their churches as apocalyptic devices that aim right at the heart of demonic confederacies and disestablish their growing reign in people's lives. They are best known for their "Die in the name of Jesus" prayers that vehemently call for violence on all denigrating forces. The MFM church takes quite seriously the "expectation, the belief, the realization that the invisible can manifest itself" and that such a quest is "a matter of accessing the underlying character—the so-called noumenal, the invisible realm—of events, circumstances and coincidences in the world."[48] From the experience of supernatural insight Olukoya had at a crucial phase of his life had now grown an international church ministry devoted to apocalypticism, turned to the affairs of revealing daily the various causes of misfortune and affliction.

When he established the church in 1989, he was several years behind pastors of other fast-growing megachurches and Pentecostal denominations, some of whom had already been operating for about a decade. However, his introduction of imprecatory forms of Pentecostal prayer and an obsessive focus on spiritual warfare cut through the rapidly growing marketplace of spirituality. His area of Pentecostal specialization was initially too provocative for his peers. For instance, imprecations in traditional societies are considered an inversion of language and are to be deployed in situations where one faces an injustice so grave that it overturns one's world. By inverting language, one can thus reinvert an inversion. It is an arithmetic of two negatives making a positive and is instinctively understood by those socialized in the culture.

However, in that same period of the late 1980s, the Pentecostal movement was also trying to fashion itself as a modern Christian formation by making a phenomenal break with practices that might associate the church with African "paganism" and traditional religious practices. When Olukoya arrived on the scene with a congregation that regularly invoked curses on enemies and occult forces through what has been called "machine gun" prayers—that is, the prayer forms that (re)animate the weapons of modern warfare with spiritual idioms such that the spiritual warrior is transfigured into an organic and sacralized killing machine—his peers balked at the lack of subtlety. They were initially uneasy with a religious imagination that dripped with blood and demanded the tearing of flesh of one's oppressors. Some even took care to distinguish their ministry from his.

Some discussions about spiritual warfare in Nigeria too easily assume that the MFM prayers that include imprecations, deliverance, and demonic encounters that are now popular in churches exist in African Pentecostalism as a holdover from some primal past. There is usually the insinuation that because Africans live in a cosmos where the supernatural is experienced daily, it was only natural that they always see an alternate reality. However, Olukoya insisted for years after he started his church that both fellow pastors and many Christians shunned him because they found his style of engaging the supernatural rather too brash. His niche of "violent prayers" was retrieving a practice of African spirituality that did not quite align with the vision of a modern Pentecostal identity. The few who invited him to their churches to minister to their congregation regretted it because, he said, there was so much pushback against his emphasis on demonic operations and the overly dramatic militant prayers that were considered unbecoming of a Pentecostal church. His peers found the prayers through which people commanded both the human and the supernatural forces that were working an evil agenda against them to "Die! and to "Die in the name of Jesus!" too shocking to even consider as prayers. Olukoya said in 1999 that, to maintain a good relationship with fellow pastors who were uneasy with his methods, he finally disengaged from other pastors or churches, never accepting invitations to preach anywhere else unless it was an interdenominational youth gathering.[49]

That his MFM prayers have today become a staple in many Nigerian churches—both at home and in the diaspora—to the point that people are intensely invested in uncovering what is not visible to the naked eye testifies to their resilience in the face of doctrinal opposition. On many prayer mountains, churches, convention grounds, and similarly consecrated spaces, millions of people sum up the forces denigrating their lives and command them to *Release my destiny by fire by force! Die! Die! Die in the name of Jesus.* It is not unusual to hear thousands of people simultaneously echoing, *All the forces calling my name from the cemetery, fall down and die in Jesus' name! All the evil from my village, from my father's house, from my mother's house, stopping my progress in life, burn to ashes in the name of Jesus! Let any evil monitoring mirror ever used against me under any water, crash to irredeemable pieces, in the name of Jesus.*[50] *Any power calling for my head before evil mirrors, die with the mirror, in the name of Jesus.*[51] *Every evil monitoring gadget, remote control device and every witchcraft coven assigned against my life and destiny, be destroyed by the Holy Ghost fire, in the name of Jesus. . . . Every spiritual screen and radar, spiritual mirror, spiritual tape, spiritual camera, spiritual satellite and all spiritual properties that Satan has set to monitor me, break into pieces, in the name of Jesus.*[52] These prayers reveal the malevolence sown into personal lives through familial connections and social relations, which they abort as soon as they are discerned. Olukoya insists on the validity of this form of prayer, saying

> Demons are real everywhere. . . . You go to church, you hear people confessing to all levels of things. . . . When you receive the miracle of open eyes, you see too many things. I think there is a reason God in his wisdom does not open too many eyes. If some people's eyes should open and see what is going on, they will be petrified. The spiritual eyes are as real as the physical. Those of us who have eyes to see, we don't talk about what we see. We just pray. There is nothing you can do that will make me tell you the extent of things that I see. Sometimes they come in revelations, dreams, or even when I am not sleeping. Sometimes, when you get to a particular level of spiritual warfare, you will be confronted physically. There are many strange things. If I tell you the many strange things that I have seen, you many get scared or find me very strange. You may even find them unbelievable, but they are true.[53]

Despite fellow Pentecostals' initial rejection of his fire-and-destruction style, he still found an audience to which his signature style of discernment and prayers appealed. During the 1980s and 1990s, when he was setting up his church, Nigeria had begun one of the most unstable periods in its recent history. The country was run by a despotic military government, and daily life consisted of the abuse of people's bodies and denigration of their humanity. As the country descended into economic chaos and physical brutality, and social life stagnated such that people could not move through the phases of life as they had been socially calibrated, the plausibility of demonic forces planting satanic seeds into the materials of history scaled up even more. People did not just want to go to church to pray "many many many many hours of prayer" against their situations; they also wanted guiding revelations that would enable them to pray the prayers that would hit right at the malevolent forces that were impeding the mobility of their personal histories.

The MFM church, with its doctrinal devotion to giving shape to the spectral characters that lurk and surveil one's life to incubate negative traits, became a crucial site of performing these rituals of prayer itself as a form of apocalypticism, to see what opposes spiritual warriors' growth and abort it. People wanted to see those supernatural forces, to visualize all those monstrosities invading their material world, and to account for how and why the spectral forces intervening in human affairs were shaping the time of their lives. By seeking the hand of God within the hands of history, they also divined the apotheosized human actions shaping the forces of their modern life, something that enhances their perception of conspiracies (and that is examined further in chapter 3).[54] Those prayers give discernible shape to their experiences, help them locate themselves in time and space, and muster the hope of overcoming the social atrophy that bedevils the social and physical environment. As Nigerian society descended into both ethical and financial corruption under the despotic rule of various leaders, people sought a supernatural reprieve from the intuitively apprehensible forms of violence that riddled society. They concluded that their prospects of social progress—and the refurbishment of their moral universe that would precede it—would not happen at the mere superficial level of civic confrontation. They sought a higher level of power that transcended politics to ultimately transform the political.

Given the large number of people who started asking to take home the prayers they prayed in church for further prayer activity and to share with others, Olukoya's wife, Sade, started hand-copying the prayer points and handing them to their congregants. Olukoya told me that when the demand for the prayers rose and it became too much of a burden for Sade to keep sharing by hand, they decided to type them out on a computer at a commercial center and print them out for their congregation members. The first two places they took their prayer materials to be typed, the computers broke down as soon as the typist-operators started working on them. The Olukoyas attributed this development to the dangerousness of the prayers. Once again, the surveilling spectral characters had seen the potential of the prayer literature if it was circulated, and they had tried to thwart it at its inception. He told me that they thus decided to buy a personal computer for themselves instead of taking their work to cybercafés, the business centers that rendered such services. By then, the age of the personal computer had commenced in Nigeria too, and they could procure one to manage the spiritual odds of producing dangerous deliverance prayers.

Later, when they decided to expand their operations and print their prayer literature on a mass scale, the machine at the first printing press to which they took the materials also broke down shortly after they had accepted the church's commission. Again, not ones to take such an incident as mere accident, they once again determined that surveilling specters had seen the threat those materials portended for the world and were threatened. The mechanical breakdown was part of the devil's means of terminating the project's progress. Once again, they aborted the demonic machinations against their project by raising funds to start their own printing press. Having now developed their own machines to produce their prayer literature, they totally dislodged the agenda of the malevolent spirit forces by producing such an abundance of those prayer materials that their production line almost never stops moving. Their prayer literature anticipates the work of the devil in multiple ways and prescribes measures to manage it. That moment in his early life amid the agony of visceral pain when Olukoya's eyes opened to see the source of his affliction thus gradually led to an enterprise that would change the social culture in profound ways.

They would go on to create a publishing house, the Battle Cry Christian Ministries, to massively print and circulate their prayer literature at an inexpensive rate. The materials are typically written in language accessible to virtually anyone regardless of their level of education, theological sophistication, or even social class. Olukoya has—at last count at least—about 650 books that reveal the names and operations of demonic agents and prescribe the rituals of prayer helpful in controlling them. These materials, always in a high demand, are mostly printed by their in-house press unless the orders become overwhelming and have to be contracted out.[55] According to one of the bookstore managers in their Lagos headquarters, each of Olukoya's classics, such as *The Prayer Rain*, *Prayer Passport to Crush Oppression*, *The Prayer of Jehu*, and *101 Weapons of Spiritual Warfare*, could sell thousands of copies across their chain of stores in a single day. Also, because they have bookshops in almost every branch of their church in Nigeria and abroad, and at various airports around the country, they can meet the demand in many places at the same time.[56]

Another reason their products are ubiquitous is their distinct policy of individually training people for spiritual warfare. They state their church policy and ministry objective as "a do-it-yourself gospel ministry, where your hands are trained to wage war and your fingers to do battle."[57] It is a practical form of theology that effectively trims down church bureaucracies by dispensing with some of the middlemen—pastors, that is—within their hierarchical structures. Rather than maintaining a vast consortium of pastors that can carry out the rituals of deliverance of thousands of congregants who need them, they thought they could use those books to teach them self-management and self-deliverance within their church (and even across denominations). If spiritual warriors could buy the prayer literature materials and exorcise demons with the violent prayers in their own private spaces, they could be "aggressive Christians," yet independent of larger church bureaucratic structures.[58] Spiritual warriors who also want to deliver their own selves from satanic pregnancies gestating in their lives are repeatedly enjoined to maintain an ethic of holiness to distinguish their bodies from those of the others in the world that regularly accumulate spiritual debris.[59] This encouragement toward taking up spiritual self-enhancement to overcome social problems is one of the reasons spiritual warriors are susceptible to the forces of neoliberalism.

As much as these apocalyptic devices of prayer have been construed as a site of resistance to forces building up against spiritual warriors' arc of destiny, and the prayer literature helps the spiritual warrior disestablish them, still, the affective economies of hope amid pain, the pleasures of creative destruction, and the daily cycles of decay and renewal intertwined with the performances of these prayers inscribe neoliberal ideas into the fabric of social life and the expressions of spirituality. Though prayer is an apocalyptic device that promises to empower the spiritual warrior—and the MFM specifically states their mission in their church's self-description as training people's hands to wage war—to battle against the metaphoric hand that capriciously shapes human history, the capitalist processes supply the apocalyptic devices of these prayers in such abundant excess that it paradoxically heightens their awareness of demonic specters. The more people buy the materials, the more demonic operations in their life are discovered and the more there are materials to be bought. One of my interviewees in Lagos told me that buying as much of the prayer literature as possible is essential to her because "one should pray before one *has to* pray." This idea of social insecurity and a fear of an even worse disaster looming amid an ongoing war keeps the machines that print these apocalyptic devices running. Several pastors, particularly those I interviewed for this chapter (some of whom I shall talk about in the next section), also conceive their production of prayer literature along the lines Olukoya established—prayer as apocalyptic devices—and which are massively supplied to help people pray to avert a disaster so they would not need to pray after an evil has landed on them.

Some of the book buyers I interviewed while doing fieldwork for this book said they buy the books regularly because "they want an answer to life questions." That line of expression, finding "answers to life's questions," was repeated to me in several interviews at some of the bookshops where people were walking in and out to buy the prayer literature. In conveying their motivation to procure these materials, they expressed their desire to understand life beyond superficial manifestations. When I asked one of my respondents what she thought those life's questions were, she said,

> Look, these things are real. They are reality. Even though we do not see them, they are true. There are demons and supernatural powers that need to be fought. You need to pull down the strongholds of these demonic powers, but you cannot do that with carnal weapons. If you have a dream where you are in a pit or where you died and someone is covering you up with sand, do you know

what it means? Some of these dreams even manifest immediately [when] you wake up. If you live to tell someone the dream, they will at least know what happened to you. You quickly buy all these books to pray to God that you don't want these things in your life anymore. You cancel it. You destroy it. You stop it from manifesting. These things are real. Those who think they are not are just trying to run away from the reality of life.[60]

The average purchaser of prayer literature wants life's questions answered and thus the prayers are devised to penetrate space and time, accessing transcendental realms where the power to disestablish the unseen forces that want to control the daily enactment of their personal histories is available. This epistemological expedition necessitates transcendence and also explains their "concern with the domain of the miraculous, the quest for the unobstructed access to divine grace as a source of power, the notion that the self arises from the interaction between a system of the invisible and the world of the empirical, and the attribution of causality to forces beyond the material phenomenal realm."[61] To know what knows them is to be able to control it, to abort the evils it portends while it is yet gestating.

Controlling time and its auspices is not an abstract affair; the idea of time as filled with malice that should be canceled is worked into clocks and calendars too. For instance, when the MFM church has its annual seventy-day fasting and prayer program between October and December as part of the preparation for the coming year, they produce a manual for use in that period, *70 Days Prayer and Fasting Program*. This book, usually procured by many of their thousands of members, could sell as many as 100,000 copies from their outlets across multiple locations.[62] A new edition of this prayer manual is commissioned annually rather than reissuing old versions. For instance, the 2015 edition was described as "Prayers that bring unparalleled favour." For 2016, it was "Prayers that bring dominion favour and divine acceleration." The following years were "Prayers that bring indisputable victory and uncommon deliverance," "Prayers that bring extraordinary turnaround and rejoicing," and in 2019, "Prayers that bring supernatural ease and double honor." These yearly fasting and prayer programs, and the production of prayers for the exercise, index how they process time as regulation of the seeds of good and evil that could potentially germinate.

They also do not just disestablish the malevolent forces against them through abortions of satanic pregnancies; they also implant more auspicious seeds in their path toward the new year. In the seventy calendar days that they fast and pray for a better year ahead, they move through social phases by disengaging with the now familiar routine they have experienced for the first nine months of the year to be introduced to visions of the new and better year ahead through the power of prayers. These prayers as apocalyptic devices help them move through the phases of time in their lives. Each new edition of the prayer book contains answers to the existential questions they anticipate the incoming year will pose, and the rituals of prayer they will use to inhabit that future after it has arrived. Similar to the modern consumerist world where cars and glossy fashion magazines are produced in a year and projected toward preparing society for another year/season, prayer literature also supplies the spiritual ethos that generates expectations of what lies ahead and bridges the time toward getting to its favorable moments. Over time, people come to "see" the truth of what underlies the transcendent reality that determines material reality and the means of controlling it. As one of my interviewees concluded, "This is not fiction. It is all about life. Everybody wants to enjoy life. Everybody wants to live well. Everybody wants to live in peace. We want to be who God wants us to be, but we know the enemy does not want that. What pastor is doing is to help people to live their best life here before they get to the next one."[63]

Another of the unique innovations of the MFM church in controlling time has been to build a prayer city in Magboro, Ogun state, where prayers go on twenty-four hours a day, seven days a week.[64] Like several other megachurches in Nigeria, the prayer city occupies an expansive stretch of land on the Lagos–Ibadan expressway.[65] The 24/7 ceaseless prayer activity that takes place there is sustained by three daily shifts taken up by church ministers who have completed some level of training in the church Bible school, and who must gather to keep the prayer chain unbroken by committing to two shifts of prayers on alternate days.[66] Over time, such abundant supplies of prayer without an interlude creates an atmosphere where people are constantly embattled and also where prayer is the norm.[67] The apocalypse in pre-Christian Africa was "a continuing process of daily fire" in the body that was intensified in significance by "great existential pressures,"[68] but was contained by custodians of tradition. In modern times, and through the works of religious leaders like Olukoya, it became a product that generates a daily raging inferno.

This unrelenting production of prayer that cycles through destruction and renewal also shows how even private rituals like prayers have to respond to life in a modern society where services are produced around the clock—such as twenty-four-hour news cycles, telematics, and the modern work economy—thus eliminating traditional distinctions between night and day.[69] The prayer city is never bereft of prayers as teams of intercessors gather to pray, uncover the darkness that rests on the land, and abort all satanic pregnancies still in gestation.[70] With different and varied programs calibrated on calendars and clocks such as these, they maximize every single day and make time's spawning of social reality to accommodate their endless and recurring expectations of a new and meaningful beginning.[71] With unceasing prayers mandated, prayer activities become a never-ending event, repeated cycles of binding, loosing, destroying, and casting out, such that people's sense of urgency toward solutions for life's unending questions get more urgent. They keep manipulating the time they feel is against them as they try to move between social phases and insist this alternative reality is no mere fabrication.

"This Is Not Fiction": Seeing beyond the Pale

Critics of Olukoya are generally amused by the fantastical worlds that he portrays—one where specters and fantastic creatures interact with humans, and humans transmute into animals, trees, and hydra-headed beasts. Beasts turn into humans, showing the mutability of evil agents. If those who live in hyper-modern societies think they escape surveillance by these forces, Olukoya shows them through the stories in the book that evil can embed itself anywhere, such as snakes mysteriously appearing in high-rise buildings in hyper-urban societies to torment their victims, or familiar spirits in Africa pursuing an immigrant in North America. Animals attack people in their sleep. Witches and occult figures meet inside refrigerators that also house commercial goods. People's bodies are penetrated by spirit beings that either have sex with them or stroll through their reproductive or digestive organs. Neighbors, kin, acquaintances, and the fellows who walk the streets every day are all ordinary humans until the Lord opens spiritual warriors' eyes to see that they are embodiments of malignant spirits. Sculptures and artifacts that are inhabited by ancient demons and vindictive spirits stroll the earth, seeking whom to devour.

Across time and space, people are remote-controlled by ancestral spirits from shrines that might appear dormant but are spiritually potent enough to connect their descendants anywhere in the world and impede their social progress. The evil undead traverse the earth, seeking people who are vulnerable because they are spiritually cold and morally lax. Mermaids and "marine spirits" take the form of beautiful women, walk the dry earth, have sex with unsuspecting men, and rob them of their destinies. These omnipresent evil forces call out the names of their victims from their abode in cemeteries until their victims are tormented into madness. There is a lot of darkness and disorder, uncontrolled border crossings by forces seeking to establish themselves in one's space and that must be apprehended and disestablished before they fully gestate. In this colorful world, neither history nor happenstance is without spiritual causality. The prayers as apocalyptic devices are protocols for controlling a coextensive spectral reality.

Despite the range of topics across his many books and messages, a universal theme in MFM prayer literature is the hyper-exposure of the body—whether an individual or the social body—to malicious spiritual forces that undermine divinely ordained potential. These unseen forces are resilient, reinvented to confront African problems as they emerge.[72] From the titles of the books to the cover graphics that promise battles, bloodshed, and victory, there is an aesthetic of excess (and this also accounts for the raucousness of MFM prayers spoken at the top of congregants' voices and in most dramatic forms).[73] Some of his books have been translated into French, because, according to some of the bookstore managers, his works are popular in the francophone countries along the West African coast where people want to pray these dangerous prayers too but do not have a prophet of Olukoya's caliber to propagate a similar vision.[74]

Their prayer literature has also been translated into Yoruba and some other local Nigerian languages.[75] According to an interviewee who buys the Yoruba books even though she understands English, the "prayers are sweeter in Yoruba."[76] Another person remarked, "When you pray these prayers in Yoruba [rather than English], even the earth listens."[77] Such prayers, having been retrieved and fashioned from the African oral mythical narratives, have a deep sonic echo that intuitively percolates through to the cultural imaginary where these stories are woven. Now endowed with the legitimacies of Pentecostal modernism, those prayers provide an "authentic" framework for narrating their histories through prayers, a resonance that compels even the ears of the earth to open. That an animated earth listens to prayers because they are rendered in indigenous languages shows how the histories and affects that have been inscribed into the matrices of culture and topology are evoked in the articulations. By getting the earth to listen, spiritual warriors collapse space and time—bringing their cultural past to the present moment for the reformation of the future. Performing the prayers cannot but be "sweet" because the cathartic pleasures derived from these spiritual rites connect to the ethical foundations of society and heighten their awareness of the sublime and the unseen. In Nigeria and other African countries where they do not speak Yoruba, the sweetness of these prayers would be their resonance with the local belief system in the supernatural. From the rural town in Ondo state where Olukoya had his eyes opened to see the forces working against his social progress, prayer—and its literature as merchandise—has disseminated around many countries.

Globally Reaching Technology and Merch of Apocalyptic Devices

The fluid nature of the global economy and the affordances of technology have further allowed the literature of prayer to penetrate beyond provincial borders and potentially reach the world. The "spirits" of globalization, modernity, and capitalism also enable the movement of the Holy Spirit and demonic forces across the globe. Such interactions with the unseen also help ground Pentecostalism transnationally, a practice whose belief systems generate the visions that transform life.[78] This section explores other means by which producers of prayer literature like Olukoya and some other evangelists also take advantage of one of the routes that open us up to opportunities of shopping globally: Amazon.com.

While someone like Olukoya represents an established Pentecostal denomination, many other authors of prayer literature enter these markets on an informal basis. Not necessarily attached to formal church institutions, evangelists take the online market as a mission field that they enter to transact autonomous prayers as apocalyptic devices divested of a specific culture to transact as universal Christian agents.[79] The format of the online marketplace and the ways it now accelerates contact allow for this individualism of creativity and charisma to not just expand one's range of choices, but to do so across time and space. Again, while it is impossible to say whether Paula White ever read Olukoya's book, its availability in a global online marketplace makes this quite feasible.

The "serendipity" of preconfigured algorithms not only helps one find certain products but other analogous ones as well. Through this sleight of hand, I found some other evangelists whose specialty was also spiritual warfare while I was researching Olukoya's books on Amazon.com. The section of the website devoted to Dr. Olukoya's works has his profile as well. I was told that if I clicked on the "Follow" button, like all authors on Amazon, they would give me "new release updates and improved recommendations."[80] On the same page popped up the typical marketing mechanism that shows similar products one could consider buying—"Customers also bought items by . . ."—and gave me the profiles of the other evangelists—Prayer Madueke, Daniel Okpara, and Tella Olayeri—that I also surveyed for this work. Each of them specializes in spiritual warfare, and they prodigiously produce prayer literature as well. I had never met them before Amazon's introduction. I followed these three evangelists through several choices Amazon offered, either because their books had more customer reviews or because they had catchy titles. Then I sought out each evangelist on social media, where I found that they were building a clique of social media followers who had found them by following the same Amazon.com route that led me to their websites. From that point, I sent each of the evangelists a message requesting an interview, and they promptly responded.

While each evangelist has a distinct ministry, their stories intersected with that of Olukoya of MFM one way or another, showing his wide influence. They had either worked as his former pastors and he had helped them launch their book ministries, or they had been members of his mentoring ministry called the Goshen Club, or they had simply been influenced by his ministry. These evangelists' books on Amazon.com, mostly electronic copies, are "cheaply" produced in the sense of their aesthetic sophistication. Two of them mentioned that they use family labor to type, edit, and upload the books. They select images online that they use as cover designs. This modest approach to packaging keeps the cost of most of the books relatively low. They claimed patronage from various countries, especially from North America and the United Kingdom. With such an expanding circle of people invested in apocalyptic devices, they frame the books' contents as appealing cross-culturally.[81] They sell to people from different countries, but their largest customer base is in the United States, the UK, and Canada. These ministers say they are contacted by people from these countries who buy their books and seek spiritual counseling afterward. In some instances, some of them established WhatsApp prayer groups to cater to this budding audience.

One of the customers who bought Okpara's *Psalm 91* from the United States noted in their review of the book on Amazon.com,

> I love this book. After having read a book about Psalm 91, I know that it only works if you actually dwell in the shelter of the Most High. As a busy person (like everyone else!), I don't always have control over my schedule and what happens during the day. I know that my relationship with God is my highest priority, but I may not always have time to silently "sit and wait for the small still voice." This book is a huge reality check for the average person trying to love their lives to glorify God. We are all in this world, but we don't have to be of it. *It's a short easy read without a lot of theology that can sometimes get in the way of getting closer to the Lord.*[82]

This observation is similar to that of an interviewee in the church bookstore at their headquarters in Lagos, Nigeria, who had said to me, "One of the things I really like about Dr. Olukoya's books is that they don't waste your time. You see the problem on one page, and you also see the prayers that you will use to solve them. You don't have to read a lot of things," speaking to the urgency of prayers as apocalyptic devices.[83] Another said of the same book in their review, "This is a book I recommend to all to read. It gives clear concise truths for Psalm 91. It's not a difficult nor preachy read. I love Psalm 91. First book I've read completely in a long time."[84] Even though the reviewers are from different places, bought books by two different ministers, spoke at different times and even through different means, they still remarkably shared similar ideas of engaging prayers as apocalyptic devices in a lesser amount of time.

For people who live in cultures where time seems to speed through the endless phases of transition occasioned by modernity and capitalism, time is a precious resource that cannot be spared to endlessly indulge in pondering one's perplexities. There is simply no time. The end point of their engagement with these apocalyptic devices is getting to the phase of social renewal after the apocalypse and doing so as quickly as possible. We live in a world of speed, where the accelerations of modernity are matched by the desire to transcend social phases with immediate effects—*now now! right now! today today!* Living in a world where science can slow down aging while being inundated with "express" services, "instant" products, and an endless spate of "breaking news" makes life feel like a time warp. There is such a perplexity of existence in modern times, when the past is still being digested, the present has not been fully lived, and yet the future already beckons. Hurried and harried thus, we are stampeded into a future that does not quite feel ready for habitation. Pre-packaged prayers sold in online marketplaces help match the dizzying speed of living in a world with all of these "future shocks."[85]

Time can be traumatic for people living through accelerated modernity, particularly those awaiting the "fulfilling [of] God's plan and *hastening* of this fulfilment" are constantly under the pressure of no time.[86] Wariboko pointed out in his conceptualization of Pentecostal time that "the peculiar encounter of economic dynamics and religious consciousness has on the one hand stretched time and on the other intensely condensed it."[87] He noted that the failures of African countries to achieve economic and social development decades after decolonization has made the passage of time seem like an endless stretch of wasteland. What Pentecostalism has done and what has impacted the sociopolitical consciousness is to deliver the opposite of this infinite extension of time—that is, "the experience of extreme condensation, concentration of time."[88] Now, Africans live in what he calls a "time gap"—the space "between the endless time of the corrupt political leaders and the condensed time of the thaumaturgical preachers."[89] Part of the genius of Olukoya and others has been to cater to that sense of "no time" inscribed in spiritual warriors' sociopolitical consciousness and to use easy-to-consume prayers as a template. Prayers as apocalyptic devices are treated as the means to urgently diagnose complex sociopolitical and socioeconomic problems. For people who want the time to the phase of realizing their destinies shortened, there is an assembly line of spiritual materials and prayer literature that fine-tunes one's sensibilities to intuit how the sociopolitical system is presently functioning and whether its outcomes guarantee their survival.

Beyond the superstition of the demonic specters are the navigational tools that chart how the sociopolitical system rests on their flesh, the way they experience it, and how they are stimulated to confront it through prayer. The desired emancipation culminates in the act of prayer. Prayer is critical to the agenda of restoration because, as Olukoya states repeatedly, everything a Christian can do, the devil can do also. The devil can preach, read the Bible, sing, and even evangelize. The only thing the devil cannot do is pray because prayer is a unique weapon of the Christian, and they must therefore innovatively devise it to abort satanic pregnancies. To some extent, this urgent redemption of time McDonaldizes prayer to make it even more efficient. Efficiency registers how the prayers race from diagnosing cosmic disaster and social disorder, to abruptly prescribing prayer solutions that will disestablish those forces in a matter of pages (and sometimes even mere sentences). There is no time for an extended reading to deliberate on one's afflictions, and so prayer literature goes straight to the point of the redemptive prayers. People just want to do battle with prayers to disestablish the forces they hold responsible for their condition, and they want to be trained for it ASAP because time is always running, and also running out, on them. Such temporal panic means constantly seeking to abridge the time to get ahead. They weave the word of God together with prayer within the moment to guarantee a future.[90]

While Olukoya might have been an outcast at the beginning of his pastoral career, his methods have now spread, thanks to various media channels and a wide congregation.[91] Many Nigerian churches, including some of the mainline ones, now pray the MFM prayers. Even the renowned pastors of the Pentecostal denominations who have typically maintained a "genteel" and "classy" outlook now pray those "violent" and supposedly "crude" prayers. "Even me," Olukoya says. "I now get frightened when I hear some of the prayers that they raise in churches these days. Everybody is now praying the MFM kind of prayers. Once upon a time, we were shunned. They said we were uncivilized, but they have started to understand that the battle is not against humans or flesh. It is against spiritual wickedness in high places. They are beginning to understand." This shift in the Pentecostal zeitgeist makes Olukoya feel justified, that he was right about his assertions against operational demonic forces all along. His church practices of a fixation with demonic encounters that Paul Gifford once described as a Pentecostal Christianity "pushed to its limits" has become the proverbial stone that builders rejected but that is now integral to the design of the house.[92] To borrow the words of literary critic Michael Warner when he described how a discourse finds its public, Olukoya had run the ideas of apocalyptic devices up a flagpole, and millions of people—eyes wide open—are now saluting it.[93]

"Redeeming the Time, for the Days Are Evil" (Ephesians 5:16)

In 2016, Reuben Abati, an aide to former Nigerian president Goodluck Jonathan, wrote a newspaper article in which he documented some of the challenges he and his colleagues faced while working for the president.[94] Abati concluded that given all they encountered while in office, some malicious spirits had truly infested the presidential residence, Aso Rock. This demonic infiltration, he concluded, accounted for a series of tragedies that happened to past presidents—for instance, the deaths of either the president or their spouse—and it was by God's grace they survived their time in the presidency without a major disaster befalling them. In a rejoinder to the article, the sitting aide, who had succeeded Abati, Femi Adesina, debunked the story of demonic occupation of the presidential villa, but he did not stop there. Adesina went on to note that evil was truly resident in the world, and it was not singularly domiciled in the presidential villa. He also said,

There was this young Christian who gave scant regards to demons and what they could do. In fact, he almost didn't believe demons existed. One day, as he walked along the ever busy Broad Street in Lagos, God opened his spiritual eyes. Some people were walking on their heads! And not only that, as they passed by other people, they slapped them with the soles of their feet. If you got so slapped, you developed an affliction, which you would nurse for the rest of your life. Yet, you never knew where it came from. As the young man saw that vision and got its spiritual explanation, he began to s-c-r-e-a-m.[95]

The story Adesina narrated about this vision is an example of how the notion of apocalypticism works in spiritual warfare: the collapse of time and space to produce a moment of astounding revelation. In Adesina's telling, this revelatory moment occurred in broad daylight, and in a busy commercial district of a densely populated urban place like Lagos. The expectations of what could be and *what else is out there* but is not immediately visible underscore an aspect of the spiritual warrior's mindset.

There is, of course, a general belief in the fluidity of worlds and the interaction of both human and nonhuman agents in daily life. This reality is shut off from the naked eye, but spiritual warriors can access this cosmological horizon through a privileged moment of revelation, such as what the "young Christian" in the story experienced. While this other world is not visible, spiritual warriors have a preeminent belief in its existence and proximity. This phantasmagoric world parallels the natural, and from Adesina's narration, some people have had privileged moments when their eyes have been suddenly opened to see into this other realm. For spiritual warriors, revelation is especially crucial because it marks phases in a spiritual warrior's progression from a young Christian to one who becomes quickly matured by having an apocalyptic insight into the order of reality that overshadows mundane life. Maturation is contingent on revelation and growing through the phases of life is a consequence of open eyes. The revelation stops time and allows the spiritual warrior to stand outside the order of social reality to clearly see the second order of reality. This belief that *there is more to this* drives spiritual warriors to relentlessly look beyond the obvious and the official reality and discern the deeper truths of existence. Apocalyptic devices of prayer offer a glimpse beyond the appearances of ordinary reality, and this enlightenment empowers them to abort its negative constituents. Spiritual warriors who turn to the prayer literature that Olukoya and others produce to explain the benightedness of the world thus expand their knowledge base, imagination, and spiritual techniques so they can manage moments where transcendent reality spectacularly reveals itself.

The unending human fascination with seeing an end to a subsisting (and debauched) order giving way to a renewed future finds an outlet in the uses of these apocalyptic devices of prayers that spiritual warriors effusively rain down all the time. As noted at the beginning of this chapter, the apocalyptic here appropriates the biblical metaphors of revelation and the popular literature's tropes of finitude to an order of existence to underscore the disestablishment of the forces that shape temporal experience. Attracted by the compelling promises of seeing beyond the obvious to understand the forces consuming the vitality of life, and to be able to creatively destroy an oppressive social order for a radically reformed one, spiritual warriors procure the prayer literature that purportedly explains the operations of unseen forces through visualizations of the mechanics of spiritual encounters. In this cycle of divining and discerning the second order of reality, spiritual warriors dwell in the timescape where the control of life, the movement from a sterile phase of life to a more buoyant one, happens through the abortion of satanic pregnancies.

In the next chapter, I look at the encounters with one's limitations that are confronted when transcendent reality opens up to a spiritual warrior. Pentecostals living in the condition of *We are at war, yet the War is coming* sharpen their discernment skills through a simultaneous rehearsal of their body, mind, and spirit. This competence is acquired through the various artifices of performance that are staged to generate certain meanings of transcendences, and they constantly rehearse to build the techniques through which they would confront the revelations of what subsists with the power they have generated. Such spiritual competence not only moves the figuration of the devil as the enemy from the remote or the abstract to the perceptible; it also trains the spiritual warrior to respond through active bodily engagement and conditioned behaviors that they continuously cultivate to discern, duel, and conquer these forces.

This perpetual sense of embattlement and revolt, and the apocalyptic devices of prayers that destroy and renew as people pray 24/7, diffuses into the social consciousness, such that notions of spiritual triumph justify whatever sociopolitical realignment is necessary to redeem secular history. The intensiveness of the activities involved, over time, curates an embodied sense of authority that entitles one to intervene to correct adversarial situations. By that, I mean spiritual warriors regularly improve their stock of competencies to the point that they are convinced that they are called—or chosen—to command and to control situations. Through prayers, they develop the identity of a protagonist, one who becomes God's angel of reshaping the time of history and begins to anticipate the imminent *War* where this status will be publicly affirmed. While such constant rehearsal of one's power and authority may give daily life an apocalyptic fervor, people also are caught in an endless loop of repeated rehearsals for a potentially big performance whose opening night gets endlessly deferred. In the cycle of expectations of the looming event of the grand apocalyptic moment, they train and hone their techniques through the different challenges presented daily to improvise and learn their authority.

2

Rehearsing Authority

• •

Spiritual Warriors as God's
Human Weapons

> *The reason so many of us are weak is*
> *because we are not armed. We are*
> *supposed to be the battle axes*
> *in the hand of God.*
> —Pastor Temitope B. Joshua

The pastor, preaching on spiritual warfare, pranced about on the altar space. The altar was set like a stage, with carpeted steps leading up to the dais, which was decorated with several colorful designs and inscriptions on faith and power. The pastor was in the nave, a wide span of space that also constituted a part of the altar and overlaid with red and green colored rugs that stopped just a few feet away from where the congregation sat. On them had been placed a glass pulpit and a simulation of a tree stump. The tree had what should have been its roots hewn off and seemed more like a stage prop. It stood on its flattened base on the altar with what looked clipped toes. On top of the stump, several vases of what looked like artificial flowers were balanced, thus simulating a tree that was in bloom. From the Bible in his hands, the pastor read out the verse of scripture that has become the grand statement on spiritual warfare prayer, the call for spiritual warriors to see the unseen, from Ephesians 6:12: "for we wrestle not against flesh and blood, but against principalities and powers, against the rulers of the darkness of this age." He then went on to talk about how a lot of Christians are currently weak because their prayer life is famished, and they have been disarmed of their warrior capabilities.

We are God's battle axes, the pastor reminded the church, and to demonstrate this charge, he stood still in front of the expansive congregation and stretched out his right arm with the Bible in front of him. He said, "This is God. This is axes [sic]." Then he made the sound of cutting down a tree, which boomed over the microphone. He paused. He seemed to have remembered the tree prop on the altar, so he turned and walked in its direction. He hit the Bible on the tree several times to mime the cutting of a tree, while using his mouth to provide the sound of a tree being hewed down ("Whoosh! Whoosh!"). When he was done with this practical demonstration of warfare, he resumed his teaching on spiritual warfare from the Bible. The mise-en-scène he set up might seem like a rather artificial manner of priming spiritual warriors for battles, but it helps them to perceive and apprehend what they are up against in the realm of the spirit. Through such a visual display with a prop and the live onstage action, spiritual warriors rehearse their skills as warriors being readied to wage battle against occult and adversarial forces through apocalyptic devices.

This chapter centers on the makings of spiritual warriors as powerful devices by looking at how they build their competencies both for the battles they face daily, and for the definitive *War* they expect to confront at some point. As apocalyptic devices, prayers are not independent of the spiritual warriors who deploy them to disestablish the operations of militating forces, but they are closely imbedded in their being. Spiritual warfare prayers are parts of the ritual processes that turn spiritual warriors into God's human weapons, deployed to carry out phenomenal mass destruction at battleground sites. In the sections ahead, I describe how spiritual warriors' prayer performances extract specific notions of a destructive God from the Bible, and then hack their psychic selves with the concepts in order to make them conform particularly to such an ideal image of God. The ideas of God that they draw from the Bible are usually His split body parts, and their self-engraftment with these parts is a fantasy of radical self-enhancement. The performance of this prayer indicates the desire to integrate God—the ultimate figure of infinite possibilities and transcendence whose power and authority escapes all accountability—into themselves.

Putting an actual tree prop in the sacred space of the altar to show that the Christian subject is God's battle axe, and demonstrating the cutting down of the tree by the hand of God, is part of an immersive process of training the minds of spiritual warriors before they launch into the intense prayer battles for which they are known. The point of the tree—a rather unobtrusive item on the altar until the moment came for the pastor to utilize it—was to galvanize and canalize their imaginative capabilities so as to make the understanding of themselves as human weapons or God's weaponized humans even more appreciable. Also, the pastor using his amplified voice to give the activity of tree cutting life through sound effects further gives a realistic texture to the spiritual contests through a visual and audio activation of the congregation's imaginative capacities. He shows the congregation that in targeting an enemy for destruction, the words spoken during the prayer are not the primary technique of warfare; the ability to candidly visualize antagonists is paramount. During the prayers, when "battle axe" is mentioned, what spiritual warriors recall is what the pastor staged on the altar rather an instrument whose uses in daily life are negligible. The tree and the pastor's act are thus part of a synesthetic process that mentally transports spiritual warriors themselves to the moment the pastor stood on the altar and then reenacts the scene in their minds. The tree-cutting is not merely for mimetic effect, but an illustration and means of rehearsing spiritual warriors' destructive ability taken directly from God. The power to disestablish an existing order, and then decree the inauguration of another one through the performative utterances of prayers, prophetic declarations, and testimonies is preceded by the ability to see—and subsequently know—beyond the ordinary.

Unlike traditional religious and orthodox teachings that take religious trainees through a drawn-out process of mastering a theology hallowed by years of discursive practices, spiritual warfare training takes place in a time of *no time* and must reflect the urgency of working with accelerated time. Spiritual warriors speed up training by going through an ethical self-rewiring—that is, the transubstantiation of the self from an ordinary human to a raging force and a weaponized human that will consume all the adversarial factors—and they achieve this effect through an engraftment of their selves with God's parts. They split God's mystique into smaller and more manageable components and haul the weaponized fragments in the direction of a situation that needs urgent resolution. Rather than an extensive or detailed learning about God and His enigmatic character, carving God up into fractions to quickly imbibe what each discrete part can accomplish saves time. It helps them incorporate the component parts into themselves so they are remade in the image and likeness of a militant God whose sovereign features of the destruction and subsequent renewal of social order they also have digested. They do not mimic divine actions; they hack themselves to become God's human weapons. By thus assuming the essence of the fragmented parts of His character, they express them in thoughts and behavior.

Designing such an imaginarium where spiritual warriors are primed with the visualization of a battle anticipates a time ahead when they will have to fight the *War*, the final showdown. This habitual expectation of a coming time when the battle actions they have witnessed and absorbed must be repeated is what Richard Schechner would have called the restoration of behavior. According to him, restored behaviors are the organized and ritualized actions and events that can be isolated from those that do them. That is, restored behaviors may be (re)enacted over time by different people. Such performances can thus be "stored, transmitted, manipulated, transformed. These performances get in touch with, recover, remember, or even invent these strips of behavior and then rebehave according to these strips."[1] The artifice of tree-cutting on the church altar as a practice of restoration of behavior to use prayers and bodies as the battle axes of God could also be taken as a practical necessity, given that the church is based in an urban center of cosmopolitan Lagos state, and members of his congregation might not easily relate to tree-cutting activities. The demonstration staged on the altar helps their minds perform the mimetics and the kinetics of prayer by giving them actions to relate to and which they could conjugate into symbolic violence while praying.[2] In this conception, future repetitions restore the meaning of the action by both deepening it and also archiving it for future use.

At the same time, as performance scholars Soyica Diggs Colbert, Douglas Jones, and Shane Vogel have shown, reenactment need not be merely repetitive or indicate the time/space between a past action that serves as a reference point and a present restaging of the same event. There could also be a more *careful* restoration of that which is lost between times. In place of restored behavior, they offer *behaved restoration* to shift the emphasis from the citational—and even linear—nature of the repetition in performances when done across time. The distance between what was enacted then and now, they show, is better highlighted through reiteration that also considers how the idea of time itself has been structured in Western history. Also, paying attention to racial histories, they show that emphasizing repetition in performance studies freezes minoritized groups in time and consequently consigns their actions between *then* and *now* into an asymptotic replay of the actions previously undertaken by dominant groups. This way of seeing the actions of cultural minorities from the prism of what has been done by dominant groups infantilizes them and prevents an appreciation of the dynamism of minorities' past actions that were suppressed or overlooked.[3]

These scholars' critique of repetitions of action by challenging the place pinpointed as the point of origination radically shifts the grounds by which restorations of social behavior are understood from that which *mimics* to that which *compensates* for past injustices. Similarly, restoration of behavior for spiritual warriors does not merely repeat actions they have witnessed (such as the symbolic act of tree cutting), nor does it merely try to achieve an isomorphism with a standard form stored in cultural memory, but instead works to steadily make spiritual warriors conform to the ideal character of God as a creative destroyer. Saying spiritual warriors are "God's battle axes" correlates them with the specific traits of God they are expected to express in their social lives. As such, their actions do not merely mimic divine actions to replicate them from time to time.

The symbolism with which spiritual warriors induce repetitions of behavior is not an iteration of a past action or compensation for what has been lost or denied through time, but is to engraft God's features into themselves, such that their social conduct is justifiably expressible as the true essence of His divine character and a consequence of their being God's human weapons.

By construing their actions as outcomes of their engraftments with God's split parts, their performances as spiritual warriors do not "fail" to measure up to an original; instead, the repetitions are rehearsals toward properly fitting God's split part into their psychic selves. Peggy Phelan noted that "the real inhabits the space that representation cannot reproduce—and in this failure theatre relies on repetition and mimesis to produce substitutes for the real. Behind the effects of the real is a desire to experience a first cause, an origin, an authentic beginning which can only fail because the desire is experienced and understood from and through repetition."[4] For spiritual warriors, the point of activities such as staging a tree-cutting is not to merely benchmark against a prior event but to animate the phantasmagorical imagination of the self as a human weapon and instigate the series of behaviors that confirm such status. In doing so, they also generate a vital content of their character as spiritual warriors and God's human weapons: moral authority. Moral authority, having the heft "to speak convincingly about what *ought to* be, as opposed to what is,"[5] needs such constant authentication through symbolic instrumentation, rehearsal, and the practice of truth-telling to establish their identity as spiritual warriors.

Engraftment as a process of simulating God's traits also speeds up spiritual warriors' training. As stated in the previous chapter, there is always a sense of urgency to spiritual warriors' prayers, because they consider time as running out on them. Engraftment is a process that bridges the time between the phases of life—from the *now* time to the *then* when the expected social renewal will come. Bringing that temporal phase even closer entails *urgently* disestablishing the conventions and habits that have accrued into oppressive establishment forces. The haste to move from a stage of social life that has lost vitality to another one that holds the promise of social flourishing intensifies spiritual warriors' feeling of being at war and impels the spiritual warriors to arm themselves through this intense performance of prayer.[6] The perplexities of living in an atmosphere of perennial embattlement necessitate prayers, but as apocalyptic devices, such prayers are not mere contemplative or ruminative solicitations of help from God. They are intense muscle work that takes some toll on the physical body because it simulates engraftment with God's body parts or aspects of his persona such as being his battle axe. The prayers are acutely gestural, and their expressions are not constrained by the ideas of social respectability, especially since spiritual warriors think of themselves as radical activists working against the norms that define social behavior. For instance, when people pray these prayers, they could fall on the ground, punch the air, scream, march like soldiers, raise their voices, swing parts of their bodies like weapons, stamp their feet, slap their own bodies furiously, and even drop part of their clothing. In one of churches I surveyed for this study, an administrator told me they take care to hold services that feature spiritual warfare prayers in spaces on a level ground because they have had situations where people got so carried away, they fell from the balcony. The architecture of the church is thus designed around the primary activities of prayers.

The performances of these intense prayers take place in the context of spiritual warriors' daily embattlement—a sense of bewilderment resulting from subsisting in a social context where the reigning ideologies mean having to struggle to express the truth of one's faith and the essence of one's humanity before a world that diminishes them. This constant struggle against the norm is seen as cosmic dualism, and spiritual warriors use these daily struggles to rehearse their ability to engage spectral forces. Generally, when a war breaks out, a society is driven to conscript its youths and hurriedly train them to fight in battle. In spiritual warfare, such youthfulness is not about the legerity of one's physical age but the agility that comes with both studying the Bible and the constant rehearsals of one's spiritual power through prayer rituals. The consistency builds anticipation and generates a repertoire of meanings that pervade social life. The experience of constant and daily rehearsals—the lack of finality or definitiveness and openness to conflicting possibilities, and continuous refinement of one's acts—makes for the proneness of their prayers to the creative chaos that generates meanings.[7]

Pastor Joshua's demonstration is also significant to understanding repeated behavior in the training of spiritual warriors because of how he cohered his physical body, the body of God, and the congregation members as he described the verse of the Bible that says, "You are my battle axe and weapons of war; for with you I will break nations into pieces, and with you I will destroy kingdoms."[8] In pointing out his right arm as a representation of God, the Bible in his hand as the battle axe (and which stood in for the warriors being trained in spiritual warfare techniques), he synesthetically reconciles several things, including the supernatural God, human bodies, and the text of the Bible that inspired the bridging of the human and the divine. This demonstration also illuminates the control and regulation of the body toward eudemonic ends through its oneness with the body of God. The technologies of self-discipline, cultivations of subjectivity, and expressions of agency derive from having been engrafted with God's body. In the next section, I will dwell critically on this technique of splitting God's body as a means of training the spiritual warrior.

Part of the uniqueness of spiritual warfare prayer is that people do not just talk to God, or even to vengeful demonic forces, as some studies of prayer and their audiences tend to reflect.[9] Their performances of prayer instead seek to imbibe and impersonate the militant features of God, particularly the vengeful, wrathful, and characteristically destructive aspects of His persona. When Joshua read out the part of the Bible that says his congregants are God's battle axe and proceeded to illustrate it to the congregation with a theatrical artifice, he strategically evoked the congregation's imagination of destruction and ethicized it with the vision of God doing the same. When he proceeded to act out what an axe swung at the stump of a tree does, he stirred their minds with an image that they will recall during their performances of prayer. This visual will transform them into God's weapons and animate them to rehearse destruction. As Dr. Daniel Olukoya of the Mountain of Fire and Miracles Ministries (MFM) noted,

> The battle axe is a weapon of warfare and deliverance. When the axe of God falls on the root of your bondage you will experience instantaneous deliverance. God has designed the battle axe for cutting off demonic trees that have been used to keep you under bondage. The battle axe is a fierce weapon. When you make use of the battle axe, enemies flee, evil powers bow. . . . The battle axe has been specially carved for serious battles. God has designed the battle axe for scattering rebellious spirits and hacking demonic agents who are bent on destroying your destiny. To deal with the eaters of flesh and drinkers of blood, you need God's battle axe.[10]

The goal of the spiritual warrior is therefore to become a human performer of savage destruction of one's enemies through prayers. Olukoya also notes, "There are prayers and there are prayers. There are prayers that if you start them, heaven will suspend all activities to answer you."[11] Through prayers, spiritual warriors rehearse their abilities to arrive at that calibrated point where their prayers are powerful enough to impel responses from heavenly forces, a point I examine in the third section. In her study of spiritual warfare among Native Americans, Elizabeth McAlister shows how training people for this form of engagement can even take the form of boot camps dedicated to both physical training and concurrent schooling in past history and interpretations of current reality.[12] In exploring spiritual warfare prayer among contemporary evangelical and Pentecostal subjects in the United States and Nigeria, Ruth Marshall critically explores the various activities of spiritual warfare such as prayers, prophecies, and testimonies.[13] She takes them up as polemical rhetoric, combative speech forms that are radicalizing, to show how their insurrectional content constructs the militant Christian.[14] As such, the dispositional truths of their faith that spiritual warriors imbibe become a psychic identity to be lived out in social life, something further examined in the fifth section of this chapter.

Though language is crucial to the devising of spiritual warfare prayers, I also show that engraftments work *with* and *beyond* words. Spiritual warriors truly harness the force of language, and for Nigerians who believe in *àṣẹ*, the power of words to invoke, evoke, and command things to manifest, utterances truly wield performative power.[15] Yet spiritual warriors also invest in the self as a phenomenon that can produce the similar force of *àṣẹ*. When they claim they are God's battle axe, the force of their conviction comes not only from utterances or their performative effects; it also reflects their combative persona. The confrontational attitude through which they challenge the forces they intend to disestablish is the result of performing prayers of spiritual warfare, because the resoluteness such prayer performances require fosters belligerence. The process of praying to rehearse their power and authority is concurrently self-transforming and self-legitimating, and the intensity of its rituals also allows the transcendence of natural limitations. By the time they have repeatedly gone through these performances of prayer, the subject comes to personify a truth conviction that is so totalizing that it does not yield to the nuances that might blunt its revolutionary ideal. In the coming sections, I also show how the process of engrafting the self with God gives a phenomenological substance to the spiritual warrior's apprehension of the self as an embodiment of God's truth. It drives the zeal with which they seek to impress it on both themselves and others, reiterating it until it becomes a potent means of self-recognition.

God's Body Parts and Human Transformations

For spiritual warriors, prayer is an elemental and fundamental ritual that works on the structures of relations, whether in the spiritual or the social realm.[16] A spiritual leader told me during a session that their activities are to "fight the evil spirits" who want to contest the authority they have been given in Christ when they became born again. Such a battle must be spiritual because social reality is determined in the spiritual realm. He further said, "We do not need to fight humans. God is a spirit. He created us as spirits with a soul in a body. For someone to win the battle of life, one needs to fight in the spirit. One needs to pray."[17] Prayer is thus the training for achieving victories by accessing powers beyond the ordinary. The activities leading up to that desired victory involve prayer, as well as developing the skill to reflexively discern threats and develop one's spiritual instincts to effectively repel them. They not only understand prayer as those ritual activities that occur when they are either in the church or on their knees in their private places. They also take what I call the "para-prayers" seriously. This consists of mundane utterances and social activities that hedge their performances of daily self and define moral character. These para-prayers could range from speaking prophetically or affirmatively about oneself to the selection of a name for oneself, one's child, or one's business enterprise.

By making these pronouncements publicly, one attracts the attention of countervailing forces who will attempt to thwart one's self-affirmation. The resulting contest will be the means by which the authority desired from prayer is tested, attested, and inscribed into everyday life. The activities involved shape the warrior identity, the one whose impulses have been trained toward a justifiable level of aggression and simulating indignation as they work toward refuting denigrating situations.

Joshua's representation of how Christians are God's battle axe also shows how the notion of God—the ultimate Warrior—and the ritual process of shaping the spiritual warrior identity work both psychologically and viscerally. By directing his congregation's imagination to think of God as his own human arm, he allows an imagination of God as an entity both divisible into parts and subsumable into the human subject to ground and intensify their capabilities. Rending God into component parts is a response to the practical challenge of the unknowability of God in His totality. Olukoya stated in a sermon on "The Weapon of the Finger of God," "there is no human brain that has the capacity of how powerful God is. The ones you and I can understand represents the limits of our knowledge. The way God operates is beyond the limits of what your understanding can tell you."[18]

To make the whole God a far more comprehensible entity for spiritual warriors to grasp, they split Him into discrete organs and functionalize each part of His body. By this notion of a "split God," I allude to Nimi Wariboko's concept of the practical theology of Pentecostals wherein they confront the highly daunting reality of God's existence by splitting Him into more manageable proportions. *The Split God* describes how "the art and act of splitting *deactivates* the traditional (inherited) notion of God and radicalizes it. By splitting, the inherited notion is not only separated from its orthodox grounding without abandoning orthodoxy, but also 'parts' and 'attributes' of God are separated from Godself and are recombined and exhibited in their separation from Godself, becoming 'spectacles.'"[19] For Wariboko, Pentecostals understand reality as incomplete. The God whose power they confront is equally immense and not fully knowable in the depths of His mysteriousness. Therefore, He must be broken into fragments that can be readily handled and weaponized against countervailing social circumstances. The notion of a split God, he posits, undercuts the systematized and coherently whole God that academics pronounced dead in the 1960s. This dead God reemerged in the 1980s among Pentecostals in the global public resurgence of religion. He did not appear whole, though. He had been radically split. Each piece was imbued with the myth of what it could achieve provided Pentecostals with resources confront the incomplete reality and thereby extend the chain of possibilities of what can be accomplished. The implication of such a conception of God is that He is "a combination of partial organs. These partial organs became means of jouissance and detachable tools to either attack one's enemies or to drive prosperity towards oneself."[20]

These partial organs could be God's hands, eyes, mouth, or any of His various phenomenal manifestations as fire, water, thunder, wind, light, and so on. It could be a mere finger, right or left hand, eyes, blood, breath or the blast of his nostrils, ears, feet, or even His footstool. What matters is that they deconstruct God with aspects of Him the Bible describes and engraft him into themselves.[21] The pieces that emerge achieve a "sacred surplus," an excess of potentialities that gives spiritual warriors even more resources to expand their universe of possibilities, thus making miracles seem ubiquitous.[22] It is not uncommon to hear Pentecostal spiritual warriors praying, saying in the first sentence that "I soak myself into the blood of Jesus" to shield themselves against unseen forces hurtling in their direction, and then, in the next sentence, demand that the hand of God descend from heaven to carry out an act of justice against an evil confederacy that is gathering. The more parts they can imaginatively divide God into, the better their armament against such forces. Their simulation of warfare does not necessarily demand knowing God as a whole; the aspects of Him that could be profaned—that is, opened to other uses while leaving its existing uses intact—are sufficient to be deployed on such dangerous spiritual missions.

The "arm/hand of God" is a crucial metonymization of the divine (counter) actions that can powerfully reshape a world in which forces prone to malice have established themselves. In popular discourses, "the hand of God" or "the hand of history" has been used to refer to providence determining the course of human affairs. Whether through the theories of economist Adam Smith or the famous goal scored by soccer legend Diego Maradona, or even British Prime Minister Tony Blair's remark about the "hand of history" on his shoulders, this divinized body part has highlighted the naturalized understandings of the role of providence, in economics, sports, politics, and social life.[23] For spiritual warriors, "the hand of God" is not merely augural, but a means of coordinated divine judgment that can either spectacularly punch opposing forces back into the earth or an intervention that picks up an embattled warrior from amid difficult situations. The spiritual warriors' idea of the "hand of God" is thus a counterpoint to the secular hand of history that can be so arbitrary that it exposes one to life's harsh vicissitudes. The Pentecostal conception of the hand of God involves control of capricious fate and a reworking of providence through the agency of the spiritual warrior engrafted with this body part of God, and whose ability to control this feature makes the operations of the hand determinedly serendipitous.

While Wariboko insists that this practice of ripping God apart and putting him back together is a function of the full incomprehensibility of God, I will argue that splitting God is also an imperative of living in an era of *no time*. There is both an ongoing war and an oncoming one, and there is no time to delve into the mystical character of God in all His details—to know God in His entirety and then to build a rounded theology of how He could work on their behalf. To abridge the amount of time necessary to understand God and the depth of His power, Pentecostals break Him into manageable pieces where He can work for them *Now now! Right now! Today today!* The process of splitting God helps to effectively replace engaged learning processes that would have covered long stretches of time with the techniques and strategies that apprehend what He can *quickly* do with his component parts. Then they seal this instrumentalization of His body with prayers.[24] As Wariboko himself described in *The Split God*, people make associative relations with language in everyday expression of theological behavior rather than logical ones. For instance, he cites the example of a prayer that says, "Holy Ghost sword, shear, shear, shear; I cut the bars of iron asunder." He notes that the person praying takes up an imaginary sword and begins to cut through the entrapment that s/he conjures in their prayer imagination as holding them down. The person even accompanies "shear" with a whistling sound of the sword blade as it imaginatively cuts through enemy defenses. Such physical demonstration by the spiritual warrior reiterating stored strips of action during prayer—helped along by dramatics staged on the altar (such as the symbolic tree-cutting)—allows them to blend the imagery of God and His destructive component parts with the perception of themselves becoming like Him even more *quickly*.

In an age where social life has been permanently altered by the supersonic speed with which things can be done, such rehearsals by engrafted spiritual warriors reflect speeded-up time. The social processes that would have taken forever to prepare, and whose instituting norms would have crept up on us gradually could happen in a matter of days or even hours, and prayers too have to be answered more swiftly. One relatable example of how spiritual warfare speeds up consequences for the believer who has been engrafted with God is illustrated in testimony shared by Apostle Johnson Suleman of the Omega Fire Ministries International (which attracted some controversy). In the testimony, Apostle Suleman had narrated how one of his "spiritual sons" wanted to go to France to preach the gospel as instructed by God but could not get on the plane because he was living in Germany without legal immigration documents. God told this person to go to the airport and join the queue of those about to travel to France. The person was worried about his immigration status, but nevertheless obeyed. While he was in the queue, God instructed him to go to the restroom. There, God asked him to pray. He closed his eyes and started praying in tongues. When he opened his eyes and walked out of the restroom and out of the airport, he found himself in France. After he had completed the mission, he asked God how he would get back home and God told him it would be the same way he got to France.[25]

While this story of teleportation looked like a scene out of D. O. Fagunwa or Amos Tutuola's fantasy novels or science fiction where characters can be magically teleported, what is reflected here is how the religious imagination is keeping up with the reality of a world where time and space can be folded and unfolded. The fact that the story took place in an airport, a place that functions as it does because of the wizardry of technology, is significant in itself. As James Bridle noted, an airport is a canonical example of what geographers call "code/space." Code/spaces describe the interweaving of computation with the built environment and daily experience to a very specific extent: rather than merely overlaying and augmenting them, computation becomes a crucial component of them, such that the environment and the experience of it actually ceases to function in the absence of code.[26] This "code" transforms the airport ethos, going from an ordinary place to a space made up through computing technology. The airport in the sermon represents a space where humans from all walks of life typically pass through to jump on the flying birds that will empty out elsewhere following certain rules and regulations.[27] Airports are liminal spaces, a zone where distinctions collapse, and time materializes space (and vice versa). They are also crossroads, places where—especially in African mythologies—all kinds of encounters become possible and that makes them a viable locale to situate the tale. Many roads—air and land—converge at the airport, and hence the place becomes a potent site for magic and the manifestation of the supernatural, a space where fantasy can take flight along with the metal birds soaring through the skies. While there are no details of how long the missionary prayed versus the time of travel of the other passengers in the queue waiting to enter the plane to travel to France, one can at least surmise that this story deliberately planted this missionary—who had neither a ticket nor valid identification papers at the airport—into the space from where he purportedly teleported so as to relativize his time of travel with that of the otherwise "legal" travelers. While those at the airport would, with the help of modern technology, travel in speeding machines flying through the air, God helped this preacher supersede their speed through fervent prayer. It is also instructive that the man was a missionary going to preach the gospel.[28] Unlike earlier centuries, when missionaries took forever to sail across the oceans to reach the people God wanted to convert to Christianity, this modern one beats space and time simply by entering an airport restroom and closing his eyes to pray. An undocumented immigrant, he finds a more efficient traveling portal than the ones modern technology has provided to shorten the time-space travel. The moral of this story is a demonstration of how God's engrafted subject can beat both natural laws and technology to abridge time and space.

This shortening of time is essential to spiritual warriors, who live their lives in a constant mode of expectation, the tussle between *what is* and *what ought to be* amid the larger context of an accelerated modernity and its appurtenances that surround us. Wariboko noted, "there is always the tension of being and becoming, the expected and the unexpected. Two models of spiritual orientation, two models of explanation, prediction, and control of history, life or social totalities appear to compete in the time gap, in the experience of time."[29] People caught in this time gap where the present seems interminably long and the future they desire seems out of reach seek the means and the possibility through which they can contract time. Those in whom God's traits have been engrafted fantasize themselves possessing the nimbleness to be teleported. Such stories are part of the spiritual techniques and strategies meant to imagine their bodies as capable of defying all gravitational reality, the belief that they could transform themselves into a bionic material that can transcend natural realities and every law of physics as the resurrected body of Christ also did.

The means and myths of self-transformation they devise rely on both narratives and theatrical contrivances that give them glimpses of how God's body behaves to absorb. Through the rituals of prayer, they rehearse their ability to act like God's component part would until it becomes part of their constitution. The hand of God, for instance, is imagined as able to reach into the battlefield of life and is either grasping, crushing, or incinerating through oppressive forces with its fingers. His hand stretches across space and time, and in their imagination, it could literally reach into the earth, into human thoughts, social situations, and realities to shield his children from the enemy's arrows, to rebuke their attackers, to intervene to extirpate evil, and even override human wit, will, and initiative. As Dr. Olukoya stated of this organ and its attributes,

> One of the most violent weapons which God has given to us for decisive victory and total deliverance is the weapon of the finger of God. The finger of God reveals God as the man of war. Whenever God comes into the scene of the battle He appears with his finger as a weapon of dealing decisively with the enemy. When God's finger becomes visible at the place of battle, the enemy will be defeated woefully . . . the finger of God is an unbeatable weapon. Every habitation of darkness in your life would be exposed when the finger of God sets your life on fire.[30]

God's hand is an organ of divine judgment, one that is well able to supersede all material forces with the force of its might, and that is who they want to become by engrafting God's parts in their psychic selves. Several Pentecostals have shared testimonies of how God's hand intervened in difficult situations in their life; they mention—especially if they had a vivid dream or a vision—its size in superlatives. They describe it as the Spirit of God or a divine presence that has come to interject itself in a confounding situation they were confronting. When such situations are resolved, they know by the spectacular manner that the intervention occurred that they were liberated by the hand of

God. When the pastors too preach about the extent of the hand of God, they talk about it as a form of power with limitless abilities and with ambiguous effects. One of the spiritual warriors told me that even though the hand of God can liberate a Christian, one has to be careful in one's social life because the same hand also punishes sin.

In closing this section, I note that the artifices that simulate the imagination of the spiritual warrior can take varied forms, but the goal is to enrich prayer with a lucidity that enables transformation. For instance, there is an ongoing church construction in Rivers state, Nigeria, called the Salvation Ministries Cathedral. A 90,000-seating capacity church, the architecture is a gigantic hand placed on the ground with the four fingers pointing out while the thumb is folded in under the palm. The builders describe it as "the hand of God," and the project boldly highlights the imagination of what God's hand reaching directly into the earth would look like. By shaping it out in concrete details, the architecture foreshadows how the people who will use the space will interact with(in) the completed building where they get to—literally—dwell in God's hand. Spiritual warfare training is thus a project of (self-)attunement and ethical qualification that happens through the incorporation of the spiritual warrior with God's partial organs—His arm, for instance—so they can become God's weapon on earth. As reconfigured human devices, they also legitimately see their transformed selves as central to the establishment of God's truth against all competing agendas. In the next section, I will focus more on another of God's constituent parts spiritual warriors frequently allude to transmuting when they pray to disestablish forces: fire.

"Our God Is a Consuming Fire"—Imagery, Sound, and Engraftment

In one of several Facebook prayer groups that I belong to, a consortium of spiritual warriors each hold forty-five- to sixty-minute prayer sessions. The Facebook groups, some of them having up to 400,000 members, are dedicated to all-day rains of prayer by e-congregants who replicate the unceasing prayer activity one might find in the prayer city (see chapter 1). These spiritual warriors—some are either evangelists or they pastor a budding church—come online at intervals to hold a prayer session throughout the day, all week, and all year round. One of the groups is dedicated to praying what they call "fire" or "hot" prayers. The number of participants that show up for each virtual service, which were well underway before the virtual prayer sessions during the COVID-19 pandemic discussed in chapter 4, could range from hundreds to thousands, depending on the time slot, the ability of the pastor or the evangelist to engage the audience with prayer points, and the perceived efficacy of their prayers. Each time I tune in to a prayer session, there is a pastor/evangelist on the screen of my digital device, seated and facing the camera directly. They hardly ever sermonize, though they might take a few minutes to sing worship songs before they start calling prayer points.

As the pastor/evangelists pray, their heads bobbing from side to side, a common gesture among Pentecostals, they get sweaty to the point that their clothes stick to their bodies. Still, they keep praying fervently. Some of the evangelists place large standing fans beside them. Sometimes their eyes are shut, and sometimes half open. Often, I get to follow the prayer sessions while multitasking with household chores. Many times, the person leading the prayer generates all the points of prayer, and occasionally they also take some that people supply through the comments page. Many of the prayers are about social transformation—to get a job, to be healed, to be victorious in one's career, to have a child or a family, to overcome the spirits within one's social and family circles blocking one's progress, and so on. For African Pentecostals, such demands are the staple contents of prayers because,

> Prayer is the pulse of the wound of existence. In existence, there is always a chasm between *what is* and *what is yet to be*, a gap between the past and the future amidst the unique specificity of the present. Prayer is humanity's consciousness of this chasm expressed as an address to God, a dialogue of humans with the divine . . . prayer is that mode and mood of engagement with God (or spiritual presences) that is calculated to initiate the new, usher in freedom, and promote human flourishing. African Pentecostal prayer—often in the form of spiritual warfare—is a way of discerning and critically reflecting, contesting, and resisting the play of powers in the ontological conditioning of being, the forces weighing down on current life, and the tensions that drag us towards death by excluding life enhancing support.[31]

Trying to bridge the time between the present and a radically reformed future requires hard work, and prayer is taken as a form of labor. With the intense embodied spiritual engagement modes through which the prayers are dramatized—and a general understanding of prayer as a formidable lethal weapon that can travel from the mouth of the spirit-filled believer—they cut through both visible and invisible worlds to land balls of fire straight at the enemy's heart.

With my earpiece plugged into my ears and the other end to my phone, I get to follow as many sessions of prayer as possible. When I finally get a free moment and sit in front of the screen as the pastor prays, one of the first places my eyes land is the virtual screen behind the person of God praying. On that screen is usually a projection of images such as a host of white angels in flaming garments surrounding a group of people praying on their knees. At other times, images of fireballs move around on the screen when the pastor's prayers get to the point where he prays, "Fire! Fire! Fire! I command the fire of God to come down! To destroy! To burn! . . . Fire! Fire! Fire!" Each time, the ambulant fireballs help me get back into the prayer mood after handling the distractions of my real world. There are times the fireballs have been distracting too. As the prayer goes on, and the voice of the pastor commands the fire of God to consume all countervailing situations, the pastor reminds us that God Himself is a consuming fire. I sometimes find myself hypnotized by the fireballs as they chase each other on the screen and circle and circle until, boom! they combust with an atomic bomb–like mushroom cloud. The screen, from that point on, goes dark and quiet until once again I hear the person leading the prayer command, "Fire! Fire! Fire!!!!" to come down and destroy all satanic forces.

The use of fire imagery on the screen is one of the ways these pastors and evangelists try to create an immersive experience of prayer so that a spiritual warrior's visual senses, easily prone to the many distractions of the social media lifeworld like Facebook, find their way back to the prayer session. With the animation of fireballs dancing on the screen, the eyes—whether only half or fully open like that of the person leading the prayer—take in the image and internalize it even as they chant "Fire! Fire! Fire!" during the endless sessions of prayers. Just like the tree-cutting on the altar, displaying virtual fire on the screen while we pray for fire to come down is a practical means of bridging the abstract gap between a signifier and the signified, and also fires the imagination of people during their prayer activities. Christians already know from reading the Bible that God is a consuming fire.[32] This attribute of God is frequently invoked in spiritual warfare prayers because its destructive operations are quite spectacular and even gratifying.

These prayers also allude to the utility of fire in the Bible in a variety of ways. From using it to keep warm to burning offerings in the temple, fire is a destructive feature of God.[33] In a contest between the prophet of God and the prophet of Baal, fire was the decider of which god was superior.[34] God said to the Prophet Jeremiah that he would turn His word in the prophet's mouth into fire, and his audience into wood so that they may be consumed.[35] When God appeared to Moses in the Bible, he appeared in the form of a fire that though raged through a bush, but did not destroy it. As the pastor/evangelist Daniel Okpara stated in one of his books, "Fire is an instrument of judgment against the works of the wicked . . . fire has no respect for faces. Fire does not beg. Fire consumes. When fire attacks, you had better stay off the way. When we pray, we can pray down fire to judge the wicked and release our blessings."[36] Thus, literalizing fire in these virtual prayer sessions is a savvy choice, because it vividly stokes the imagination to conjure a practical idea of what God is when people pray. The artifice of fireballs dancing on the screen as the pastor commands fire to appear makes the experience of prayer even more memorable, expands the mind's range of imaginative capabilities, and is encoded into the memory because it stands out among the stream of chores one does every day. Just like the pastor who simulated tree-cutting on the altar, fire is used to give people images that will continuously replay in their minds long after the service is over. These are the ways strips of behavior are created and stored for future use.

In that moment of intense prayer where people become fired up and their senses are acutely primed as they throw punches against spiritual oppression, spiritual warriors become more expressive and tend to be extremely loud. As Dapo Asaju noted, the fire of God they invoke also comes with noise. Both fire and noise are "vehicles of God's awesome revelation," although while "noise is discernible by sound; fire, with its accompanying effect, has audiovisual effects."[37] At church campgrounds or prayer cities where thousands of spiritual warriors simultaneously wage war through prayer rains, their practice of disestablishment of demonic confederacy relies on generating a sonic universe where humans reach proximate worlds by stretching their voices in prayer, sometimes carrying technologically amplified music and prayers emanating from the altar all over the extensive campground. However, in the Facebook prayer groups, "noise" is just the voice of the evangelist leading the prayer, chanting "Fire!" or sometimes pausing the prayers to ask the congregants to "share" and "like" their prayer sessions. Noise and its aftereffects are therefore simulated through the images of fireballs that appear on the screen. The fire that features in the Bible as a vehicle of divine revelation appears in this virtual arena as a simulation, both foregrounding and intensifying the existing beliefs in the phenomenology of God. At church campgrounds where thousands of people simultaneously pray at the top of their voices, noise is neither ephemeral nor anomalous. It is part of the immersive experience of spiritual warriors whose prayers have to be disruptive to be effective in disestablishing the forces militating against them. The prayers are loud and noisy, and such raucousness is part of spiritual warriors' means of rehearsing their becoming God's human weapons. Noise is "a kind of . . . anarchic proliferation of audio occurrences,"[38] and prayer itself is "an irruption of the senses."[39] Noisy and riotous prayers are the presentational means of piercing the ears of forces lurking from the earth to the farthest parts of the cosmos to violently disestablish them through disruptions.

The unruliness that people demonstrate during prayers is encouraged by the pastor or evangelist leading the prayers. During a live sermon when he was about to begin one of his prayer sessions, Olukoya enjoined his congregation to fully yield their physical bodies to what was coming through prayers. He stated,

> So many transactions are about to take place now. But everything depends on you. You must strike while the iron is hot. There is an envelope of God's power and presence around this place. Make sure nobody's voice is louder than yours. Let your head know that you are praying. Let your hand know that you are

praying. Let your hand know that you are praying. Let your legs know that you
are praying. The kind of prayer that I want you to pray now is not the kind of
prayer where you stand still and you are just shaking your head like this [bobs
head side to side]. You won't get far with that.[40]

By telling the spiritual warriors to drop all propriety, he alerts them to the spiritual transaction to negotiate with their body parts. He says, "This is not the
time to play the gentleman or woman.... Pray like a man or woman from
another world. Focus your attention entirely on what you are saying. Don't
allow your mind to go here and there." The body, he says, had to be free to make
the exchange possible. A part of God's body—this time, His finger—was in the
assembly, and they needed to transact with it with their bodies. He adds, "That
finger [of God] that disgraced Goliath, the finger that introduced worms into
the life of Herod, the finger that parted the Red Sea is here now. It is just for
you to access it. These are not normal prayers at all, they are actually strange
prayers. Whether you understand the prayers or whether you don't understand
the prayers, just pray them." Prayer was their access card to another realm,
and the impropriety of their bodies set free would launch them there.

The prayers, "strange" in their contents and unruly in their enunciation,
will irrupt their senses but will also generate new impulses as they are engrafted
with God's body part already present in the assembly. Noise is a staple of
this activity because it productively heightens the immersive experience of
prayers, especially when done by a large congregation, and that is why he further
entreats them, "make sure nobody's voice is louder than yours." Especially in
the campground, people pray to cultivate a rich sonic space where they groan,
moan, cry, murmur, make guttural sounds, inhale air, and ecstatically expel
it. The attendant noises show the intensity of their engagement, not simply
registering "a source of aesthetic reinvigoration and revitalization";[41] they also
require the full concentration of each spiritual warrior. Famed for its affective ability to perturb, the irruptive force of noise is a part of designating sites,
occupying spaces, and reinscribing their spiritual authority against the forces
they seek to evacuate. Noise is part of the productive affect that also curates
prayer sites.[42]

When Olukoya instructed people to shout to the point that nobody's voice
was louder than theirs, he pushed them to build a mass of sonic disruptions
that also established their authority against those observant unseen forces, thus
making such auditory contests part of the process of reorganizing the world.
Given how loud and how much of a nuisance such shouts can be, particularly
when done by thousands of people converging on the prayer grounds at
the same time, and who fight to raise their voices above that of anyone else, the
experience can be quite overwhelming. Noise contests spaces because it forces
an audience to listen to its effusions. At the top of their voices, people pray in

the church, *I command! I destroy! I pray! I break! I smash! I arise!* as well as other similar commands that percolate both human and supernatural territories. The voice they primarily perceive in that universe of sounds is their own, not that of another agent. While listening is "an activity, an interactivity that produces, invents and demands of the listener a complicity and commitment,"[43] individual spiritual warriors hear and overhear their own voices, and this is even more true even when their numbers are multiplied in those extensive campgrounds. Each person hears their own voice in a defamiliarized and objectified manner that sounds as if it comes from an external agent that has taken them over.[44] Those moments of stepping out of the self to command target forces in every part of the cosmos forced to listen to them, but the overall effect of the noise is spiritual warriors' self-authorization, speaking to their own selves at a most instinctual level.

The engraftment of the spiritual warrior with God's attributes is ultimately achieved through an immersion in this multisensory atmosphere where "fire and noise" and the attendant sensations irrupt. Birgit Meyer's study of sensational forms of Pentecostalism looked at how the link between the human and the divine is facilitated through aesthetics as Pentecostals work through the "religious structures of repetition" to "convince religious believers of the truthfulness of the connection between them and God or the transcendental."[45] Also, studies of immersive experiences in theater also emphasize how space and time are skewed to create an effective response, "a graded and temporary state defined (somewhat paradoxically) by the existence of its boundary."[46] Similarly, the intense activities taking place in this atmosphere rarefy the space and the moment, and the transactions of the human-divine body works through vivid visualizations of the self being transubstantiated with the component parts of God. The aesthetics of the moment work to convince them such transactions are taking place.

Once, while at a prayer ground in Lagos with thousands of others, the voice of a woman fervently praying beside me cut through others who were similarly engaged in loud prayers. Everyone around was yelling various prayers at the same time. Some stood. Some knelt. Some rolled on the bare floor. This woman had her hands raised straight to the sky and her eyes tightly shut. Her body heaved as she prayed intermittently, "Lord, turn me into fire! Lord, turn me into fire!" She would pause and mutter some prayers and then loudly—and repeatedly—shout to be turned into fire. Her closed eyes must have been open to another realm where, in that moment, her imagination of herself becoming the fire trait of God was vividly perceptible. In that liminal moment, surrounded by thousands of people whose voices and shouts of "Fire!" "Power!" reverberated throughout the entire place, she must have been seeing herself as the fire of God—blazing and reducing denigrating situations and conniving human agents into ashes.

Turned into Human Weapons: Using Power in Daily Life

Studies of prayer and the body of the supplicant during the ritual note how the human agent becomes a mediator between natural and supernatural realms. Sometimes, studies of prayers emphasize them as means of communicating with God and attuning oneself to perceive His presence and the ways it might manifest.[47] At other times, studies of prayers that dwell on the spiritual warfare genre argue that people also perceive demonic activities during prayers, and they work to both repel those forces and to deliver themselves from their diabolic influence.[48] This dichotomous way of considering which of the forces the body connects with while engaging in prayer—God or demonic agencies—is also a function of which genre of prayers people are engaged in.[49] However, the emphasis on whether what is sensed during prayer is God or the devil—whom they want to divest themselves of—literalizes the idea of the body as a conduit through which spectral forces pass or as an access point to another realm too much.[50] Truly, when the body is heated up by the intense activity of prayer, it also opens people up to another order of reality where they perceive either God or demonic forces. Spiritual warfare prayer, however, acts as more than a channel that reaches transcendental realms. It also engrafts parts of God into their psychic selves and refashions their consciousness so that even their day-to-day activities evoke a sense of power to disestablish reigning powers.

This sense of self-perception is perhaps the most significant consequence of spiritual warfare prayer, because spiritual warriors acquire some of the various attributes of God through the rituals and events of these prayers, and this assimilation produces a sense of power and authority in them. When they pray and ask, "Oh, Lord, thou consuming fire, turn me into fire!" they take their bodies and their minds through an intense ritual activity, recalling visceral images such as the fireballs of the Facebook prayer sessions or the symbolic tree-cutting on the altar, and get fired up with the phenomenally destructive energy that God portrays and through which He has previously landed judgment against some people. In those same prayers in which they ask to be made into fire—or they ask for God's hand or finger to touch them—they display various kinetic actions such as jumping, rolling on the floor, crying, groaning, sweating, and even making some bodily emissions. These ecstatic moments where the body is let go are also the instants in which they visualize themselves enacting certain kinds of actions in the spiritual realm to contend for the body part of God that they want engrafted into them during the activity of fervent prayer. These moments are significant because they are liminal—their bodies are open to influence from otherworldly realms, and they vigorously battle with opposing forces to be victorious. As Olukoya said in the excerpt from the aforementioned sermon while prepping people to battle through prayer, the minds and bodies of the congregants need to be fully engaged in this activity. Their going through this phase of "hot" prayer takes them into a transformative state where they are engrafted and their conviction of themselves as warriors of God—authorized to disestablish the orders of truth the world subsists on—gets burnished into them thoroughly. When the prayer activity is done repeatedly, it does not merely repeat or restore behavior, as Schechner might describe it. It affirms their status as spiritual warrior, ingrained with God's body part.

As the cases of Joshua who demonstrated the tree-cutting on the altar and that of the church complex designed as "the hand of God" show, God is metonymized everywhere the spiritual warrior occupies to furnish engraftment so that the processes of disestablishment are naturalized. To the sliced fractions of God's ontological features, the split God, spiritual warriors attribute the myths of functions they internalize during the immersive experience of prayer and culminate the process by being engrafted with God's genes. To normalize the initiative of people who go through this process and propel them toward simulations of victory, spiritual leaders help the imagination of the congregation along with visual aids and various engaging performance techniques. These devices help with their engraftment as well as the efficient use of the reinvigorated body to disestablish demonic confederacies. Through frequent rehearsals of prayer and preparations for a coming *War*, they acquire the spontaneity and the impulses of a spiritual warrior. When they are shown a tree being cut, they can translate the metaphor of pulling up evil forces into concrete action. By also showing them fireballs while they pray, the symbolism of consuming fire can be imagined, with themselves at the center of destructive action, manifesting this aspect of God. By engaging in this form of prayer repeatedly, they rehearse and expand the repertoire of actions of supernatural power and authority. The spiritual warrior emerges from these rites fully convinced not just of God's indwelling presence, but that they are conveyors of the specific traits that can ultimately inscribe a moral vision.

Becoming fire like God, or being sutured with His hand/finger, is tested through social agonisms that could be physical humans, social situations, or spiritual forces. In churches during "testimony time," or even in prayer literature where pastors collect these stories, people tell various stories of their victories against the forces that would have stood in the path of their social advancement. Some of these forces are humans and some are established bureaucracies, but they are all quantified as evil that must be disestablished through spiritual warriors' power and authority. As a certain brother Chukwudi's "visa by fire" testimony in Tella Olayeri's *Fire for Fire, Part 2: Double Thunder, Double Fire* demonstrates, this enemy against whom one's authority is confirmed need only be a factor hindering one's social progress. Chukwudi stated that he read Olayeri's book on spiritual warfare, *Fire for Fire*, and "I thought I need to apply the missiles and bullets in to face white men that, six times, refused me

[a] visa. I used it for seven days as directed but later considered to go for another 14 days night vigil before my appearance at the embassy. This I did. Before I knew it, my visa was approved. My conclusion is, they fired me six times and on the seventh time, I fired them. It was a battle of fire for fire of which I won. Praise the Lord."[51] For the testifier who is said to have reported his victory from where he is now based in Holland, visa refusal six times in a row took on the coloration of a spiritual contest through which he could discharge the weapons that he had acquired when he prayed, first for seven days as the book prescribed, and then for another fourteen days that he added for himself to strengthen his armory. The consulate officials at the Dutch embassy might not have known him personally to have denied him a visa, but the fact that they stood against what he needed to move up the social ladder made them an enemy whose fire-power he could finally resist with the superior firepower that he had found.

The enemy could also be spectral, in which case the regress toward a second order of thinking gets even more acute, where people discern the spiritual chain of connections between realistic events.[52] Unlike the impersonal models of scientific techniques modern society employs to account for events, spiritual causality in the second-order thinking of a spiritual warrior features stories of demonic encounters with ancestral spirits, spiritual spouses, familial relations, and close encounters that make the wide expansive global world which one inhabits shrink to a level where one is hypervisible to a malevolent attacker. Rather than blaming abstract factors for one's misfortune or attributing the perplexities of modern social life to the hand of history, seeing one's enemies within existing social chains of relations reduces and relieves the complexity and the mental work of navigating a globalizing world. These demons linked to one's authenticities such as kith and kin, especially the ancestors that connect one's roots within a world whose spatial bounds keep expanding, make one visible enough to be a target for malevolence. Nigerian Pentecostals themselves refer to such demon forces that knows one intimately as "familiar spirits," a use of language different from its standard meaning of a close friend or associate. This suggestion of a prior acquaintance with them based on antagonistic relations facilitates the rehearsed practices of negating and expelling them, and further empowers one to face multifaceted world situations. To say that the global is political is rather too obvious an axiom here. Instead, the global—with its complexities—is personal because a nuanced web of events and social forces is summarized into a suite of concrete enemies, and familiar enough for one to test one's engrafted abilities.

The evil that engrafted spiritual warriors must wrestle against is frequently presented through intimate family relations and close alliances. One's attackers never come from outside; they are mostly people one already knows. Consequently, the evil that the spiritual warrior is up against feels up close and personal, and, in fact, visceral. The various materials church leaders produce to shape the appearances of evil for their congregation—from live or recorded sermons to prayer literature—not only point an arrow toward the enemy figure in one's life; they could go as far as creating dialogues between both human and supernatural agents, developing elaborate "acts and scenes" of events such as instances whereby an afflicted person sees a supernatural figure in a dream or vision. When the person wakes up, they do not confront such an enemy in real life even if they are familiar with them. Instead, they pray or consult their pastor. When they go back to sleep afterward, they could return to the vision to continue the contest with the haunting figure.[53] For instance, in Olukoya's *Victory over Satanic Dreams*, after instructing Christians that their not recalling their dreams is dangerous because they could miss divine ministration or a warning of demonic attack, he goes on to narrate the story of a woman who prayed to God to be granted access to "certain secrets." As she prayed, God opened her eyes to see a "great king" who told her to be careful who she listened to. When she woke up, she consulted Olukoya, who told her that she had a "strange king" ruling over her life who must be dethroned for only Jesus to reign. The next time she prayed, this woman found herself before the throne of the same "strange king" once again. This time he was angry with her for having consulted the man of God. This king said, "What nonsense is this? I know how to deal with you. I will remove your spiritual memory so that whatever you see or hear in a dream will never be remembered." A remarkable part of this dream is the continuities of time and space—the dreamer wakes up, has a conversation with her pastor, and then goes back to sleep to confront a nonhuman character who has omnipresent abilities to surveil his victim.

This rather elaborate dramatization of how evil syncs across spatial and temporal dimensions notably does not suggest confronting one's enemies in the physical realm. The battle has to be restricted to the spiritual realm, where spiritual warriors can effectively activate the power and authority they bear. Living in a milieu where the apocalyptic is an everyday affair, they have the second sight to see into the other realms where the spiritual shapes the physical, and that is the realm they have to stay in to effect a transformation. Since the enemy is not limited by either temporality or spatiality, and their malice can even breach spaces such as one's dreams, the warrior too must be able to pursue these forces into the otherworldly realms where they might be dwelling to annihilate them. A physical battle against such a familiar enemy does not guarantee victory, but it could diminish them in other ways. The spiritual realm is where the enemy is summoned to the battleground.

The descriptions of enemies are written in simple language, formulaic, and often brief. They seem more like oral dialogues than elaborate theology.[54] For instance, in Olukoya's *The Mystery of Water Cure*, we find the story of a brother who rented an apartment "in a strange building." The brother was unaware that all his neighbors were either witch doctors or fetish priests, but he did notice a heavy human traffic passing through their apartments all day long. He did not know that the crowd of people he saw came for "demonic consultation." This brother, unaware that he was the only one in the apartment complex who was not part of the occult, was already tutored in what the book describes as "the science of spiritual warfare." This Christian brother, we are told, was the type who wakes up at midnight every day to pray aggressively. When his conspiratorial neighbors could no longer take the spiritual salvos he fired in their direction, they begged him to reveal the source of his power. They admitted that they had been trying to launch spiritual attacks on him every night, but each time they came to his apartment, they saw him surrounded by rings of fire. The brother told them it was the power in the blood of Jesus and the fire of the Holy Ghost.[55] In this story, the demonic agents are the neighbors who live close enough to him that even though they are not blood relations, the function they fulfill is an affirmation of his status as a spiritual warrior who embodies the raging fire of God.

A similar story was told in Olukoya's *Too Hot to Handle*. A woman who had miscarried for the seventh time in the fifth month of her pregnancies was pregnant for the eighth time. She always dreamed that a cow ran into her, and then she would lose her pregnancy. Her friend invited her to a church crusade where she prayed and held on to a verse of the Scripture. As she and her friend left the church, the pastor warned the same friend who took her to church to desist from what she had been doing. The pregnant woman had no idea what had transpired between the pastor and her friend, but she kept meditating on the Bible. When she dreamed again that a cow was rushing toward her, a stone appeared and stood between her and the cow. The cow smashed into the stone and broke its horn. The following morning, the pregnant woman was told that her friend who invited her to a crusade had died. She was found with her head smashed, and no one had any idea how it happened.[56] These accounts heighten the sense of the pervading apocalyptic by mistrusting even intimate acquaintances and characterizing them as incubi or a miasma of foul air.[57]

All of these stories have in common a pattern in the apprehension of the enemy figure that must be disestablished by spiritual warriors now aware of their powers. They are not random forces, but composed of friends, family, and acquaintances whose nearness and establishment in one's personal life and social network make one even more vulnerable to their mischief. The central factor here is anxiety about daily existence—susceptibilities to the social circumstances of suffering and exposure to the global economics that exacerbates despondency. The malevolence of witchcraft preys on intimate relations, but the prayers offer an antidote that regulates the fear through reassurance from a higher power. This level of order to reality eventually establishes the world as a giant conspiracy, and the gradual cultivation of one's consciousness of their interventionist role in this world order impels the fighting instincts of the engrafted spiritual warrior.[58] Having been engrafted with the source of ultimate power, they can—and they do—act as God in situations they see as transforming of the world. As Amando Maggi stated of the contemporary interest in exorcisms and demons in U.S. culture, they are "less a reflection of a persistent religious creed than a fascination with a set of beliefs that in many people's view used to explain and grant order to reality."[59] Spiritual warriors' ability to grant order to reality deploys violent means, frequently rolling out the battle tanks of prayer.

Also common in the literature of prayer is how the enemy to be vanquished is rendered as a faceless archetype. Olukoya, for instance, tells many stories where the antagonism between supernatural forces and human agents typically occurs between demon-possessed people, or "the enemy" working against "one man," "one woman," "one sister," "one brother," "a minister of God," and similar nebulous descriptions. The stories could have happened "some time ago," "months ago," or "recently," or even "many years ago," and about the only sense of location one derives from where these attacks happen is mostly rural areas or any unnamed place. As some of the enemies from which people should seek to be delivered are one's close family members, evil gets couched in intimate interpersonal relationships and the atavistic fear of exposure to occult forces heightens. At the same time, by rendering the enemies as faceless, ahistorical, and acontextual, radical evil appears timeless and universal. Their ability to exist without history or any apprehensible context does not defamiliarize these "familiar spirits." It makes them commutable into a universal standard of evil and applicable across time and space. Such figuration helps spiritual warriors to see that evil and demonic agents are not limited by the complexities of history. They, in fact, trigger history and personal destinies into action through their wickedness.

Their lack of historical identity or discernible motives means these unseen agents of evil can possess an unending source of power. There are no nuances to their actions, and therefore no basis whatsoever to empathize with them. To accommodate any sentiment would mean mere carelessness, making oneself susceptible to enemy attacks. The enemy has to be depersonified. Without being assigned a narrative identity, their superficiality makes them both incorrigible and irredeemable, and the only logical resolution is to destroy them in prayer. Enemies to be considered have no discernible motives to their wickedness, nor is there ever a nuanced appraisal of their actions. They are characterized as mere archetypes and devised to initiate sacred power toward the establishment of justice in the world as quickly as possible. Prayer is crucial in these battles because its language resolves a disordered universe where virtually every factor militates against meaningful existence. Prayer is the battle cry; prayer is also the means by which people become the battle weapon and also test their dexterity in using it. While they are available to all, those prayers also require elaborate preparation and bodily discipline. Prayer teaches concentration, bodily training, mental acuity, and the acquisition of knowledge to discern and direct affairs. It crushes communally felt experiences into mental images that everyone will be stimulated to battle with in the ritual action of prayer. The spiritual warrior's instincts are refined through this rendering of evil forces as they go through routines of prayer to rehearse their authority to deploy battle weapons. Having been taught the techniques of commanding and taking authority through prayer, they build a projection of strength for themselves to fight, win, and establish their authority as God's commanders in the world. As a pastor told me of his church and spiritual warfare, "It is the enforcement of our victory in Christ. We are training people to be war machines here."[60] To be a spiritual war machine is to be a human subject who has been engrafted with the body parts of God through prayer and supplementary artifices.[61]

Spiritual Warfare and Unending Rehearsals

This chapter has chiefly dwelt on the spiritual training of spiritual warriors, forging themselves into a weapon of spectacular destruction, especially as God's battle axe. Going forward in the next chapter, I will look at how this paradigm of self-enhancement has the ultimate end of self-legislation, the idea that one can effectively fashion oneself into a human weapon to undertake the urgent mission of disestablishing powerful forces of authority by acting above authority. The spiritual warrior fights to de-anchor themselves from the restraints of some of the norms and legalisms to which they are subject. In his analysis of the rhetoric of Islamophobia in an American right-wing think tank, the Center for Security Policy, Jonathon O'Donnell identifies some of the tensions that underwrite Islamophobic conspiracism as part of the tension between the sovereignty of subjects and the societal structures that produce and restrict that sovereignty. Locating his argument within the context of the series of the fallouts of neoliberalism, the tensions between self-sovereign individuals and the larger socio-political structures that constitute and contain them, O'Donnell shows how Islamist conspiracism is borne of the fear of the Muslim subject who is a threat precisely because they cannot be disciplined and ultimately absorbed into western models of ideologies of freedom.[62] Spiritual warriors share similar ideas of the self as powerful precisely because of their radical inassimilability. Social and secular disciplinary forces, composed of man-made traditions that can be self-serving and ethically corrupted, limit the potential of the spiritual warrior from achieving social flourishing. For God's battle axe to be as sharp as necessary and be destructive, it must diverge from entrenched paths as they are composed of the moral corruption that structures contemporary society. The spiritual warrior must, as much as possible, strive to distinguish themselves, extricate their selves from the moral forces of secular social structures and disestablish them.

As a case study, I start chapter 3 with the story of a spiritual warrior and the circumstances that reconciled her apocalyptic vision with the phantasms of heroism as a powerful device. God's human weapon, Dr. Stella Immanuel, became a viral sensation during the COVID-19 pandemic. Like a classic drama performed in different theaters over time, the plot of a story might no longer hold suspense or offer surprises. However, there are times when the same play is restaged against the backdrop of a phenomenal historical event, and the ongoing social and political currents in the society supply the force that *retells* the story and reenergizes the plot. Such was the case of Immanuel, who had spent many years rehearsing her spiritual authority in the place of prayer, and one day, suddenly, went viral worldwide. Her public performance as a medical doctor who believes in supernatural agents added cadences to the convergence of science and the spiritual. She would become a unique yet representative figure of the millions of spiritual warriors worldwide. As she became a viral phenomenon, Immanuel made a telling declaration about herself: "I am God's battle axe!" Like other spiritual warriors with similar instincts, there is a sense in which the object of that declarative sentence—battle axe—falls off, leaving an idea of oneself made in the image of God and therefore able to determine and instrumentalize the mind of God on public issues. Immanuel's conduct in the wake of her newfound fame also aptly illustrates how the continuous rehearsals to fight and be victorious in the coming *War* found a battle arena in the politics and contests that attended the COVID-19 pandemic. If, as Olukoya theologized, the battle axe is a weapon that is specially crafted for "serious battles," to hack down "rebellious spirits," "demonic agents," the "eaters of flesh and drinkers of blood," it is telling how she conceived of her role in the politics of COVID-19.[63]

The politics of COVID and the spiritual warfare that underwrote it for spiritual warriors like her provided a real-life example of how the expectations of the *War* heightened the political stakes of the pandemic. Spiritual leaders have constantly emphasized preparation for *War* even while rehearsing for it through daily battles, as discussed in this chapter. COVID-19 as the *War* is an event during which our bodies are exposed to malevolent forces that either want to enter them, or for the ones already inside them to expand their presence. The coronavirus proved the near-perfect real-world manifestation of this endemic fear of the unseen overturning an entire world order. It was perceived as the *War* that has been long in coming, the one for which people fought endless ongoing wars as trainings. When the entire world reacted to the news of the outbreak with varying degrees of panic, the impulses of spiritual warriors to disestablish the forces responsible and affirm their status as God's human devices were triggered to the highest degree.

Prayer had been the apocalyptic device of these spiritual warriors, and their performance of prayer—frequent rehearsals to engraft parts of the split God into them—have prepared them for how they might interpret and react to the epidemic as God's human weapons. Prayers, daily deployed to confront the vagaries of life, expanded their minds as to what their roles would be on the battleground of COVID-19 politics. As prayers are also generative, the constant rehearsals against the enemies within familial or social circles exploded their imagination about the nature of the attack. The idiom of prayers mapped onto politics and the skills of explaining, predicting, and controlling events attained through spiritual competence facilitated political partisanship as people chose the side of "good" they belonged to against an "evil" that needed disestablishing. With the prayer anchored to the polarization and the polemical nature of political situations, the urgency and imperative became even more self-evident. Immanuel's case will also show how the ubiquity of technological resources in our modern life has broken down fourth walls such that the former boundaries between the relatively private spaces where the rehearsal of prayer happens and the public stages where the authority of spiritual warriors is attested and received. There are no longer rehearsals that are not part of the public staging of the performance itself.

With COVID-19, the uniqueness of an event like a global pandemic coincided with the rehearsed practices of spiritual authority and political partisanship. Already enmeshed in the social relations where claims of a privileged relationship with an omnipotent God structure the definitions of "good" and "evil" in partisan politics, these spiritual warriors could not resist the inclinations toward anti-elitism, anti-expertise, and anti-science driven by an urgent sense of the reenchantment of politics. Personal conviction as God's human weapons in an unfolding war supplied the impetus for a moral confrontation against the prevailing order of the universe, with the machismo derived from fighting supernatural forces all day and all year long. Drawing most of its radical performatives from religious pieties and supernaturalism, the Manichaean ideology of the self as "good" and the other as "evil" animated the imagination as to the nature of the disease outbreak and compelled the persistent suspicion of a lurking radical evil force that must be resisted even unto death.

3

The Noisome Pestilence

• • • • • • • • • • • • • • • • • • • •

COVID-19 Pandemic
and the Conspirituality of
"Fake Science"

*I watched something yesterday on the
Frontline Doctors in the USA. . . . If
somebody comes out and say we have
treated 350 people with this drug and none
died, they say, No, that's not necessary. So,
what's necessary? To kill them is necessary
or to force your demonic vaccines on
human race? Who knows what you have
inside it? To turn human beings to
properties for wealth sake, for political
reasons? The same way Pharaoh perished
because he won't let people go, these evil men
will disappear into shame and ignominy
wherever they may be and whatever forces
are behind them. It's [COVID-19] mere
noise. The Bible calls it noisome pestilence.
It just came with noise, zero.*

—Bishop David Oyedepo

In the seventh month of the year 2020, when the COVID-19 pandemic was still raging and the uncertainties high, a Black female doctor, along with some other White doctors, appeared on the steps of the Capitol in Washington, D.C. The video of that event went viral mere hours later. Organized by a conservative political group, the Tea Party Patriots, the event, "White Coat Summit," had the stated mission of addressing what they described as the loss of American lives to "a massive disinformation campaign."[1] Each of the doctors was wearing a white lab coat patched with the logo of "America's Frontline Doctors." One after the other, they stepped forward to speak. This Black person among the team, Dr. Stella Immanuel, stepped out too and faced the cameras. Everyone would later find out that she was an immigrant from Cameroon, lived in Houston, was a Texas-based physician, and was also the pastor of a church with a niche in spiritual warfare, Firepower Ministries in Katy, Texas.[2] She also used to be a member of the Mountain of Fire and Miracles Church (MFM), a Pentecostal denomination overseen by Dr. Daniel Olukoya (see chapter 1).[3] Immanuel spoke on the use of the drug hydroxychloroquine (HCQ) as a cure for COVID-19, and a means to end the seemingly interminable lockdown of public spaces, part of the effort to break the transmission chain of the virus. She claimed all the deaths from the disease were needless, and masks were unnecessary.

The U.S. president, Donald Trump, had been promoting the medicine as a cure as well, despite vehement warnings by medical experts who stated that HCQ had no visible benefits in the treatment of the disease.[4] Consequently, HCQ had become highly politicized, and its proponents' public stand on its benefits became more telling of their partisanship than informed knowledge of the science of its efficacy. Laypersons claimed to have read medical journals and proclaimed their expertise on HCQ to the point of directly challenging trained experts' authority on the ability of the drug to treat the COVID-19 infection. This Black woman in a white coat—a universal symbol of credentialed learning in the medical sciences, of expertise, and of purity of purpose— buttressed the claims that there was indeed a cure for COVID-19 and Americans did not have to die. She even likened her fellow doctors who refused to use the drug to the "good Germans" who stood by and watched the Holocaust happen.

Her assertions about the politics of a viral disease would soon make her go viral. Within hours of the video live-streaming on the social media pages of the right-wing conservative-leaning media outlet Breitbart, it was picked up by multiple right-leaning blogs and news sites, circulated, and downloaded onto an indeterminate number of television and computer devices. Within eight hours of watching the video as it streamed live, it gathered 17 million views on Breitbart alone. In Nigerian churches, where pastors had been alleging that the COVID-19 pandemic shutdown that began on March 30, 2020, in major cities was part of a secret conspiracy by certain elites to denigrate social life, Immanuel's video became part of their sermons.[5] One of those who took the video of Immanuel to heart was megachurch pastor Bishop David Oyedepo of the Living Faith Church (a.k.a. Winners' Chapel), whose sermon about the video was excerpted as the epigraph to this chapter.[6] He saw the pandemic as a conspiratorial scheme targeted against the church so it could be locked down indefinitely.[7] He described the pandemic as a "noisome pestilence," a term used in the Bible to describe a form of evil from which God's elect are shielded.[8]

From Nigeria to the United States, this woman adorned with the symbol of institutionalized trust in medical authority became a figure of the antiestablishment, a defector racing toward instituting a truth that self-interested capitalists, political corporations, and their scientist allies did not want known. In litigating her claims, the media dragged out the convergence of her beliefs in spiritual warfare with her conspiracy theories, what I will later call "conspirituality," about the politics of the disease, to insinuate that she might be delusional and therefore not a reliable witness. The *Daily Beast*, for instance, published an article, sensationally titled "Trump's New COVID Doctor Believes in Alien DNA, Demon Sperm, and Hydroxychloroquine," about what they described as her "history of making bizarre claims about medical topics and other issues."[9] Without explaining what these ideas of the supernatural entailed for spiritual warriors, the eccentricity of her beliefs in supernatural agencies seemed ridiculous. For a spiritual warrior, though, such dismissal by establishment figures only reinforced the conviction of the truth she was telling.

Focusing on the role faith and spirituality played in the public reactions to the disease and the economies of knowledge, science, and truth seeing, this chapter explores the devices of spiritual warriors during the pandemic. Their fixation on disestablishing establishment forces found an outlet in their generation and circulation of spiritual warfare rhetoric, condemning scientists, and circulating conspiracy theories and partisan ideologies. The global pandemic activated the disestablishing impulses of spiritual warriors to confront political hegemonies and the (global and globally visible) science-based institutions associated with them, such as the World Health Organization (WHO). The everyday anxieties that have necessitated prayer as an apocalyptic device, as discussed in chapter 1, suddenly coincided with a momentous global epidemiological crisis. The enterprise of science became a target in the battles that followed because its epistemes and established truth propositions had created the same norms of social reality that spiritual warriors found oppressive and contested. Ideologies from scientific institutions had grown into global hegemonies that validated political hierarchies and structures of power, an arrangement spiritual warriors sought to invert. They articulated their discontent by illuminating diabolical confederacies conspiring against humankind. The confluence of ideological hegemonies and demonic powers believed to be incarnated in these powerful institutions of science found an archetypal destructive character in the person of President Trump. Spiritual warriors perceived him as a battle axe (chapter 2)—an antiestablishment occupant of a formidable political institution who would use his position of power to effectuate the takedown of these diabolical forces. In the sections ahead, I will show how his politics became the node through which spiritual warriors and conspiracy theorists connected to dislodge certain dominant influences in global power dynamics.

Using a singular individual like Immanuel as a gateway to analyze the confluence of conspiracy theories and spiritual warfare can also clarify how the truths that both religion and science proclaim can deepen social cleavages. Beyond the identity categories of race, gender, class, nationality, and so on, that typically divide society, there is also the agenda of righteousness. The ideological contests boil down to a radical conviction in the truth that would better organize society. Spiritual warriors, for their part, moralize those political contests with symbols and idioms steeped in their faith beliefs. When conjoined with their prayer practices, their persuasion of truth against any contending authority becomes zero-sum. These truths not only attach to contingent ideological political platforms, but they also become controlling by promising total freedom from other controlling political ideologies. With the high emotionalism that defines partisan divides, spiritual warriors see their disbelief in facts dispensed by scientific authorities as moral and political resistance, an assertion of self-autonomy in a world of human and nonhuman influences. Politics is also personified through individuals like Immanuel because, as she demonstrated, the evil villain hiding in darkened shadows must be made seeable. This perennial fixation of spiritual warriors to make the unseen seeable thrusts them into the public. Under dazzling stage lights, they enact their God-given authority to pull opaque forces into the light of revelation and consequently annihilate them. It is not enough that prayers are apocalyptic devices through which they see beyond apparent reality, or that they seek to engraft themselves with God to enhance their abilities; they must also seek the limelight to stage the battles so their status as spiritual warriors is self-affirming. As Simon Coleman notes, spiritual warfare's dualism is not only about good versus evil, but also about reaching out to the world while also constituting one's personal spiritual agency.[10]

Spiritual warriors are consumed by the spiritual economy of seeing. Seeing, however, entails *seeing against* a background. Structuring perception means the objects—human and nonhuman—that appear in the line of sight must be stripped bare of all their opacities to reveal their true significance to the beholder. In exploring the operations of spiritual warfare, Ruth Marshall asserts that spiritual warfare is "waged through language, through the performative and rhetorical force of speech (which are not identical, but which both refer to an order of truth beyond the order of the predicative or constative)."[11] While language is truly paramount in spiritual warfare as she noted, encounters of sight precede language because things have to first give up the truth of their phenomenality so they can be rightfully countered with utterances. Appearances of phenomena come before the utterances that apprehend or counter them, and that is why spiritual warriors are deeply invested in seeing *back* the forces that see them.

Countering the gaze of surveilling forces is not done entirely through spiritual means, but also through physical confrontations, especially if the antagonists are renowned secular institutions, politicians, or corporations. Countersurveillance is a means for the layman to audit the processes of organizations whose activities are otherwise shrouded in the obfuscation of specialized knowledge. The truth the spiritual warrior publicly proclaims against these organizations in a bid to disestablish their legitimacy can be quite forceful, especially since such expressions happen through the distinct personas of spiritual warriors whose combativeness as God's battle axe confronts other secular truth contenders. What is seen, and how they are seen, is quite crucial to waging spiritual warfare. As powerful devices who make the unseen seeable, spiritual warriors do not only want to see beyond the pale. They also want—and, in fact, need to be—seen by as many witnesses as possible. In the age of global communication technology and models of digital capitalism where public exchanges on social media thrive on adversarial content, being seen—especially by "going viral"—is also a means of testing and attesting to the truth the spiritual warrior proclaims. Without the congregation of eyes that turn such public battles into a social phenomenon and raise the stakes, declarations of truth will lack the generative force and carryover power that give it a self-confirming legitimacy. With manipulative algorithms that run a feedback loop on these electronically driven interactions, assertions, and contentions of truth between opposing sides become resolute and circumscribe their respective free wills.

In an atmosphere where mutual suspicions of malice were rife, accusations of "fakeness" by spiritual warriors thus analogize diabolization and articulate battles between the establishment forces and those who want to dislodge them. For instance, about ten days before leaving for Washington, Immanuel's Twitter account was already becoming combative. She had denounced some assertions by CNN's Dr. Sanjay Gupta—a trained neurosurgeon—(and later, Dr. Anthony Fauci, presidential chief medical adviser), vowing not to be "chained by fake science."[12] It is instructive that Immanuel attached "fake" to science in the same way Trump attacks and delegitimizes journalists critical of his presidency by labeling them as "fake news." The term "fake" was already shaping up to be a sleight of hand through which apparitions of malevolence can be projected onto public institutions and also induce visceral revulsion toward them. In their study of "fake news," Johan Farkas and Jannick Schou showed how the term is variously used by political contenders within the larger context of political struggles to attack and delegitimize. They argue that "fake news" is not an objective description of the contents of news reports but a discursive category that draws the battle lines between political contenders, articulates discontents, and launches antagonisms between hegemonies. Rather than encapsulate a standard definition of news report that is genuine, "fake news" is a signifier floated into public discussions and expected to accrue meanings through repeated usage and ultimately repress other versions of narratives.[13] Their discussion of fake news is expectedly secular, but their treatment of the concept as power politics is analogous to how demonization works as a hermeneutic of suspicion and contestation. People demonize to accuse others of malevolence. In the high-stakes arena of politics, such finger-pointing is a means of contesting the knowledge of an expert by dragging the issue at hand into the realm of spirituality, where their own expertise lies, so they can spar on those terms. Through demonizing as "fake," they challenge and discount the opaqueness of the specialized knowledge that empowers the expert. As such, "fake" is the new demon.

Just as spiritual warriors can accrete various threats under the banner of the demonic to conceptualize the nature of the threat they sense, "fake news" too enters a public discourse to introduce a focal point in political battles. The term "fake news" is floated to demonize an opponent whose established role of news reporting and public agenda-setting threatens the truth convictions of the spiritual warrior. As Farkas and Schou noted about the phenomenon of fake news and the control of social reality, the "fake" that qualifies "fake science" too is not about which of the details in contention are factual or not, nor is it merely about the quality of knowledge that authorizes the scientists.[14] Instead, "fake science" designates another category of power (like the establishment power of the media) whose dominance has given them the privilege of determining reality and whose social force has been bestowed through knowledge that can be questioned, destabilized, and renegotiated on what the contenders consider more favorable terms.

The signifier of "fake" applied to science takes off from the process of diabolization that Trump activated by wielding his political power at his opponents. "Fake science" expands the battleground beyond the realms where the elite knowledge of science has bestowed social power and authority on a clique of experts. Thus, the scientific enterprise and its institutions of knowledge production and world-making are turned into a battleground and can become a casualty in the contests of what and whose knowledge could and should define reality. The politicization of technocratic knowledge by calling it "fake" also makes it possible for otherwise ordinary folks to define their identities within the politics of the COVID-19 disease by taking on notable scientists and invalidating their knowledge. Just as the rise of the phenomenon of "fake news" was coterminous with the technological means that affords ordinary folks the chance to make their own news, calling a category of science "fake" also demarcates a social phase where non-elites and nonexperts who can also access the vast repertoire of specialized knowledge that has always given scientists the edge seek to usurp their roles. To establish themselves as authorities whose arguments against either media or science are legitimate, they must also clear the ground by demonizing them as fake and appropriating their techniques. This is not to say that either the proponents of "fake news" or "fake science" come up to the level of the knowledge base of established authorities in those fields. Instead, the attitude about garnering basic knowledge signifies how political contests necessitate acquiring the means and methods that both the media and science use to validate themselves in their bid to usurp these establishment figures. For the proponents of "fake science," disestablishing experts requires possessing some of their knowledge because rational-legal culture is a language of its own, and understanding its basics legitimizes the claims of those who say they have discerned the malevolence of the established experts steeped in the culture. When conspiracists claim the knowledge of science to allege scientists' malevolence, they put a sturdy base under their conjecturing of reality.

Conspiracies, whether secular or spiritual, are about perceiving reality as it appears, and that is why spiritual warriors claim their ability to see beyond the pale. Like conspiracists, they interpret events by looking at factual details along with speculation in a bid to overcome the limits of what the obvious, the publicly available, and even the empirical can divine. While such understanding of events is a fallout of a post-truth world where emotion and gut instinct tend to displace facts, and the ever-shifting borders of truth and falsehood can imperil democracy, the conjecture is also a problem of a crisis of certainty.[15] The option of knowing fully now meets the practical limits of what can ever truly be known, and both spiritual warriors and conspiracy theorists fill the gap in reality by engaging their second sight, their ability to link discrete happenings into a singular narrative of cause and effect, explored further in the next section. Conspirituality reconciles the perceptual activities of conspiracy theorists and spiritual warriors.

Prayer as an apocalyptic device reframes how Immanuel's coming to global consciousness as a militant Christian, a firepower whose claims asserted the conspiratorial logic of people who had suspected all along that there was more to the whole COVID affair. Immanuel herself told me with what was tantamount to a chest-beating conviction, "I am God's battle axe!"[16] This identification of the engrafted self as God's battle axe, discussed in chapter 2, reveals a hero mentality in a grand plot that features her as a seer of hidden truths. The ability to see *back* is an important component to how spiritual warriors use conspiracy theories, which is further explored in the third section. With her white coat, she was perceivable as an expert who could see into a realm where invisible viruses move through matter to enter human bodies and wreak havoc. As a spiritual warrior, she also sees beyond the natural world into the spiritual realms where demonic forces operate. Quite importantly, she also sees how these insidious agents—both demons and viruses—map in the material world and operate through institutions. With her second sight unavailable to most other humans, whose perception of social and political reality is tyrannized by the obvious, she could therefore demonstrate the judgment to interfere in political contests and steer the country in the direction of redemption.

Her calling out other institutional figures from scientists to media networks, and labeling them as "fake," was an exercise in self-establishment—enacting the disestablishment of the forces of elite knowledge that shape social reality to assert a new and favorable order. It was not enough to have discerned the demonic forces ruling over the United States during the pandemic; she also needed to be seen bringing them to light. In her pre-Washington tweets, she would tag news anchors working for the conservative media network Fox News—such as Tucker Carlson, Laura Ingraham, and Sean Hannity—all of whom had broad viewership for their shows and whose partisan politics were well publicized. Tagging them could have led to being selected to make an appearance, thus giving her a chance to stage a public battle. None of those anchors, as far as her Twitter profile showed, ever responded to her in all that time. Yet she was not dissuaded. She remained convinced that there was a demonic plot against America and that there was a looming battle that needed to be publicly fought.

On that day when she was leaving for the nation's capital to speak her truth, she said she prayed, "Lord, if I perish, I perish." That day, she said, "I spoke with boldness and it was like my voice"—at this point she clasped her two cupped palms together and pushed them forward to pierce the air in front of her, mimicking a battle axe—"cut through the darkness in the whole world. It was a watershed moment. It was like when I spoke that day, something broke in the spirit all over the world. That cage that had been all over everyone broke. It was a moment to. . . ." Her voice trailed off briefly. "It is something they will talk about in generations to come."[17] The video of Immanuel talking about how Americans had been duped to lock down most of their public places when there was an immediate solution to COVID-19 virally circulated through various social media networks and an indeterminate number of devices worldwide. Trump retweeted it to his 80-million-plus followers. His son, Donald Jr., did as well. Iconic pop star Madonna posted—although she later deleted—the video on her Instagram page. Madonna called Immanuel her "hero" and echoed the sentiment prevailing among conspiracy theorists that some powerful elites rejected HCQ so they could make money from a drawn-out search for a COVID-19 vaccine.[18]

Even though Immanuel appeared on millions of screens worldwide in her viral video, she was not uniformly perceived by observers, showing how bearing politicized truth can unite as well as divide. While some who had hesitated to believe there was a conspiracy afoot found the corroboration by a physician—a Black one to boot—too compelling to resist, some thought otherwise. At the time, the United States had recorded around 150,000 deaths from the disease. It was almost unbelievable that a First World country with all the gadgets of modern medicine and a corpus of medical and scientific knowledge like the United States would be so badly beaten by a disease, and people grappled with a crisis of reality. How could the country with the greatest military power on earth and some of the most advanced medical systems struggle against an invisible virus? From denials to conspiracy theories about a supposedly "liberal agenda" using the pandemic to ruin their nation and making their president—a White man who had indulged and helped cultivate nationalist sentiments—look incompetent, people struggled to rationalize the times.

When this Black woman in a team of otherwise all-White doctors emerged to explain with all the indignation she could muster that "nobody has to die," she provided a moral meaning to the moment. For those who supported the incumbent president and wondered why so many lives had been lost under his watch, she helped them revalue their partisan choices. Indeed, conspiritualists were especially attracted to Trump and receptive to those who, like Immanuel, defended him, a concept further examined in the fourth section. For the spiritual warriors who wondered about the continuity of the potency of U.S. exceptionalism, she lifted their dark mood by repatriating responsibility elsewhere. She was God's battle axe, but her discernment of the malevolence behind the moving hand of history was not just an opinion to them. Her training as a physician and as a spiritual warrior gave her the ability to see reality outside of what the laws of nature allow everyone else to see. She could also make authoritative proclamations on how events should subsequently unfold. And once the wave of apocalypse passed over Africa without the death and destruction predicted by the scientific elite, it seemed as if the type of discerning diabolic forces and disestablishing institutional regimes had worked, which is the subject of the concluding section of the chapter.

Conspirituality: Conspiracy Theories, Spirituality, and Disestablishing Power

Conspiracy theorists are also likely predisposed to believe in the agency of unseen forces like spiritual warriors because they are similarly attracted by Manichaean narratives of good and evil, and are more willing to believe that some happenstances, such as the COVID-19 pandemic, are acts of intentional mischief by malevolent powers.[19] Throughout the pandemic, especially in the early days, this belief that the disease was the handiwork of some powerful and vengeful characters was prevalent in the social sphere where news of the disease circulated. In the case of Immanuel, however, this belief was no longer just about conspiracy theories as some form of reasoning motivated by dwelling in a social milieu that supplies traction to the paranoia of those beliefs.[20] It was also about spiritual warfare, thus lending a critical (re)direction to the study of "conspirituality" as proposed by Charlotte Ward and David Voas in their study, in which they described the convergence of conspiracy theories with New Age spirituality in social culture.[21] They noted that both conspiracy theories and New Age spirituality are modes of apprehending social realities jointly underwritten by denying coincidences, finding patterns in seemingly random events, and believing in the agency of unseen forces. While conspiracy theories tend to be male-dominated, conservative in ideological leanings, pessimistic, and fascinated with current affairs, New Age spirituality tends to be female-dominated, liberal, self-consciously optimistic, and mostly focuses on social and personal relations.[22] To sum up, while conspiracy theories mostly express a reading of historical development, New Age spirituality tends to supply answers that "awaken" people to perceiving and responding to it.

While both divine the means of apprehending events of history beyond official reports, I should clarify that the New Age spirituality Ward and Voas described is not synonymous with Christian forms of spirituality. Spiritual warriors would, in fact, vehemently reject New Age spirituality's focus on holistic and harmonious practices as demonic or "paganistic" and ontologically opposed to their own beliefs. In their study of the paradox of self-enhancement, Roos Vonk and Anouk Visser noted that spiritual trainings might ironically boost a feeling of superiority and create pride in spiritual endeavors.[23] Spiritual superiority can thus ambush the goal of spiritual trainings by producing feelings of narcissism, hedonism, and overconfidence, thus undermining the goals of attaining humility and a common humanity. But such an outcome is also where Christian spiritual warfare differs from the practices of New Age spirituality and similar spiritual trainings. Spiritual warfare does not have the end goal of humility, forging a common humanity, or harmonizing with certain energies latent in the atmosphere. Rather, it boldly asserts the radical differences between spiritual warriors and New Age spiritualists.[24] Spiritual warfare does not disguise its aims of producing a human who is precisely superior to every other human's claim of superiority because spiritual warriors embody specific personality traits of God that have been engrafted into them. It is not a paradoxical outcome of spiritual training; it is the point.

What is not deniable is that both spiritual warfare and conspiracy theories operate in the same public domain, and the ideas that underwrite each bounce off one other. While drawing these broad strokes about the convergence of conspiracy theory and spiritual warfare will make for an informed generalization, analyzing a distinct individual like Immanuel, a certified physician who combines the means of knowing things through rational means and visions into the supernatural, can also be acutely clarifying as to how conspiracy theories and spiritual warfare truly meet. "Conspirituality," a neologism, suggests that conspiracy theories and New Age spirituality are discrete strains of thoughts and expressions being interlocked as people express them. However, a look at the internal logic contained within the two—the ability to see alternately—shows why they cannot but interact and how they borrow motifs from each other. For instance, it is not hard to see the similarity between the famous conspiracy theorist David Icke's ideas about reptilian elites running politics and Immanuel's sermons about the same human–reptile hybrids running politics.[25] As Asprem and Dyrendal noted, conspirituality itself is not altogether novel. Historically, the phenomenon has recurrently manifested within the cultic milieu of Western esotericism.[26] Taking into account the intermittent emergence of conspiracy and spirituality in various phases of history, "conspirituality" thus applies in this chapter as a study of contemporary practices. The term describes the extent to which conspiracy theories and spirituality converge in the politics of power and knowledge, and how both are mediated by a metaphoric eye behavior—seeing beyond the pale of what is obvious, official, and orthodox. Conspiritualists, as expressed here, specifically reference Christian spiritual warriors who traffic in conspiracy theories.

For Immanuel, being a spiritual warrior means that she had long been predisposed to believing that some unseen forces of good and evil are in conflict, and that there was a higher force that could intervene and deliver judgment. Conspiracy theories generally chart the causality of events as incidents beyond mere quirks of history, and they satisfy certain ideological and psychological needs of people who need to account for reality beyond official accounts.[27] Their ways of seeing alternately can be hugely political, because their stringing together what is factual with the fictive to generate the probabilities of what could also be true is typically underwritten by their partisan ideologies. They apply the outcomes to phenomena, and this mode of divining reality subsequently works on them as sociopolitical subjects whose performance affects the public sphere. Immanuel, for instance, told me in a private interview that she had prepared for a role as America's prophet long before she became a sensation online. She had had a series of apocalyptic visions on the state of the United States and the spiritual intervention the country urgently needed. She referred me to a sermon she had delivered earlier on the demonic siege on the United States where she talked about being locked up in a prayer room for a hundred days straight. On the ninety-ninth day, she had a vision of some monstrous beings that walked into her backyard. She said,

I started beating them. I mean when you are spiritually strong, you do exploits in the spirit. I was practically picking them on the leg and knocking them on the tree. Picking the two of them together and jamming their heads, flinging them up. I mean they were regular human beings in my size and I was picking them, throwing them around as if I was playing with dogs. I was beating them, knocked one on the tree. I will pick them, use one as a cane to beat the other. So, I was beating them for almost twenty minutes. And then they said okay stop, stop, you cannot kill us. We are genetically modified human beings. We came to check out what you were doing.[28]

In that same sermon, she talked about how she observed in that vision that America had been zombified, how she called on pastors all over America to pray, but they did not heed her because they were "busy running their churches." She eventually found someone, and they began to pray for people's liberation. One by one, they would pray for someone, "slap the person out of the trance they were in and they will wake up and join us. Then we will go around and slap another person, we will pray and pray and the person will break through and when they break through, they will now wake up." This vision she had about America, she claimed, had long shown her the true condition of the people, and God had given her the tools to free them. What she lacked was the means of reaching the whole world. After going viral in 2020, she linked her visions about America's moral degeneration and her soteriological desire to see the truth of that moment. The deliverance of America from demonic forces that was once only probable in her dreams and visions was now happening: "I had prayed for years that God should give me the microphone and I would call America back to Him. What happened did not just happen. God has been working in me for a long time."[29] She further explained to me, "When I went viral, that was what I did. I prayed."[30] Prayer bolstered her resolve in the crucial moment she went viral—when she had been acknowledged by the president of the most powerful country in the world while the news networks dug into her beliefs for salacious stories to share with their prime-time viewers.

For her, even the media attacks on her beliefs were part of the politics of power struggles with spectral forces that dominate reality; standing up to them would disestablish their cultural power to fix her with a defining identity and diminish her truth. Marshall noted, "Charismatic truth is only truth because of its performative, engaged, committed, and *partisan* position, as a decision for Christ. Without this, it has no radical transformative power at all."[31] For Immanuel, the radical force of the truth conviction she bore also manifested in her counteraction toward the journalists who mocked her beliefs by mocking their efforts at mocking her. As she narrated, she left Washington without any idea she was going viral. She landed at the Houston airport only to find that her phone was blowing up and her social media accounts were besieged with

thousands of messages, some people calling her a "witch." Friends called her to
tell her they were worried about her, as they were destroying her in the media.
Her house guests from Nigeria, who were also Christian ministers, however,
told her to brace herself for her moment had come. She said she thought of
Olukoya and became emboldened enough to confront all of them. "I realized
that I was trained for this. God trained me for this. Can you," she asked me
with a sharp questioning look, "ever imagine Dr. Olukoya backing down? I am
a daughter of Dr. Olukoya. I am a daughter of the king!"[32] She confirmed her
royal authority by responding to the journalist from the *Daily Beast* who had
written the well-circulated article about her, which had drawn from her old videos on spiritual warfare that had lain dormant on the internet. She tagged the
journalist's Twitter handle with a post that showed a woman wearing red box-
ing gloves, her arms outstretched in victory. She captioned it, "round one." The
next day, she granted an interview to a local news station in which she stood
her ground on her beliefs, especially when the reporter brought up the issue of
demon sex.

In the same interview with the news station, she noted her thanks to the
Daily Beast's article and CNN's relentless focus on her videos. She added that
she had become famous and that even though the media crew were demon-
possessed individuals, God had used them for her in a way she could never
have imagined.[33] Everyone, she said exultantly, was now watching her. With
such bold declarations and a refusal to be shamed for her seemingly outland-
ish beliefs, she took the power the establishment media, a.k.a. the "fake news,"
would have wielded to fix her as an object of fun and used it to establish herself as God's warrior.[34] By making light of their ridicule of her beliefs and declaring that their pillorying of her was ultimately a victory for her, she achieved
two things in the moment. First, she pushed back against the force of the media's
establishment power that allows them to direct a public discourse. In her case,
that legitimacy extended to the media's ability to ridicule people as the article
about her beliefs in "demon sperm" did. Second, by refusing to cower and fighting back at them while she was surrounded by a cheering crowd of her own
supporters, everyone could see the limit of the media's establishment power to
demean.

Spiritual Warriors as Battle Axes against Global Conspiracies

The COVID-19 pandemic made the familiar fears that the ideologies of spiritual warfare had always espoused—the hyper-exposure of one's body to the
invisible evil forces that could somehow penetrate it—quite visceral, and other
conspiritualists responded accordingly. With the news of a viral disease that
could enter one's physical body and result in—among other named symptoms—
gasping for breath and the necessity of being hooked to life-support machines,

people grappled with the fear of losing their bodily autonomy. In the various conspiracy theories that circulated worldwide, especially ones around 5G technology and vaccines, there was a recurring fear of the invasion of one's body by foreign bodies—either a virus or a mechanical device like a microchip, or both—and subsequent zombification. Spiritual warriors who had always anticipated the *War*, an imminent showdown with a spectacular supernatural force, saw the onset of COVID-19 as the expected moment. Conspirituality apprehended the diabolical agenda, the means of characterizing the nature of the threat and preparing the spiritual armament with which they would confront the moment.

For Africans, this crisis was frightening on another level. It was clear that as they increasingly participated in global affairs and opened their borders to the rest of the world, the continent's vulnerabilities would no longer be limited to the abstract problems of economic or political issues, like globalism, neoliberalism, capitalism, or any ideological isms that have always affected daily living. The 2008 financial crisis, for instance, acutely showed up the global financial systems and accentuated the fear of a connected world.[35] The reality of the COVID-19 disease induced even more trauma. Physical bodies, now potentially linked with billions of others worldwide through the networking capabilities of an invisible virus, made everyone's susceptibility to the malevolence of modernity intensely visceral. Because their bodies and what could be done to them—or with them—were quite implicated in the pandemic affair, the conspiracy theories that sought a connection between the pandemic, impending vaccines, and 5G network technology that ruled social media at the time made immense sense to some people, including spiritual warriors.

The conspiracy theorist is typically paranoid about the processes of modernity.[36] Like the spiritual warrior, their second-order thinking makes them believe there is always more to reality than what is stated, and that a momentous historical or social situation unfolds because some morally suspect powerful people who navigate an unseen world are keeping everyone in the dark to carry out a sinister agenda.[37] Michael Barkun described conspiracy theorists as people who probe beyond the official report to explain evil. Since much of conspiracy reasoning is conjecture, the force of evil and its motives tend to be hyperbolized in their account of evil.[38] This outsized projection of the power of evil affords them the chance to create a grand narrative of cosmic dualism—good and evil locked in a showdown—and sometimes to implant themselves into the story as a hero selected by superior design to win a victory on behalf of others. Thus, when the news of a looming epidemic from a powerful country like China broke, there was, expectedly, fear on the part of people in the developing world who had no idea how they would fare. There were no clearcut answers for their befuddlement; the anxiety of the moment and the instability of familiar epistemes in the face of the pandemic traumatized them.[39]

From China to Europe, a deluge of news of a crisis of certainty flooded everywhere, heightening the fear of what the months ahead would bring.

In the midst of these developments were experts who claimed the power of science to predict Africa's looming fate in the pandemic. As experts saw what would befall the continent, Africans also saw themselves through their eyes. For instance, in February 2020, Bill Gates warned that the effect of the disease in Africa could be "very dramatic."[40] In early April 2020, during a television program that featured two French doctors, one of them suggested using Africans as guinea pigs to test a tuberculosis vaccine to see if it would be effective against COVID-19.[41] The cofounder of the Bill and Melinda Gates Foundation, Melinda Gates, further added to the fears of Africans by telling CNN in an interview that the disease situation would be intensely bad in Africa. According to her, "When I saw what China had to do to isolate an enormous part of its population, my first thought was Africa. How in the world are they going to deal with this? . . . It is going to be horrible in the developing world. Part of the reasons you are seeing the case numbers still do not look very bad is because they don't have access to many tests. Look at Ecuador. Look at what is going on in Ecuador, they are putting bodies out on the streets, you are going to see that in countries in Africa."[42] That a spectacularly rich White woman singled out Africa to raise a specter of mass deaths was not only irritating; the perverse fantasy of corpses on the streets also intensified the existing fears and made for probable connections of White institutional power, the mischief possible because one possesses specialized knowledge, and the dispensability of Black bodies. These predictions of Africa's fate in the pandemic might seem disparate, but they connected to a historical resentment of Western imperial violence on the continent and fueled conspiratorial fantasies about neocolonial exploitation that would be perpetrated through mass deaths.

Barely a week after Melinda Gates "prophesied" African deaths, a media report stated that the U.N. Economic Commission (UNEC) for Africa "expected" at least 300,000 Africans to die and about 29 million more would be further pushed into extreme poverty. UNEC thus called for a $100 billion safety net for the continent, saying that without such intervention 1.2 billion Africans (out of 1.4 billion people) could be infected and 3.3 million could die in 2020 alone.[43] About a month after Melinda Gates's interview, the World Health Organization (WHO) Regional Office for Africa stated that as many as 10 million cases of infections would occur within six months and 29 to 44 million within a year. Given the low level of medical facilities available in much of Africa, they stated that as many as 190,000 Africans, less than what UNEC predicted but still serious, could die from the disease within the year.[44] As the stories circulated in both the media and across social media platforms, the fear of a diabolical scheme against Africans became even more probable. Churches, already well placed to interpret the assertions of these high-ranking global(ized) institutions with idioms of demonic attacks, raised the level of paranoia and conspirituality and amplified the stakes to the level of a cosmic battle between good and evil. The *War* had finally come.

Conspirituality gave a discursive frame to a matter of epistemic crisis, but did so within the context of contemporary politics and the crisis of trust in authorities.[45] Recent works exploring discussions of fake news and conspiracy theories (a task that became more pertinent, especially given the QAnon phenomenon in U.S. politics) locate these issues within the larger frames of post-truth and post-factuality politics.[46] Context is crucial to the generation and circulation of conspiracy theories, these writers tend to emphasize. While both conspiracy theories and post-truth's prioritizing emotions over objectivity is not a new development, the present political milieu and particularly the event of the pandemic gave fresh currency to conspiritualists' alternate reading of history and signs. The symbolism of some powerful people in globally visible positions predicting a woeful fate for the continent during a pandemic was taken as evidence of conspiracy. Such perceptions approximated the insensitivity of the commentators and also characterized their expertise as acts of malice that could be canceled through the power of prayers.

As the specter of mass deaths in Africa loomed, conspiritualists responded by initiating supernatural power to challenge the body of knowledge and the certainty with which these institutions paternalistically predicted the fate of humanity. As the pandemic was global, the crises of both knowledge and institutional trust that underwrote the mass circulation of conspiracy theories were shared across borders.[47] Conspiritualists' accounts of Western mischief through conspiracy theories also did the cultural work of disestablishing the power structures these institutions had built through an economy of knowledge. The cliché "knowledge is power" seems aphoristic but it also hides the power dynamic inherent in the enterprise of knowledge. Everybody has a degree of knowledge, but the power aspect comes from the asymmetric privilege of knowing *more than others*. Knowledge is only power because its concurrent constructions of reality and the establishment of ideological formations is premised on the exclusion of certain people based on knowledge—what they know and how they know it. Thus, whether designating "fake science" like Immanuel or deploying conspiracy theories like spiritual warriors, the goal is to quarter the massive influence of elites' privileged knowledge in the making of social reality and doing so on the familiar grounds of prayer warfare.[48]

Conspirituality was thus a part of the rituals of countersurveillance, the act of *seeing back* those who denude with their elite expertise and cultural power acquired through their elite knowledge. Conspiracy theories were an economy of sight—a spiritual gaze to counter condescending scientific gazes, hold gazes, and also stare the experts down. The idea of an evil agenda that needed to be met with spiritual armament allowed exercises of creative imagination to connect happenstances, and also locate the internal logic that could lend credence to the conspiracy theories.[49] For instance, the association of a viral disease and the innovative technology of 5G was not all that random, because their arrival happened around the same time. Typically, new technology generates a moral panic, especially if it will change the structures of relationships to time, space, people, and even religious beliefs. The 5G technology was no different. Its potential of connecting virtually everyone and everything—humans and machines—and at a supersonic speed would reorder the world as we know it. While this "future shock" was still being processed, the pandemic hit the world with a suddenness that highlighted human vulnerability and disoriented temporality.[50]

The crushing level of uncertainty over our collective fate contributed to the high level of stress, and the psychological, situational, and political factors that also intensified conspiracy theories.[51] A technology like 5G, described as capable of enhancing the connections between space, time, people, and cultures, also metaphorized the hyper-connection of bodies equally linkable by the technology of a disease. One could now easily die from a disease ignited in a faraway country, exported from a land one had never even heard of, just as one could connect to its inhabitants through speeded-up internet technology. This heightened sense of exposure quickly spawned many desperate explanations from those nonexperts conjecturing reality and arriving at the possibility of humans living in a supposed "new world order" or a "unified world order," where wizard scientists would manipulate everyone to compliantly live under one government. These all reflected how people, including spiritual warriors, had been forced to examine their bodies' weight(lessness) against the larger forces of late modernity.

There was some irony to people wracked by the fear of hyper-connection sharing affect through technological devices that facilitated connection to a global chain of humans through which they networked to build and reinforce the ethos of disestablishment. It was not just people's bodies that could be connected through disease; even the anxieties and rites of conspirituality became linkable across space and time through their mobile devices and the apps stored on them. For instance, WhatsApp, which had greatly helped families, professional colleagues, and even old schoolmates to stay in touch, played a role in transmitting these tales.[52] With the ubiquity of mobile phones and easier access to technological resources such as cellular data, social networking apps like WhatsApp have become commonplace in Nigeria and many African countries, and changed communication from earlier versions of electronic media to which they listened to ones on which they actively create and circulate content. While social media networks such as Twitter and Facebook have structured political literacies and social empowerment through their comparatively democratic nature of creating and circulating information, the WhatsApp domain has added the advantage of intimacy.[53] Often limited to close circles of family, friends, and known associates, the ease of accessing people in one's private networks—you had to have their phone numbers—made WhatsApp a veritable means of circulating what had been made seeable to them among their close associates, who also transmitted them to others who needed to be able to see as well.

During the early days of the pandemic, it was through both news reports and the mis/dis/information circulated through the WhatsApp medium that the death anxiety and the impulses to cancel the agenda of demonic conspiracies that had been triggered by a looming "new world order" in the wake of the pandemic traveled far and wide, gaining strong appeal. Truth-tellers made and circulated YouTube videos in which they claimed they had decoded the conspiracy behind the pandemic, and were proving their power of discernment to the public by making videos of themselves that would be transmitted through mobile devices.[54] Some of these truth-tellers did not make visual appearances, but typed their exegeses on the evil behind the pandemic, appended their names, and sent the material to others to freely share. Some merely narrated their accounts in audio recordings. It was through this means that perhaps one of the most popular conspiracy theories that linked 5G and coronavirus spread, a recording by a voice who claimed to be a former Vodafone executive—and therefore privileged to know about the technology. He was later unmasked as "Jonathon James," an evangelical pastor in the United Kingdom who had worked for Vodafone as a sales associate for less than a year.[55] A Nigerian, simply identified as "Kunle," who claimed to be an IT engineer who had worked for the WHO (and therefore was privileged to access their schemes against humanity), narrated a similar tale in an audio recording in the Yoruba language. After purportedly breaking down the complex link between 5G technology and COVID-19, he encouraged Christians to pray and also recommended some supposed scientific resolutions to blocking out the radiation from 5G towers. Because he spoke in a local language, the information traveled far into the hands and hearts of virtually anyone who carried a mobile phone and could speak the language.

Conspiracy theorists' efforts at educating the public against "fake science" like these showed how they feverishly and hurriedly sought access to the power that knowledge had given the likes of Bill and Melinda Gates the edge to make authoritative pronouncements about how the world would fare in the pandemic. In present-day society's models of digital capitalism, knowledge is content and content is the new extractive resource. Posturing possession of knowledge is a means of generating topical content across one's social media accounts. The heightened stakes around a sensational issue like the pandemic gave a number of these content generators room to project themselves to the public, test resolves, and "go viral" by being seen as punching against the larger

The Noisome Pestilence • 97

authority of science and its global elites. Having admitted themselves into an elite club of esoteric knowledge production, conspiritualists and truth-tellers appeared on social media platforms to narrate the diabolism of "fake science" to others still battling with the opacity of what had befallen the world. They take advantage of the suspicion and distrust people have for "big" corporations and institutions by posing to know the truth that is obscured from everyone else. In a time when terms like "Big Data," "Big Pharma," "Big Tech," "Big Meat" metonymize the rise of corporations whose operations are increasingly beyond the access of the regular guy and therefore unaccountable to the public, the retailers of remote knowledge like conspiritualists, who are able to connect a web of possibilities outside the official and obvious narrative, earn trust. Yes, they earn this trust as a result of confirmation bias, but also because they are considered "small" actors pushing back against the enormous organizations whose gigantic size means they are above the control of the populace and have therefore become monstrous. People queue behind these individuals because they promise a deviation from the monstrosity of "big" institutions that have embodied oppressive bureaucratic traditions over time. The conspiritualists are far more accessible, and their smaller-scale operations are seemingly transparent. Also, because their epistemologies are penetrable (and therefore relatively uncorrupted) and they do not seem to have any corporation behind them, they have no obligation to anything but the truth.

One of these local retailers of "truth" during the pandemic was a Nollywood actor, a conspiritualist called Joseph Okechukwu. He typically made his You-Tube videos by sitting behind an office desk with sometimes two laptop devices opened before him as he narrated embellished stories of a global elite conspiracy. Part of what he shared were stories that had already been bandied around on social media by other entrepreneurs of truth, such as when far-right U.S. conservative Rick Wiles urged Christians to stand and fight Bill Gates.[56] Okechukwu's videos too would be circulated by those in search of the truth that had supposedly been hidden from them by the "mainstream media" and "globalist media" beholden to the agendas of so-called establishment figures and globalists—or global icons—such as Bill Gates, Barack Obama, Hillary Clinton, and George Soros. Sometimes the truth Okechukwu shared came from QAnon, but coming from a Nigerian, those conspiracy theories had a vernacular scaffolding that resonated with a local audience. From talking about the pope as part of a global conspiracy to discerning the "evil eye of Horus" in the Nigerian version of the reality show *Big Brother* that took place during the lockdown, he built an audience. He not only took advantage of models of digitality to build an enterprise of distributing the truths hidden to the public, he also initiated an "Africa for Trump 2020" campaign, parading T-shirts and baseball caps he had produced for sale. He urged fellow Africans to "evangelize" by sharing his videos and wearing his T-shirts to campaign for the "most non-racist President of America" that he had ever seen in his lifetime.[57]

For his audience, Okechukwu, allegedly a professional actor, did not just intuit the truth. He created an impression of "diligent" research into science and history, ostentatiously evidenced by the laptops on his desk, his supposed gateway into a world of infinite information and infoteering. Since other conspiracy theorists' battle cry has become *Do your research!* as discussed in the introduction, Okechukwu grandly exhibits his bona fides in these videos by displaying the props of modern technology—two opened laptops—to show his technological connection to the world of unlimited information and data.[58] By making these videos, conspiritualists like him were purportedly standing up to the power of the knowledge of scientists and politicians and demonstrating to these elites that they do not have a monopoly of seeing and asserting truths.[59] Thus, the intricacies of science are explained by people without expertise in science, but in possession of the truths they had seen on YouTube, read from blogs, "researched" by themselves, or learned from dissident scientists such as Immanuel—who would go on to set up social media accounts across multiple platforms and dedicated them to counseling the public against vaccines, nefarious liberal agendas, and support for Trump, particularly in the months before the presidential election. These abundant supplies of knowledge from people who needed to be seen became a part of spiritual warfare because they claimed knowledge of malevolent global forces and promised empowerment to resist both demonic forces and their human collaborators.

Sometimes, conspiritualists justified their legitimacy to disestablish the structures of power and knowledge through travel and professional expertise. Just as Immanuel never failed to add "Doctor" to her name, conspiracy theorists who explained the links between the disease, vaccine, and the looming dystopia were appended with local descriptors such as "Arinze, a pharmacist in Manchester," "Kunle, an IT expert who works with the WHO," "Biodun, who currently lives in the USA," and so on. Their combination of local descriptors with the international sites assumes the credibility of truth-telling conspiritualists because it highlights the rational factors that legitimated these informed individuals to narrate those truths. Their conspirituality was to prompt an eternal vigilance against a diabolic agenda, and its corpus of narratives moved across various regions of the world through social media apps and digital devices. Pushed by both spiritual warriors and conspiracy theorists, these accounts steadily absorbed the existential anxieties of those it encountered across its digital routes and sometimes ended on the church altar, where pastors turned them into inspired visions and rites of disestablishing incarnate demonic forces.

Like Okechukwu, who uses the props of two opened laptops to validate his videos, adding secular details such as having worked at a globally visible corporation or having traveled through famous world cities to the account was essential to building credibility. Similar to Immanuel at the Capitol, whose white coat and professional training made her a renegade, these local ones too exhibited their logical connections to rationality. They were eager to prove that they did not just intuit the truth, but that it had a rational basis. While they appropriate the symbolic power of institutions, they also make an ostentatious show of disengaging from its institutional legitimacy and the traditions of oppressiveness it had come to represent, so they could be seen as nothing more than an individual who embodies no other interest but enlightenment. The institution that props the conspiritualist recedes to the background, only useful as a backdrop at the moment of disengagement, such as wearing a white coat to compare fellow medical doctors to the "good Germans" of the Hitler era.

Trump: Disestablishing Demonic Confederacies through Politics

As much as conspiritualists distrust size because they correlate it with invincibility, obscurity, and ethical corruptibility, their support for Trump was proof they do not totally reject it as a battle axe in their task of disestablishing the forces of power. In their study of political ideologies and conspiracy theories, Miller, Saunders, and Farhart observed that "knowledge exacerbates motivated conspiracy endorsement (and turns off the positive effect of knowledge) *among conservatives.*"[60] Conservative politicians and pundits, they noted, more readily motivate their base through conspiracy theories than liberals. What makes the politicians succeed is not the ignorance of those who receive the message as much as the audience's existing lack of trust in authority.[61] Many studies of political partisanship and conspiracy theories, of course, were written before the pandemic in the year 2020, and in retrospect they fall short of explaining why Trump, who craves political power and authority, so much appealed emotively to the anti-authority instincts of conspiritualists during the pandemic. The perception of Trump as the battle axe against the established world order, which, ironically, inverts the crisis of authority and trust that typically defines conspiracy theories in his favor, were the main factors that reconciled conspiritualists in different cultures and historical contexts.

Ideally, Trump, with his radical departure from the norms that have structured political establishments in the United States and beyond, has been a fascinating object of study for scholars, especially in performance studies, who take disruptors from the norm seriously. Christopher Grobe's analysis of performance studies' fixation with radical resistance to norms and the liminal breaks it affords, for one, explored how Trump and his band of alt-right supporters and trolls, who also construe their online pranks as habits of disruption to normativity, become an ethical and methodological conundrum of sorts for performance scholarship, which typically valorizes disruptions.[62]

Richard Schechner admitted that "as a performative, Trump is exceedingly fascinating," but he still considered his emergence as president as part of an ongoing
crisis of ethics and morality, not of viable political resistance.[63] Trump and his
horde of right-wing followers paradoxically disrupt the norms of disruption
with pranks and trolling that have significantly impacted the cultural landscape.[64] Like Grobe, Tony Perucci also explored the various ways "performance
art" is now deployed in discussing Trump in popular commentary.[65] Designating
him a performance artist passes off his actions as mere play or pranks to discount
the reality of their effects, and sometimes characterizing him thusly is a means of
managing the dizzying reality of having such a disruptive figure as president. Presidential performances are generative of power, and politicians' simultaneous production and manipulation of that power give the public a basis to relate to the
presidential figure.[66] With Trump and his radical difference, some of those per-
mutations changed significantly. His supporters' valorization of his refusal to
accept the normative aesthetics of presidential performance added another layer
to their contestations: the will to perform power, to ostentatiously beat down
opponents wedded to the norms by disrupting political symbolism.

Trump thus figures as a barbarian—the archetypal "outsider" standing
at the gates of civilization, whose values are antithetical to the standards that
foster stability in the empire—who disrupted the norms of American politics
through his unruly performance as a political contender and as president. Maria
Boletsi shows that the barbarian trope that has encapsulated an external threat
in Western politics was similarly applied to Trump, to designate him as an outsider, but ambivalently. Rather than a threat that would destroy U.S. civilization, his outsiderness profiled his relative lack of aesthetic sophistication, his
departure from established norms of public conduct, and also how these factors
might have contributed to his appeal. To be labeled a barbarian affirmed him
as a disruptive figure whose deliberate refusal to act in consonance with other
political actors would denormalize extant traditions and the political structures
that have instantiated the oppressive political establishment.[67] The desire to see
an end to the existing political order and its complex institutions was evident
in his followers' persistent invocations against the "deep state," a term that
connotes the shadowy elite and conniving bureaucrats who actually run the
political system and whose unending powers are not subject to democratic
accountability.[68] While conspiracy theorists seem to take the existence of the
"deep state" as factual, their expressions of its insidiousness highlight an
objectification of the administrative customs and bureaucratic expertise that
uphold political establishments. These expert and professional administrators'
contributions to the formidability of the political establishment that conspiritualists seek to disestablish have been continuous even when political power
has moved across ideological divides. Trump's nonconformity to normative standards thus made him—to them, at least—a veritable wrecking ball, a

figure of anti-normativity in the top spot of political power, who could demystify the performances of traditions that make politics so formidable and oppressive.

His nonconforming behavior as politician and president showed the limits of the disciplinary norms that constrict politicians' public conduct and through which they derive the authority to order other people's lives. By abjuring behavioral standards socially prescribed for those who inhabit elite institutions of power—speaking in colloquialisms, shunning genteelness, and embracing the instinctive habits of "bad taste"—he broke down the establishment power of the subsisting norms, their hubristic means of determining lives, and let people see the limits of these institutions' ability to enforce discipline. It also helped that he was a billionaire, because in addition to other factors that made Trump appealing to his voter base was his seeming autonomy. Unlike his fellow political contenders, he did not seem morally or financially beholden to the institutions of power they want disestablished. For people such as conspiritualists, who find politics' legitimizing forces in textual and abstract knowledge acquired in "liberal" spaces of advanced learning institutions rather complex and thus alienating, his unconventional public attitudes also let them see that civic ineptitude need not disqualify one from inhabiting spheres where elite knowledge is required. Trump is, of course, also an embodiment of several legitimating social factors—Whiteness, social class, gendered power, and elite formal education. However, his self-posturing as the quintessence of an elitist who chose to become the representative of the "real" Americans—conservative people who are the certified opposite of the "out-of-touch" liberals—made him seeable as a class traitor and a defector to the authentic American cause. It was this trope of barbarianism and outsiderism that made him appealing to conspiritualists, who saw him as God's battle axe that would penetrate the high places of authority they want humbled.

Trump as candidate—and later as the president who would personify the power of the most established and powerful institution in the world—also represented a figure of liminality. In 2016, he won a rather improbable victory to make it into the Oval Office as a norm breaker, social transgressor, and flag hugger who was disdained by the same establishment figures that conspiritualists hold responsible for the many things wrong with the world. More than his opponent in that historic election, Hillary Rodham Clinton, he perhaps better understood how America itself was the religion—rather than the ethics of right-wing Christian conservatives that he publicly pandered to—operative in his followers' minds. The national flag they fervently adulate was a totemic symbol of America as religion, the cross of their nationalist salvation.[69] For nationalists and "patriots" who consider themselves the soldiers of Christ, the U.S. flag was emblematic of compounded victories of the nation-state and the transcendental-ethical forces that upheld the country.

Trump's embrace of the flag was thus not just an ostentatious demonstration of his patriotism; it was also the equivalent of a public conversion to their nationalist cause. Having established that crossover to the "right" side in the minds of his followers, every other sin he committed—or could have committed—in office was not only forgivable but was forgiven in advance. His adamant refusal to conform to the established ethics of seeking political office was a form of performance activism. So unconventional was it that it helped him stand out and appear as an authentic figure who would not merely repeat the ethical traditions of power they wanted disestablished, and a promising candidate for the agenda of implanting righteousness.

From a theological point of view, his political trajectory as a billionaire who had descended from the height of Trump Tower to rescue the "ordinary" American folks parallels the narrative of the supreme God who loved humankind so much that he became an ordinary man in the person of Jesus just so he could redeem humanity.[70] One of the repeated assertions of Trump supporters was that he is "one of us" and he is "fighting for us." Although that statement shows their relationship with him is hierarchical and even utilitarian, it also illustrates their self-categorization and how they imagine what and whose interests the almighty power of the U.S. presidency should serve. "One of us" is a theological language that shows a collapse of hierarchies between God the supreme being and ordinary humans. Other studies of Trump's performance also clearly show how the years of his acting bossy on the reality show *The Apprentice*, which he hosted for a long time, contributed to perceptions of him as a figure of power.[71] His performance as a "barbarian" politician was not all there was to his "performance art." The years of performing a serious-minded and efficient CEO foreshadowed his clowning during the electioneering in 2016, and those who supported him had genuine reasons to look beyond his "unseriousness" on the campaign trail. Reid, describing the sociocultural circumstances in which Trump emerged as the archetype of a tyrannical boss and capitalist folk hero, identified the socioeconomic crisis that helped his rise as a public figure of power as an era when the "interplay of economic and non-economic humiliations and indignities encountered in daily life under globalized market economies and the endless War on Terror."[72] Within a social context where economic power further delineated people's sense of self-worth, his gratuitous cruelty as he performed the boss became laudable.

His performance of barbarianism in the high-stakes arena of Washington politics could not have tanked his political chances because those acts as a politician had been prefigured by his performance as a powerful CEO who wielded what was tantamount to godlike powers to decide the fate of subordinates by hiring and firing them. Within the context of America's corporatized politics, the brute power of an economic overlord that he dramatized on the

screen for years was appealing to his followers because it promised to be efficacious enough to disestablish the self-serving agents that have formed the order
of ruling political authorities. For conspiritualists who frequently rehearse
battles and victories, he was an extension of their desire to see political orders
disestablished. Even better for practical and spiritual purposes, he was not ethically beholden to the norms of the institutions of power they want to see
disintegrated.

By the time he played the barbarian for the 2016 election, his followers rationalized his performance as a parody of both himself and the procedures
through which his fellow politicians construct their power, and lauded his pre-
emption of his predictable political opponents who would play by the rigid
dictates of the political rule book. His followers insist his characteristic vulgarity and brazen acts were an aggressive means necessary to enact the hostile
takeover of political power from its present holders in established institutions
of power. A person who could promote cruelty and endorse violence to assert
his sovereignty from social regulatory structures was thus the right candidate
to carry out the work of destroying the established order. He was the right
human weapon through which conspiritualists could vicariously achieved their
desire to see political orders disestablished. The perception of his autonomy was
also boosted by his claims of self-funding his campaign. They surmised that having freed himself from all the ethics of social respectability through his so-
called "barbaric" behavior, he would be an effective battle axe swung at the trees
of political establishments. Such a person could negotiate virtually anything—
the Constitution, trade deals, health insurance—and with anyone, including
Vladimir Putin and Kim Jong-un.[73]

For spiritual warriors who had always prayed obsessively to see power change
hands in their favor, this candidate was their political weapon. His confounding
alterity from the norms of political culture and inability to feel the constraints
of social shaming would be effective in doing the work of creative destruction
and bringing the much-desired radically reformed order closer. He would smash
the traditions that had instituted present conditions; he would not be incom-
moded by confining democratic ethics, and he would not have problems applying an iron hand—or a battle axe—when necessary. In that sense, he was a
battle axe in *their* hands who would achieve what they prayed for through
political means. By not yielding to sentiment, he would also be expectedly
merciless and vicious with his enemies. When writing on spiritual warfare,
scholars cannot help but note the associations between its practices and neoliberalism. For instance, O'Donnell and Sean McCloud respectively wrote about
how neoliberalism impacts spiritual warfare from the angles of contemporary
realities.[74] While O'Donnell looks at spiritual warfare narratives as interventions
in a neoliberal crisis of consensus narrative that are expressed through "post-
truth" politics, McCloud sees how the structures of neoliberalism reverberate

spiritual warfare through the ideas of capitalism and individualism that are prioritized.

The kinds of desires transposed to Trump by conspiritualists also show that the continuities of spiritual warfare and neoliberalism include how their politics of survival at the expense of others become zero-sum. Prayers and political actions that seek to disestablish the forces they hold responsible for their diminishing seek to eradicate the *others* perceived to be standing in the way of their flourishing, and activities of spiritual warfare tend to justify heavy-handedness or outright cruelty to those others. Characteristically optimistic about their ability to survive any strangulating conditions on account of their faith and their ability to determinedly press their bodies in service to the disciplinary regimes of prayer, conspiritualists also tend to take the fallouts of social engineering—the human casualties from its adverse side effects—as the consequences of personal choices and moral weaknesses, a point Adam Kotsko crucially notes about demonization and neoliberalism.[75]

As an outsider who was able to cut through the thicket of political machinations that the conspiritualists see existing in the highest corridors of power, Trump thus earned the trust of those who had a crisis of trust in the government. By claiming to also be fighting a Christian agenda against the radical evil represented by the Democrats, media, scientists, and so on, and all the structures of power that sustain their power, he became God's anointed candidate in high places. For conspiritualists, he was the ultimate anti-authority authority, the anti-normative figure with the right vibe of triumphalism, machismo, and bravado to enact the political confrontations that would make spiritual warfare efficacious. His unruliness was also quite entertaining. Those who consider themselves God's battle axe derived a vicarious pleasure from watching Trump smash the structures of establishment politics. With his supposed authenticity, typical disregard for the norms of public conduct, brashness, vulgarity, spectacular talent for stoking conflict, and the way his political victory confounded the political experts, most of whom did not give him a chance, Trump humbled the social ordinances they wanted disestablished.

They perceive him as a warrior who would not easily succumb as other politicians are wont to do under pressure. This promise of a lack of compromise appealed to conspiritualists, for whom truth is truth, and like Immanuel, would stand by their convictions even when the rest of the world tries to shame them for it. By being an "unshameable" public figure who would not capitulate to the dictates of the establishment that expected him to conform to rules of political conduct, he became even more credible to antiestablishment conspiritualists. His refusal to "act presidential" even while campaigning for the presidential job suggested he would not simply go along with the norms that had constructed the oppressive order they wanted to see disestablished. To those who have come to believe that at the base of all politics is mere theater, that politicians put up a contrived front before the public, Trump's acting out of the script was far more compelling and sincere than his pearl-clutching, predictable, and safe "opponent" wedded to the rule book of public political conduct. His disruptiveness, they envisaged, would deconstruct the architecture of power politics and usher in a new and radically reformed order that would be more favorable for them. The constant reference to Trump's refusal to "act" like a president, and the challenges his administration faced from those deemed establishment figures over his policies, only further proved the existence of those shady elites. They—the deep state, as these shadowy figures came to be labeled—must truly exist in the highest places of power and be committed to an agenda of decimation against him. This conjecture spurred their combative instincts to resist these forces so that he—and they, by extension—could be established in place of those spectral forces.

Trump's willingness to use the gravitas of his office to promote ideas of "fake science" by circulating conspiracy theories about the disease—and subsequently divest himself of moral responsibility for the massive scale of death the United States was experiencing—did not throw off the resoluteness of his conspiritualist supporters, who saw themselves as part of a cosmic war against evil; it only sealed it tighter. His mere existence in politics had yielded a valuable category of participation for them to attest to the truth of their conviction against oppressive power, and those dead from COVID—if they truly even died at all—were battle casualties.[76] The many conspiracy theories about how Trump faced many dark forces because he was holding up the truth of Christianity, and how much he deserves their prayers of support, were part of the efforts of moral mobilization by his followers who needed his resounding victory in the political sphere against the "deep state," "fake news," "fake science," and so on, to vicariously proclaim theirs too in the spiritual sphere. These conspiritualists proclaimed the many threats to Christianity if he lost by criticizing every phenomenon that threatened his political success. They demonized everyone—Democrats, Islam, China, pharmaceutical companies, Bill Gates, socialism—all in a bid to establish the truths of their faith and disestablish counteracting factors.[77]

For his African conspiritualist supporters, his performance as an unconventional president was also a valuable weapon of warfare to disrupt established traditions of democracy, the lofty requirements for political participation, and the false gods of orthodoxies that leave many of them behind in the arrangements of global modernity when it insists on viewing their lives and experiences as an alternative to Western realities. For instance, the contention between Malagasy President Andry Rajoelina and the WHO over an herbal potion to "cure" COVID-19, pitting an African leader against establishment science and expertise, further bolstered African conspiritualists' suspicion of the pandemic as a global conspiracy, especially against Africans.[78]

Trump—about the most visible figure of authority standing up to institutions like the WHO during the pandemic by threatening to cut U.S. funding for them, diminishing their expertise, and alleging they colluded with China against the world—made him the perfect enforcer of conspiritualists' instincts to remove the political and social traditions that built the structures they want diminished. Trump was their human navigator in high places, the one whose radical difference and inability to fit into the ennobling traditions of political leadership made him fascinating and effective in disestablishing structures.

His xenophobic accusations of China infecting the world with the virus also resonated with his African supporters because of preexisting anti-China sentiments and the heightened racial awareness that followed the global Black Lives Matter protests of 2020. It did not help China's image that when the COVID-19 issue was generating a moral panic in March 2020, Western news media sites carried increased reports of Chinese racist attacks on Africans in China. For example, some stories reported Africans being chased down the streets and forced into quarantine by the Chinese police because the Chinese believed that Africans were importing COVID-19 into China. In another story, a McDonald's in China barred some Africans from dining because they alleged Africans were carriers of COVID-19.[79] Africans were also angry because they already thought of China as either thoroughly careless or malevolent in inflicting COVID-19 on the world. What Africans read in the reports was that China was trying to offload the burden of guilt for the disease onto Africans, who were victims of their machinations.

The blend of a pushback against a condescending West and its institutions' superciliousness, a pushback against the Chinese who transferred the shame and aggression of being responsible for a global pandemic onto Africans by drumming up anti-Black racism, plus the growing anxiety to assert oneself in the world also created tension, solidified attitudes, and further redrew partisan lines.[80] By the time conspiritualists were repeating Trump's labeling of COVID-19 as the "China virus," they were more than merely echoing his racist attacks. The accusations of malice by China resonated with them because it coincided with the resentment of racist disrespect of Africans by the Chinese.[81] As many of the conspiracy theories circulating on social media that alleged the disease was created in a laboratory in Wuhan, China, gained more traction, conspiritualists who needed a demon onto which to offload the anxieties of the moment found a ready one in blaming China for the "China virus."[82]

These circumstances prepared the ground for when Dr. Stella Immanuel exposed the truth hidden by "fake science" and propelled conspiracy theorists who were seeking to know what lies beyond the pale. For African conspiritualists, her beliefs in both global and spiritual conspiracies were credible because she was an African like them and was also a trained medical doctor who worked in the United States. As an expert in the realms of the unseen mediated knowledge of science or specters, it was easy for them to juxtapose her assertions with global health experts like Bill Gates who had earlier said that life would not be the same until a vaccine was created. The latter became not just a purveyor of "fake science," but was also denounced as an agent of evil who had manufactured a disease so he could sell the cure. Some pastors urged prayers against him and his presumptive attitudes about humanity.[83] Conspiritualists praised Immanuel for her truth and even circulated memes comparing her to Bill Gates. In one of the memes, they juxtaposed the two of them and noted that while she was an actual medical doctor, Bill Gates was a mere "college dropout." In another meme, her head was photoshopped onto the image of a woman putting a machete around the neck of a White man; the head on that neck was that of Bill Gates.

Noisome Pestilences and Noise-Some Victories

Despite the grave predictions, many African countries thrived far better in the COVID-19 pandemic than global experts predicted, lending credence to the suspicion that the science that predicted woe for Africa was truly "fake." In a continent of 1.4 billion people, the number of recorded cases went up to around 11.2 million, with South Africa alone accounting for that the bulk of them.[84] There were high rates of recovery too, much more than expected. Despite the paternalistic vision of dead bodies littering the streets of Africa, the death rate stayed at roughly 2.16 percent. In contrast, relatively powerful nations of the world such as the United States, the UK, India, Brazil, Spain, Italy, Russia, and France have had far higher casualty rates. The United States alone has had more than 850,000 deaths as of January 2022. There is a strong possibility that the African COVID-19 cases are undercounted, but that will also be true of every other country. In whatever manner the COVID-19 infections are totaled, Africans have still performed better than all the gloomy forecasts predicted for them. The continent that was infantilized at the beginning of the pandemic turned out to be the one that triumphantly emerged with far fewer casualties.

Conspiritualists felt justified by the outcome and doubled down on their claims that COVID-19 was part of an evil agenda, and that they had preemptively thwarted it by being able to see it and cancel it through superior power. The lower death figures became their victory against the elite scientists who conspired against them but who were defeated through the power of God. As it has turned out, the scientists who foretold their grim fate by presuming their helplessness turned out to be the ones with limited vision. The Western media that African conspiritualists had demonized as "fake media" for their pejorative reporting on Africa could not hide their surprise at the turn of events.

Western elites did not help matters when they asked questions like, "Why are Africans not dying?" or attributing the eventual low death rate to the resilience of their poverty—the same poverty they said at the beginning would be Africa's doom![85] People like Immanuel celebrated how their spiritual vigilance had undercut and triumphed over technocratic malevolence. The befuddlement of scientists and their fellow "conspirators" in the global media channels was a victory that announces itself.

The aftermath of the pandemic also showed that though the COVID-19 pandemic might have been a war, it was also not the *War* they had always strenuously expected. People did not die as predicted, and the definitive end surely did not come. As such, the pandemic was taken as a major rehearsal toward that *War* that was still coming sometime in the future. While the fear of mass deaths that wracked people at the start gradually dissipated (and diffused into other social contests), the incident of a global pandemic and the lockdown did not leave social relations untarnished. The liminality of this unique event disrupted existing social orders, affirmed the identity of some spiritual warriors, and also inverted it. In the next chapter, I will explore how the sense of fear and doom that developed at the time became oriented toward ideas of state persecution, the paranoia that someone somewhere with an anti-Christian agenda wanted all churches shut to diminish the force of their faith, and how that sense of embattlement enhanced existing ideological polarities among groups of Christians locally and internationally.

With algorithms having now been effectively configured to maximize the reach of outrage-inducing rhetoric and the subsequent fueling of chaos, people became more resolutely locked into their polarizing bubbles, where the good they now personified resounded in the echo chambers of like minds. As examined in the next chapter, the various activities of the conspiritualists who dominated this period were consequential in testing the existing and established power dynamics between the state and the church so the latter could become autonomous of certain strictures of governance. As it happened, some church leaders and their congregations who were emboldened by Africa's victory against the virus pushed for the immediate reopening of their churches that had been shut (along with all other religious houses) in March 2020. They grew weary of preaching to empty auditoriums while their congregations watched remotely via the internet. They insisted that the costs of the pandemic to every sphere of the economy, including churches, was not worth the continuous shutdown. Their sermons through which they pressured the government to reopen the churches were also a campaign for autonomy from the democratized order that they felt subjugated the essence of the church under the authority of the state. They more or less attacked public officials and fellow pastors whom they portrayed as dupes of a malicious Western conspiracy.

4

Churches Going Virtual

• •

Empty Auditoriums and the Essential Services of Prayer

If you refuse to open church for fear of being infected, you were never a believer! This is a great concern because there were churches that were thought to be churches until recently. We find a lot of ministers who were thought to be advocates of the gospel advocating for shutting down the churches because they cannot guarantee safety. It is pressure like this that reveals what is a church and what is not. Do they really believe in God, the same God of the patriarchs in the Bible? When you get to that point where you are afraid of opening churches for fear of being infected, you have denied the faith. You never believed!
—Pastor Chris Oyakhilome

About six days after the Dr. Stella Immanuel outing, four adults and two children met in a private residence in Ibadan, Oyo state, Nigeria, to hold church services. At the time, religious houses were on full lockdown in the highly populated states of the country.[1] There was growing restlessness about the lockdown, and in some quarters there was agitation that their churches would not be the same after being shut for an extended period. There was fear that people would discover they could do without church after all, which might lead to a decline in church culture. These six people from two families decided to meet, in defiance of both COVID-19 and the state regulations that barred gatherings in public religious houses. According to one of those who gathered in that house, their obedience to government regulations was disobedience to God's instruction that Christians must meet regularly. In an article he wrote about the meeting, "How John McArthur Inspired a Gathering in Ibadan," blogger Deji Yesufu stated that many churches in most parts of the world have, for too long, enjoyed such considerable stability that they no longer know what it means to be a Christian in times of turbulence:

> When we read in scriptures that trying times will come on the church and the faith of many will fail in the end time, very few of us would have imagined that what would try our faith would be a germ or a virus. And with the threat that we may contract Coronavirus and die, many of us do not think that commands like "... do not neglect meeting together ..." (Hebrew 10:25) is worth obeying anymore. Perhaps if I remind us that these times are trying times, like times of war, we would realize that the way we respond to the times is somewhat a reflection of our faith and that self-preservation is not anything different from those whom the Lord warned against saving their lives and in the process losing it (Matthew 16:15).[2]

The John MacArthur he mentioned was the pastor of the megachurch Grace Community Church in Los Angeles, California, who had taken a similar stance on the shutdown of churches in the United States due to the pandemic.[3] MacArthur had reopened his churches during the pandemic, saying he would "rather obey God than Caesar," and Yesufu's reference to him is significant because it shows how the disruption of the social order occasioned by the pandemic generated a Christian moral dilemma of either submitting to religious instruction or to Caesar (secular political authority), and stirred a victory quest that resounded internationally.[4] From Nigeria to the United States, people took on a supposedly secular government whose strategies of governance, power, and regulation construed religion as a matter of mere belief that could wait while the more urgent crisis of the pandemic was resolved rather than as enlivening practices of community.[5] Christians in both countries who watched their churches close while other so-called "essential services" remained open saw an opportunity to disestablish the legitimacy of extant political arrangements that gave politicians power to remove prayer and church fellowship from the social practices that are considered crucial to running a society at material and moral levels. They interpreted the extended lockdown and restrictions on their public gatherings as tyranny, an abrogation of religious rights, a satanic plot, and an insidious state agenda against the autonomy of the church that must be resisted with both spiritual force and political power. A conservative pastor like MacArthur, standing up against the supposed dictatorship of a Democratic governor, Gavin Newsom, in liberal California, made for an archetypal story of Christian persecution, giving spiritual warriors an enhanced sense of identity generated from such contention. This was war, to be fought with political and spiritual weapons.

Already making national news in the United States, MacArthur would not only reopen his church after weeks of initially complying with the government rules; he would also resist health inspections. The church meeting in defiance of the state rules also took place in the context of the Black Lives Matter protests that roiled the United States (and other countries as well) that summer. Given how thousands of protesters defied the guidelines against mass assembly to protest in cities across America, MacArthur's congregation thought it was unfair to disallow faith gatherings. To make this point determinedly clear, his congregation construed their gathering as civic marches and "Jesus's Life Matters" protests, saying they were well within their rights to gather for such matters.[6] Over the next few months, MacArthur further mocked orders by state officials, stating "there is no pandemic" and that "there is another virus loose in the world, and it's the virus of deception . . . the one behind the virus of deception is the arch deceiver Satan himself."[7]

In Nigeria, megachurch pastors such as Chris Oyakhilome of the Christ Embassy Church had similar issues both with state officials having and exercising the power to lock down churches, and with the church leaders who complied with regulations.[8] Similar to Yesufu, the blogger who said that the historic moment of the pandemic afforded Christians the chance to assert the truth of their faith, Oyakhilome too thought that the period should have been a chance to defy both the threat of a virus and the state's authority to regulate church meetings. Unlike MacArthur, though, Oyakhilome did not reopen his network of churches as an act of "civil disobedience." Like other Nigerian pastors, he streamed services online. In those services, he would vehemently criticize his fellow pastors who did not object to moving their church online. Sitting among a group of up to six people and with a microphone in his hand, he would preach and pray, veering into political commentary that would be reported in the news, and then preach and pray against all kinds of satanic devices some more. During those sessions, he made biting attacks on both fellow pastors who willingly opted for online transmission rather than push for church reopening, and the government authorities who gave churches a list of regulations for how they should operate.[9] In one such instance, he said that when government officials had a meeting with prominent church leaders and pastors, trying to get their cooperation on health and safety regulations, the church leaders should have told the government officials to give them some time to pray. He said if pastors had used the opportunity to come together to pray, they would have seen "the hand of God." As noted in chapter 2, to a spiritual warrior, "the hand of God" is a counterpoint to the whimsical hand of history, a divine (and spectacular) intervention in the chaos that defines human affairs. Other pastors' willingness to submit to state regulations, to him, showed that God's house was never their priority. He taunted his fellow pastors who did not protest the move to online services, saying, "I hope you have enjoyed your time so far where *only you* in the cathedral did online transmission."[10]

Beyond the spiritual and political efforts to disestablish the confederated forces in global institutions during the pandemic, examined in the previous chapter, there were also attempts to disentangle the power structure that gave the state so much power over the church. This chapter examines how, by framing church activities as "essential services" and God-mandated rites and practices integral to their Christian identities, Pentecostal pastors like Oyakhilome resisted the attempt to cast religion as dispensable activities. The sacramental services that the churches provide to the populace have blended into the structures of congregants' social experiences, and stopping their gatherings during lockdown was tantamount to chipping away at the sources of life itself.[11] The battle to make the state recognize this essential quality was also necessary to perform their power in the political arena, where the degree of legal and moral maneuvering possible raises both the emotionalism and the stakes of such confrontations. For Pentecostal religious leaders, antagonizing the government was essential to reasserting their power, given how they had been severely ridiculed for their inability to either foresee or stop a global pandemic despite their frequent claims of possessing supernatural powers. In place of dealing with the fallout from not being able to supernaturally intervene in the pandemic, they devised political and civic battles allegorized as diabolism.[12] Conspiracy theories of satanic machinations, anti-Christianity, and Western scientists' plot to alter people's DNA through vaccinations became a battlefront that redirected the embarrassment of religious leaders who were blindsided by the pandemic. With the combined weapons of prayer and the invocation of modern jurisprudence, spiritual warriors argued for their right to remain on the grounds of their churches to worship.

This chapter will also show that church–state relations during the pandemic were not simply about confrontation, but also about taking advantage of the various social changes resulting from the pandemic lockdowns. As the rest of the world moved to video conferencing and similar means to keep social rites going in the early days of the pandemic, some pastors and churches, such as Senior Prophet Jeremiah Omoto Fufeyin of Mercyland Deliverance Ministry and Pastor Temitope Joshua of Synagogue Church of All Nations (SCOAN), saw the means to expand their operations virtually. Not all the arrangements they made at the time have been permanent—some have kept those worship formats and even improved on them dramatically while some have not—but they were astute apprehensions of ways to keep worship activities going in the time of the pandemic and lockdowns, including revising the sensational experience of in-person services when they went fully digital. A pandemic changes the structures of all human relationships in different ways, and what COVID-19 did with religious relations is but one example. Historical analysis by Adam Mohr illustrates how a global pandemic affords an instigation of religious fervor among people of faith who choose to look outside the official channels of medical aid (or scientific authority) for survival.[13] Churches that, in a bid to prove their social responsibility, are too compliant with government directives during a pandemic thus tend to lose their chance to assert their prophetic capability during the uncertainty of the times.[14]

In the Nigerian context, I argue that whether churches put up a fight with what they perceived as the demonic confederacies of institutional authorities, or simply complied with state directives, both attitudes reflect perspicacity—a reflexive insight into the order of things and the shrewdness to distort them to advantage. It is crucial to note the difference between the reaction of those churches that resisted and those that embraced a move online not as opposites, but as consequences of their perspicacities. As powerful devices themselves, spiritual warriors not only see demonic operations, satanic forces, and occult powers; they are discerning enough to also see opportunity and use it to judicious advantage. Though closed, church services were not banished. Like many other social services and businesses, they could continue their operations online for the time being, which both those who argued against closure and those who willingly moved online did. However, some churches turned this shift to virtual operations into a polemic and a source of aggravation by alleging that they were being exiled from the sure terra firma that forms a part of their identity and is a source of spiritual strength. In both Nigeria and the United States, some churches pushed back against the prolonged closing of their auditoriums and the conjoined matters of public health concerns by framing the directive to close in-person worship as a matter of Christian persecution. By seeing satanic machinations in the lockdown and even appealing to Trump, they promoted their identities as spiritual warriors, and in aligning themselves with the political power of the U.S. president, also signposted them as a politically privileged class.

Those who argued for reopening felt that to go *fully* virtual was tantamount to being sent into exile from one's native land, which in this case was their physical churches and their insistence on remaining on the physical—as opposed to virtual—grounds of their church, indexing how much of their identity as spiritual warriors is tied to physical territories and bodies. The fight to meet physically at all costs shows how the spatial territories that they occupy, the activities that take place in them, and the bodies that come together in those places facilitate the sense of intimacy and connectedness of Christian brotherhood that nurtures their spiritual and political identity. The physicality of worship also asserts their groundedness and their primal connection to the ethical forces they invoke during worship in physical spaces. Through togetherness in a place, they produce the "spirit" of the place, which Nimi Wariboko describes as generative of their performative repertoire.[15] Physical gathering is essential to generating their affective force and social power because congregants filled with the power of the Holy Spirit while still being connected to a physical, tangible ancestry of familial and cultural relations constitute the axis mundi—the sacred site where the social and the spiritual touch. Their practices of faith are thus inseparable from both the physicality of their space and the assemblage of the embodied histories that gather to offer an invocation to God and assert dominance over the spiritual forces that exist within the universe of relations. Physical gatherings thus facilitate a continuous dialogue between time and space, a means by which they codify information.[16]

To go online fully—and abruptly—to worship was asking pastors to interrupt the connection of spaces and bodies, yield the collective effervescence of their gathering, alter the arrangement of the symbolic resources that organize their Christian identity, and start working to establish such an ethos in the semi-accustomed realm of cybersphere. They would also have to interrupt the assemblage of the specters they regularly call up and destroy and replace them with the buzz of the reticulated wires of internet technology. As Willie Jennings shows, displacement from the familiar comforts of the land contributes to an identity crisis as the surrounding social vestments that protect one's body on one's land get stripped away.[17] While the claims of indigeneity being alluded to here are a moral standpoint for native populations to stake their claims against colonial displacement, a similar assertion was invoked by religious groups who wanted to maintain in-person worship during the pandemic. Claims of being autochthonous encompasses even the flora and fauna of a place into a composite and reified domain of paternalistic interest, ethicizing all the components to the point that attitudes of patriotism descend into a parochialism that sees the *other's* "groundlessness" as a moral deficit that must be surveilled through spiritual vigilance. The idea of being native to a spatiality can also feed the construal of self as an original—the more authentic national specie—and one against whose values everyone else would be defined. In this case, the basis of standing one's (church) grounds was that the familiar rites of physical meetings had become an inalienable property of the Christian collective. The ritualism and spontaneity of the sensory relations within the physical space were integral to both worship (as discussed in chapter 2), and the constitution of the social. Thus, asking them to leave the storied precinct of their church for the bare land of the internet was tantamount to an epistemic erosion.[18] Yet some pastors recovered from the abruptness of the request to move online temporarily and began to plan how to replicate the in-person experience online.

For the churches that protested closing in-person services, their opposition was about standing their ground—metaphorically and literally—to maintain the social and spiritual resources that nourish their gathering and establish their Christian identity as native or natural to their church territory. To be confronted with the sight of empty church auditoriums is equivalent to dislocation from the physical sites of the Christian commons, and to be banished into a machine where their display of charismatic authority would be lost in the tide of endless chatter that exemplifies modern forms of electronic communication. In signifying his rejection of online church services, Bishop David Oyedepo stressed the importance of physical meetings. In a sermon after churches were finally reopened, Oyedepo restated his grievance against the decision to ever lock down the churches. He stated that there is no virtual substitute for fellowship, and that

> You can't lie down with your computer and be warm. When you stumble, your computer cannot lift you up. Whatever stops God's people from worshipping in Church has destroyed their strength; it's only a matter of time. Wake up. To pose to be smarter than the truth is simply playing the fool. I know those who thought at a time that going to Church is not necessary . . . you know there are some people, they call "Twice Dead": dead raised to power two. You will never know that they were partakers of a revival before. Why? They disregarded the place of their strength: Fellowship.[19]

Oyedepo's dismissal of the computer as soulless hardware incapable of delivering the warmth that actual bodies can generate when bunched together is not sheer Luddism—a phobia of the uncertainties of new technology and how it might take away the sensory effects of Christians being together in a place physically.

Scholars who have studied the new media and Pentecostalism, such as J. Kwabena Asamoah-Gyadu and Rosalind Hackett, showed that Pentecostals were the ones at the forefront of the embrace of internet technology in Africa. They enthusiastically embraced internet culture in the early 2000s while it was still novel and made the sacralization of virtual space part of their mission.[20] Asamoah-Gyadu also noted how these newer-generation Pentecostal churches made their participation in internet culture part of their distinguishing character from traditional churches. In one of his essays from 2007, Asamoah-Gyadu quoted Oyakhilome, claiming that extending his ministry online was divine instruction: "God told me, Get on the Internet if you want to win more souls for me."[21] The internet was a part of the appurtenances of social mobility, and moving a church online was crucial to establishing their identity as churches for young, upwardly mobile, cosmopolitan, professional, aspirational, and trendy people.[22] It was also a "virtual arena for spiritual warfare," where they could ameliorate the impact of the devil and increase the global influence of God.[23] With internet technology, they affirmed their interconnectivity to global cultures; its borderlessness emblematized the limitlessness of the Pentecostal spirit. More than a decade after Asamoah-Gyadu's essay, however, some Pentecostal churches were not so amenable to moving their church fully online while the country tried to control the pandemic. Yet this reluctance cannot be merely labeled conservatism because, in recent times, the interfaces of contemporary Pentecostalism have gone beyond churches using social media to multiple initiatives such as spiritual warriors organizing prayer communities on the internet, something also touched on in chapter 2.

What those pastors rejected during the pandemic was an evisceration of the space where they manufacture their ethos, and the move online became the grounds for civic and spiritual resistance. For one, the rejecters had grown more conservative; from being nomads in search of new virtual lands to colonize for God, they had now become settlers and landlords with grand cathedrals. Such privileges had to be protected. Also, their decision to reject online churches was pragmatic: they were realistic about the logistical factors involved in running an online church. Churching online requires mobile devices that can be expensive. Despite the number of people who have eagerly embraced the internet in Nigeria, millions of people are still potentially cut off. Even regular church members might not be able to afford the cost of streaming church online. Over the months I monitored the Sunday service of several megachurches that streamed during the pandemic, they never seemed to have more than 10 percent of their congregation watching their services on all their social media accounts plus their websites.[24] Oyakhilome, overhyping the potential of their reach through the internet, claimed that his livestream was being watched by "3.25 billion in 227 countries, apart from those watching from over 400 television stations around the world."[25] Those who accepted the move to online pending resolution of the pandemic did not rely just on virtual technology since only relatively few people had the technological devices necessary to connect to online churches. The acceptors sought practical ways to maintain their audiences. Some of them increased their existing church broadcasts on local television channels, radio stations, and even satellite broadcasts.

Despite all the practical changes possible to church leaders, those who still fought for church reopening demonstrated how much their identity had been tied to where they meet and how the bodies that meet curate the sense of ownership and belonging in those spaces. Meeting in physical churches had become like a community possessing land and its histories, memories, and culture all tied to the interactions of the feet as they tickled the face of the earth, as I will examine in the next section of this chapter. Within those "indigenous" territories and the webbed system of beliefs and ethics that ring it, people generate the social and material resources that invariably organize the techniques through which they take their cases to the Lord in prayer.[26] In building a network of support for their causes, the alliances they form are tribalized, because politics becomes comprehensible when expressed through the framework of us versus them. Yet such dualistic confrontations with the others that spiritual warriors want disestablished is not always seen in monolithic terms; neither is the conception of the enemy ever static. In the third section, I show how spiritual warriors who insisted on physical worship used Trump as a key ally despite their anti-authority sensibilities, demonstrating their ability to split authority and relate to each fragment accordingly. They not only split God, as indicated in chapter 2; Pentecostal political astuteness also splits political authority itself. Associating with potent political power such as Trump represents helps the authoritative pronouncements spiritual leaders make become efficacious, while resisting some other (liberal) politicians helps them to simultaneously frame narratives of embattlement and anti-Christian persecution.

Other leaders who willingly migrated online afforded themselves a chance to further reflect on the practices of their theology to meet the challenges of practicing fully digitized worship.[27] On one side were pastors who rationalized moving online as a temporary measure, and even though their decisions positioned them against fellow pastors, they maintained their own essential necessity through other social actions. As examined in the fourth section, Jeremiah Fufeyin created prophetic giveaways of cash on social media, demonstrating the dynamism of religious leaders who take existing structures of social media relations—where celebrities and other minor benefactors frequently give away cash to their followers—and fold them into church activities. T. B. Joshua used the opportunity to develop a new church model that brought people of different nations together under one roof. Joshua's show is the subject of the fifth section. SCOAN's healing program through digital technology was different from how healings take place on "traditional" media such as radio or television because it was far more interactive. By using the spectacle of miraculous healing to gather people from all nations, he also gives us a glimpse of other possibilities of transcending nationalities. These pastors saw opportunities to relate with others worldwide through miraculous exploits.

As the model of performing church took place on the computer, it inflected the ideas of liveness, presence, retrievability, aura, and audience experiences that have been debated in the studies of performance and mediation, which performance scholars like Phillip Auslander, Peggy Phelan, and Rebecca Schneider have variously examined to explore how technology impacts how performances are witnessed, enjoyed, or even recalled.[28] Though Auslander's well-known argument refuted performance theorist Phelan's construal of performance as consisting of a distinctive internal character that makes it irreproducible, he asserted that performance is both a medium and a technology, one of the diverse means of conjuring presences The questions of being a live presence at sites of performances that scholars have studied have mostly been examined in performance studies that mostly looked at shows primarily designed to entertain. Churches, physical or virtual, would define presence primarily in terms of the invocation of a transcendental force that effects radical changes in the material world. For spiritual warriors, the idea of presence is about the extramundane forces that join their gathering, the aura of God's presence that they themselves bring with them as subjects engrafted with God's split parts, and how the interactions of these beings effectuate miracles. By looking at church services on social media during the pandemic where miracles were the primary activity, I thus demonstrate that the activity of spectacular miracles replicated the technology of prayer as communication with nonmaterial beings and still fought against supernatural forces through online media. By formatting the ontologies of prayer into modern technological forms, they augmented their contests with spiritual forces with social media technology and further naturalized those contests when answers to their prayers instantly materialized through miracles being watched on the screen.

Standing Your (Church) Ground

Despite Oyakhilome's taunting of fellow pastors who willingly stood in their cathedrals all alone and transmitted their sermons to a congregation they could not see, the emptied spaces of those church buildings were integral to the larger debate about the status of the church. Pastors like Oyakhilome pushed for recognition of the church as autonomous, free from the whims of secular laws and the politicians who regulate them. Another matter at stake, which also contributed to turning the churches' reopening into spiritual warfare and proxy political battles, was the practical matters of finances. If members could not gather in church to listen to sermons, pray, and enjoy fellowship, the affective means of stimulating them to give their donations, then the churches would have a hard time surviving an extended period of lockdown. As most churches relied on members' donations through tithes and offerings to stay open, the shutdown hit their finances and threatened the survival of the churches and the pastors who led them.

In my interviews with Dr. Daniel Olukoya of Mountain of Fire and Miracles Ministries (MFM) (see chapter 1), who supported closing churches during the pandemic, I asked him about welfare projects the church could carry out at such a crucial time to support indigent people who were badly affected by the crisis. At that time, Nigerian pastors like Sam Adeyemi of Daystar and Poju Oyemade of Covenant Christian Center were supporting their church members with large sums of money, and people were sharing their generosity on Twitter by showing proof of bank transfers. Olukoya told me that apart from church members, their church had even had to support fellow pastors. He shared with me stories of pastors of smaller churches whose livelihoods were severely impacted by the effects of the lockdown. Most of them, he stated, had no prior online presence or even the infrastructure for raising money online.[29] They were smaller, numbering only in the tens and hundreds, and never had enough resources to squirrel away for uncertain times. Given that all of these churches were shut down suddenly and did not have time to prepare ahead and put in place the necessary infrastructure that would have helped them transition to online, they greatly suffered from lack of finances. The MFM's Goshen Club (see chapter 1), he said, had to create a fund for them so they could survive the period. This reliance on in-person gatherings and member donations seriously affected the Pentecostal denominations whose church administrative processes were corporatized—that is, a network of church branches, chains of businesses that financed church operations, salaried employees, and various moving parts of church business that required regular infusions of capital. The experience of churching online can also be distracting. Besides, church leaders understand regular attendance as a habit that, if broken, would be hard for some of their parishioners—especially those on the fringes—to restart. The threat of financial breakdown due to the corporatized structures Pentecostal churches run underwrote their indignation about the lockdown more than other religious houses (including orthodox Christian denominations and mosques) in their insistence on affirming their autonomy.

For instance, when the Nigerian government started proscribing large gatherings and instituting other lockdown measures in the middle of March 2020, it was a general rule every organization had to observe.[30] Schools were shut, and, where allowed religious organizations—whether churches or mosques—were not to have a congregation of more than fifty. For a country with a landscape sprinkled with thousands of churches and mosques, the lockdown was going to be hard to implement. However, given that the fear of the virus was still fresh and palpable, people were generally cooperative. The Sunday after the lockdown began, Oyedepo's church, one of the largest churches in Africa, still held church service. Oyedepo told the congregation they would fully subscribe to whatever measures were necessary to protect the lives of congregants, but they would continue to hold church because they had a "covenant responsibility to be in fellowship," and they "would jealously guard it because that is where our strength is . . . and shutting down churches will be like shutting down hospitals. There are many places that will never have medical solutions but in church."[31] Media reports stated that he had been warned by state officials not to open his church, but he did anyway. Oyedepo was severely criticized for the move. The following day, the church issued a press statement that they were not being deliberately defiant, but they had to hold the service to sensitize and mobilize their congregants who might not be literate enough or aware of government directives "regarding the danger of this deadly virus."[32]

After Nigeria closed its borders on March 23, 2020, and a week later implemented a lockdown of two states and a territory—Lagos, Ogun, and Abuja (and the entire Federal Capital Territory)—in a bid to slow the spread of the virus, they also announced the restriction of movement across state lines and a shutdown of all businesses.[33] Over the following weeks, the news of the arrest of some pastors who defied the lockdown by the COVID-19 task force enforcement team, and who were disgraced out of their churches for holding church service, circulated in the news. On one occasion, when the task force arrived at a church, a pastor, his deacons, and church workers scaled a fence to evade arrest.[34] On another occasion, a pastor, sighting the task force team, hid among his own church members, and when questioned denied his ministry.[35] In a country where Islam and Christianity struggle for supremacy, it was not long before Christians generally began to compare the crackdown on their churches with the relatively reverential way the Muslims who also defied the rules were treated. Worse, the sudden disruption of social and spiritual life brought tedium, anxiety, and decreased earning power to Pentecostal churches, which exacerbated their impatience with regulating institutions. Some people turned to so-called alternative medicine, and spiritual warriors intensified their search for religious meanings in the moment.[36] By May 2020, people like Oyedepo had become fully combative. He had gone from describing COVID-19 as a "deadly virus" to insinuating that it was mostly hype, that the dangers were exaggerated, and that it was a "noisome pestilence" and mere "corona noise" (see chapter 3).[37] By June 2020, he delivered another sermon in which he described COVID-19 as "a golden calf that the world must worship," a precursor to a dystopic world where the government would dictate how much time they should spend on worship.[38]

The major business districts in parts of Nigeria at the time remained shut down, people's movements were regulated, and public economic activities were massively disrupted to the point that people who were already living below the poverty line and those at the margins slid further down on the social scale. In one of Oyedepo's sermons, which he was now forced to deliver in one of the smaller chapels on the same expansive church grounds that contained his megachurch building, he argued that if people could be allowed to go to the market for six hours daily, why not spend two hours in church? Why could they not open churches? He said,

It is an upside-down way of looking at things. Which one is more orderly? The market or the church? I can smell a rat. The Lord spoke to me on it yesterday.

I can smell a rat. . . . Behind all these is how do we stop the church from exploding? All the demons in hell! The people that are involved don't know it! What held down Israelites in Egypt was not Pharaoh. They were the Gods of Egypt! The greatest headache worldwide is the growth and expansion of the church. Worldwide. . . . No civilization has ever endured without a foundation in Christ. Where are the philosophers of Greece? Gone! I can smell a rat.[39]

In the sermon, he further claimed the forces of darkness were influencing people at various levels, and they were targeting the church because the exponential growth bothered the devil, but they would eventually triumph. Since the pandemic did not affect only the church, saying that some preternatural force wanted to slow down church growth seemed a stretch, but as one of the effects of the pandemic worldwide was that it forced people indoors without an answer to such a perplexing situation, the boredom combined with uncertainty and curiosity, and what looked improbable began to seem believable.[40] In the absence of coherent and satisfying scientific explanations for what was going on and their general resistance to and suspicion of establishment science, many spiritual warriors turned to their religious leaders to provide an intellectual and spiritual rationale for what they were experiencing. Both leaders and members turned online to search for information and found conspiracy theories.

Pentecostal pastors, finding themselves in a situation like that of their congregations, were both bewildered by the crisis of meaning, and at the same time had to provide some spiritual illumination for the public on the pandemic. In the combination of their situation as the people of God exiled from their church land and their roles as pastors who must frame the narratives, plus the disorientation from the destitution that a lot of people were suffering as a result of the shutdown, the devil soon emerged from the combination of distresses as the enemy to pummel. Now that they could more easily reach their counterparts in the rest of the world through modern technology, spiritual warriors went through different figurations of the anti-Christ they could fault for the apocalypse. Bill Gates, a global icon who had successfully predicted a pandemic from the scientific viewpoint (chapter 3), would become the personification of the evil that not only afflicted the world but also shut down the church. His traducers reasoned that a man who possessed such arcane knowledge as to accurately predict a disaster with such gigantic implications could also develop a god complex to penetrate the secrets of nature and become as malevolent as the trope of the "mad scientist" typically features. His intervention in global health matters despite being a private individual provided a fertile breeding ground for conspiracy theories.

Oyakhilome was one of the biggest propagators of the conspiracy theory linking COVID-19 to 5G technology (examined in chapter 3) and other shadowy agendas of the world's elite, and he frequently held services in which he reiterated these ideas.[41] His promotion of the pandemic as satanic attacks on the world by a conspiratorial elite attracted a lot of controversy. As a pastor who preached these stories as inspired truth, he drove the circulation of the conspiracy theories circulating online on both fringe websites and even the circles run by groups such as QAnon.[42] According to academic researchers who used Crowdtangle, a tracking technology, to chart the global circulation of COVID-19 and conspiracy theory, Oyakhilome's part in retailing those 5G and coronavirus conspiracy theories was quite impactful in disseminating those claims across African regions.[43] For pastors like him who had always claimed the power of healing and miracles, COVID-19 blindsided them. Conspiracy theories became a means of controlling the narrative, because their contrarian stances translated the anxieties of and dissatisfaction with the moment into spiritual contests.[44]

As Oyakhilome insisted, rather than merely complying with government directives, pastors instead would enhance their identity as God's children (or even as a people of faith being persecuted or martyred) by praying.[45] With public health at stake, state agencies would, of course, not have tolerated defiance of their directives and descended on defiant spiritual warriors with the force of political power. The resulting clash framed a narrative of martyrdom, of Christian persecution by a Nigerian government—led, incidentally, by a Muslim president.[46] Such accounts were framed as narratives of martyrdom, where the weaker party, here the Pentecostals, possessed the inner strength that "subverts hegemonic powers, providing a language of, and hence a means for, resistance to those facing similar violent circumstances."[47] Unlike Christians who saw themselves as responsible and law-abiding citizens, Oyakhilome saw an occasion for the church to resist the overwhelming powers of the state, to be central actors in an unfolding tale of oppression that would rally other Christians to make something give in the political order. In times when the dividing lines between the social and the religious had largely blurred, the period was also a chance to bracket the distinguishing traits of Christians amid the fluidity of the modern world. They would be *seen* as the people who would rather obey God than yield the biblical standards of what makes a Christian.

During the lockdown, state government officials had Zoom meetings with religious leaders across the spectrum, including Catholics, Anglicans, Aladura, Seventh-day Adventists, and Muslims, to deliberate reopening religious houses. I was reliably informed by two different church denominational leaders who were present that the Muslims agreed not to reopen their mosques since the times were not conducive to worship. It was the Christians, specifically the Pentecostal leaders, who made the biggest issue out of the lockdown. A church locked down along with every other religious house because of a virus was an embarrassment for spiritual warriors who established themselves in the social sphere by claiming miracles, signs, and wonders. The various materials through which they had indexed their power and social significance—such as large auditoriums and gatherings—had become inconsequential in the months they were empty. For Pentecostal churches, especially those that needed a steady stream of finances to keep their facilities running, much was at stake. To incite their members to a similar level of urgency, pastors alleged malicious attacks on the church, and some state officials had to meet them to defuse the tension. In July 2020, during a live sermon, Oyakhilome condemned fellow pastors who not only failed to take a decisive stand on the lockdown with the government at this meeting, but also surveilled other fellow pastors to ensure their compliance with public directives. He told them they were "never Christians" and had merely deceived themselves over the years:

> Some of you that are making money out of this situation, you have never known Christ. Otherwise, you will stay away from it. Look at what is happening. They banned Holy Communion. You are not supposed to take Holy Communion in this new church system they want to create for the churches. . . . You are not supposed to baptize. You cannot sing . . . and you think it is about COVID 19? It is not! Hear what they are telling you, it is about "infection" which means that apart from COVID 19, it is a new way of keeping the churches clean of infections. It means so as not to have other people infected in the church, we must not sing out, have communion or baptize. . . . These are lunatics. I think they lost their minds.[48]

In that sermon, Oyakhilome went on to say they would obey the commandments of Jesus to baptize, take holy communion, worship with their mouths open, and "pray as they did in the Book of Acts," whether anyone liked it or not.

The regulations that he denounced, according to my informants who attended the Zoom meetings with government officials, were conditions proposed to religious houses of worship to safely reopen. They were given a maximum number of people who could be in the building at one time, so that mega-congregations could not have more than 500 people in the church at once. They also should not have more than an hour of service per session and must fumigate the place afterward. The Muslims at the meeting agreed to wait out the pandemic, saying that the conditions were not conducive to their modes of worship. The Christians in the meeting, coming from diverse denominations, doctrines, and movements, were more divided on the issue. One of the pastors present at the meeting was Tunde Bakare, the senior pastor of the Citadel church. According to my informant, he brought up examples of churches in other countries such as South Korea where the worship services they held in defiance of health guidelines became superspreader events and advised that Christians too should wait out the pandemic. When I called him to discuss these details, he confirmed them. He said the conditions were not practical for those who run megachurches like his. "They said twenty to fifty people [in the church] at a time. How is social distancing practical when you have a congregation of 10,000 people? They said between each service, they said you must fumigate. How is that practical? They said we must only meet on Sundays, and there should be no vigils. Why meet then? Noah did not prove his faith by going out to swim in the flood. The Lagos state health commissioner already stated to the public that the infection would peak in August [2020]. So why reopen churches and then enforce restrictions?"[49]

This line of argument did not go over well with several of his Pentecostal colleagues, who insisted that churches should, no matter what, be kept open as "essential services."[50] They argued that if public markets that are by nature dirty and disorganized could be open, how much longer should the churches where people gather to meet and worship God in a cleaner and far more organized environment be closed? Fueling the grievances further, the Christian Association of Nigeria questioned what "sin the church committed" that public places like open markets could be open but not churches. They asked, "In what way are the open and roadside markets more organised than the church which warranted their opening? Is it not our members in the places of worship that do go to markets and other sectors opened? Why are they allowed to go to markets and disallowed from going to places of worship? Is it because the marketers cannot contract the virus in the markets and airports?"[51]

Ironically, the church renowned for spiritual warfare, the Mountain of Fire and Miracles Ministries, was one of those not in a hurry to reopen. Dr. Olukoya, the general overseer, told me he predicated his decision on the supremacy of science, an area where he has authority due to his Ph.D. in microbiology from the University of Reading in the UK. He said not every matter is a demonic attack, nor should they all be approached that way. He said he found it rather embarrassing how some churches skewed the issues at stake as evil conspiracies. He had had the prayer city (see chapter 1) locked up because he did not want people who should go to hospitals or isolation centers when infected with the virus to come to the church in search of either a miracle healing or deliverance. COVID-19, he stated, was not a matter of deliverance. The kind of violent prayers they pray in MFM, he further stated, were not practical in a pandemic.

> Some of those pastors who don't know how science works kept asking why they should open markets and close churches. If they understand science and know how viruses work, they will be scared! Because they didn't do science, they don't understand the difference. They fail to note that the market is an open place and people do not stay there long enough like church where people stay

for hours and it is enclosed. I told them [the pastors] just like I told the government the difference, but they don't listen to anybody. They will tell you God spoke to them. How do you argue with a man who insists he heard from God?[52]

While some church leaders framed the issues at stake as an anti-church agenda and framed their resistance thus, they were not merely looking to be validated through martyrdom. They also astutely took advantage of the instruments of jurisprudence.[53] Given that Nigerian churches operate in a society where the contending forces of other religions (a.k.a. Islam) is strong, they were self-conscious about being perceived as weak people who could be bullied and beaten. Rather than be at the mercy of their supposed persecutors, they saw the supposed anti-church sentiment as constitutive of their salvation and also an opportunity to test their mettle against the architecture of state power.[54] By thus enacting modern persecution, they also enlivened the narratives already enshrined in the scriptures.

God versus Caesar versus Caesar

Despite how some religious leaders framed the issues around church closures as dissent against political power, the clash over whose authority—that of God or Caesar—should determine church operations was not all antagonistic, because those who supported reopening churches got the support of Donald Trump, who made a case for reopening churches in defiance of regulations by state local authorities by virtually commanding them to "allow these very important, essential places of faith to open right now."[55] Overriding democratic processes in favor of religious consideration resonated with Christians everywhere who saw him as a battle axe (chapter 2) against the evil machinations that surrounded the pandemic to overrule them by executive fiat.[56] Church leaders' centering Trump's "Caesar" support of their anti-authority dissent shows perspicacity—the political power that enables their theocratic moral vision for society. Spiritual warriors' practical politics also do not necessarily see an opposition between God and a monolithic Caesar as construed in the trope of God versus Caesar. Instead, they split Caesar into components and relate to each pragmatically: the part that could directly imbue them with political privilege (as Trump does), and the one whose persecution of them also earns them a moral legitimacy (such as the authorities who insisted churches stay locked). For instance, a couple of days after Trump's announcement, Oyedepo said in a church service that "Trump has declared places of worship open across the US. That is how God has been humiliating this noisome pestilence."[57] Oyakhilome's church reported in their bulletin that the [U.S.] President stated unequivocally that places of worship are essential places that provide essential services. Therefore, it is injustice to allow liquor stores and others to open as merchants of essential commodities or services and still lockdown places of worship. Trump stated clearly that this order takes effect beginning this weekend and all Governors must adhere to it. This is not a chance occurrence rather, it is a direct result of answers to the prayers of the saints around the world and the fulfilment of the prophetic word declared by the man of God, Reverend Chris Oyakhilome. At the May, Global Communion Service, the man of God, Reverend Chris Oyakhilome, by God's Spirit, declared May, to be "the Month of Opening." Truly, God's Word is the ultimate. The Church is marching on the gates of hell shall not prevail against it.[58]

By linking how Trump's declaration and presidential override of state governors' authority on the church lockdown with pastoral pronouncements, they show how religious and political power are mutually bound up in their imagination, and religious authority uses political commandments to effect prophetic declarations.[59] Trump's populist tactics in an election year were worthwhile because they affirmed that spiritual warriors' spiritual power, which they had been using to battle during the pandemic, was efficacious.[60] International politics became a means for Nigerian church leaders to realize victory in their contest with oppressive local authorities, and the lines of the "good" in high political authority contending with the "evil" in other political contexts were further drawn across time and space.[61]

In October 2020, while the United States recorded an accelerated wave of infection and death figures were well above 200,000, MacArthur—who had inspired the Ibadan blogger—made a video, "Open Your Church."[62] The video featured shots of him walking in an empty auditorium, its vastness accentuated by its emptiness. He accused Democratic politicians like Joe Biden, Kamala Harris, and California state officials of trampling on their right to worship "under the pressure of manufactured fear." After noting that "abortion clinics, strip clubs, and marijuana clinics" remained open and BLM protesters were allowed on the streets, he stated that the lockdown was "obviously targeted discrimination. Leftists and secular government have no tolerance for biblical Christianity, and [are] using COVID as an excuse to shut us down. We have to stand firm on the reality that the church is essential." Many of the video clips were shot in the church, and the video featured icons of American identity conflated with those of Christianity—the flag, the cross, the Bible, and buzz words like freedom and the Constitution. By putting the Bible together with the Constitution, he pushed Americans to see their nationality and faith as synthesized to the point where the desire to shed one's blood for one's faith becomes inextricable from doing so on behalf of one's nation.

By compounding the icons of faith and the nation such as the cross and the national flag, MacArthur concretized the symbolic content of a utopian American freedom with that of Christianity that promises freedom through faith.[63] For members of his congregation, especially those who had their fighting instincts sharpened through prayer rituals, the flag was an emblem of American victories—world domination, imperialism, exceptionalism, and ideological triumphalism, all of which are owed to a transcendental force. Juxtaposed with the cross, everything America symbolized to them—and which the flag affectively evokes—takes a transcendent turn. By staging this act a month before the presidential election and adding the faces of Biden and Harris—Trump's contenders for the presidency—he could effectively ground the ideas into a singular ideal of conservative ideology and iconize liberal politicians into the faces of evil to be exorcised through prayer and the ballot. By sharing this video on a forum like Facebook that links Christians worldwide, he could potentially inspire others to see spiritual warfare in national politics. While every outcome might not be similar to those inspired to hold a church service in Ibadan like those at the beginning of this chapter, circulating a video like that could still arouse a possessive investment in the U.S. presidency for Christians transnationally.

In Nigeria, much of the lockdown battle similarly played out through challenging state authority and compliant pastors. Those who found inspiration in a figure of power like Trump's support of the church's dissent vicariously shared in the promises of America's triumph over the dark forces of political malevolence. It was inconsequential that they were not Americans; faith was their basis of imagined nationhood. Nationhood is also about "shared memory of blood sacrifice, periodically renewed," and those who "share such memories often but not always, share language, living space or ethnicity," but "always share . . . the memory of blood sacrifice."[64] Those who see themselves as jointly embattled with their counterparts elsewhere accentuate ontological similarities through such memories of anti-Christian persecution, suffering like Christ, whose shed blood ties Christian identities together everywhere. The nation that spiritual warriors imagine is a global church where the memories are shared through means that include electronic technology—while, ironically, condemning devices like laptops as unsuitable for worship—even as they are being constructed. America—at least as Nigerian Christians tend to see it—has built a stable and iconized system of meaning-making regarding God and Caesar. Nigerians' investment in this established order also demonstrates a *covetousness* of what the United States represents: a country that almost fully bases its symbolic social and political structures on the Christian faith, one where the figure of the president fighting for churches to reopen stands for an undifferentiated political and religious authority—God and Caesar both using spiritual and political power to work toward their desired ends.

Miracles, Spectacles, and a Virtual Auditorium Full of Humans

As some churches kicked up a storm over moving their church services to the virtual sphere, some others moved online and stayed there throughout the lockdown period without fuss. They rationalized their decisions with the Bible and interpreted their ability to adapt to virtual reality as a victory for Jesus over Satan. To effectively operate a church in cyberspace, they reinterpreted church traditions, and their theological reflexivity helped the transition to virtual worship. Some said that when the devil poured the virus out into the world, he intended to stop the children of God from meeting, but God was always ahead. He had already prepared the technological equipment ahead of time to keep his church going. Those pastors pointed at technologies that allowed them to livestream as proof that God had already preempted the devil's schemes. The flexibility of those who adapted to an e-church is as telling as those who insisted on meeting in physical churches. The differences in their attitudes go beyond standard ideas of responding to technology in terms of conservatism versus progressivism and defiance versus compliance to accent their perspicacity based on what they want disestablished. During the months of lockdown, the churches with a virtual infrastructure and that had transitioned online made use of the interactive features of the internet to make church streaming close to the physical experience.[65]

At first, the abrupt move online brought a confrontation with the limitations of the medium. Truly, the internet had the ability to bridge space and time, but there were practical difficulties to holding services solely online. Generating the sensory qualities of close human interactions that worked in their physical churches would be hard, and to register their presence in a manner that blended with the attention-grabbing nature of social media would require some creative tactics that would be continuous with social life and the nature of interactions on social media. Technology, some argue, allows us to transcend human limitations.[66] In this case, they needed to deploy an already familiar technology beyond its much-vaunted features of public interaction, evangelism, and networking to meet other limitations that arose. Also, a creative adaptation of the technology was needed to generate the sensations that curate a worship space and that are integral to the invocation of supernatural forces during worship and warfare prayers. For spiritual warriors, physical gatherings are not only biblical instruction, but they also generate affective power when the Holy Spirit descends among the congregants and connects with the parts of God engrafted within them. But first, they modulated theologies underwriting physical meetings to justify moving online. Bakare told me about the decision to go online during the pandemic, that when God said "tablet" in the Bible, he knew the day would come when they would reach Him through electronic tablets.[67] He also said of his choice to take his church online:

God wants us to worship Him in Spirit and the Truth, and that is not determined by location. Let us stay safe and keep each other safe. When it is safe to
gather, we will gather. Livestreaming is not unbiblical. We just don't take note
of these things enough. When God said, "Write the vision and make it plain
upon tablets," he knew the day would come that we would rely on our iPads
to meet as a church. The people that have scattered can be gathered through
livestreaming. When God asked us to hear his word, how could we have heard
from Jerusalem to everywhere in the world without the technology to transmit
it? The churches that are suffering the most are the ones who did not put
technology in place to speak to their people. I pity them, but they have learned
from this episode.[68]

Comparing stone tablets mentioned in the Bible with technological modern devices shows that assisted means of soliciting the divine are timeless, and
it was prudent to recognize that. Several other church leaders I spoke to during
the pandemic looked at the internet to also see its ability to collapse time and
space and (un)fold reality as compatible with the nature of transcendence itself.
It was not surprising that someone considered the devices through which internet technology functions as ancient stone tablets retrofitted with electronic
buttons. David Noble noted, "modern technology and religion have evolved
together and . . . the technological enterprise has been and remains suffused
with religious belief."[69] While some pastors used such theological reflexivity to
absolve their use of technology to temporarily replace physical church, others
added sensational miracles. If the nature of communicating on the internet was
an exchange premised on a presence existing at the other end, then its mode of
communication also corresponds with the nature of prayer, where the goal
of communication is to make a psychic contact with that spectral figure.
According to Jeremy Stolow, "Buried within the Internet's drive toward instanta-
neous, disembodied information exchange one finds the ancient desire to approximate the unblemished rapport of angels, spirits and other divine beings."[70] For
Africans whose ideas of power are symbolized by the force of the invisible and
the spell it can cast on one's existence, there is always another realm where the
contending forces encounter to tussle either on behalf of or against the human
agent. The prayers of warfare, myths, accounts of visions and revelations, and
practices of faith are largely a human envisioning of how the battles take place.
Thus, the metaphor of internet technology and its interplay between what is
seen and unseen, known and unknown, blended into the nature of Pentecostal
faith practice, with its fixation on deriving religious experience out of intangible
reality. In addition, technological devices also intensified the urgent commands
of *Now now! Right now! Today today!* that typifies prayer forms.

Seeing how people have become so enchanted with the "magic" of the
internet that the techniques of soul-nourishing and quests for meaning

have become gradually networked to its mechanisms, some pastors drove people to the internet with promises of enchanting miracles. This mode of enlivening virtual reality through phenomenal displays included giving away cash on social media. Shortly after churches went into full lockdown around April 2020 and their expansive church auditoriums emptied, people were uncertain of the future, and the economic hardship was biting, and some social media influencers and celebrities gave away money to indigent people so they could cope. Richer pastors disposed to similar demonstrations of generosity also gave away money in lottery-like manners. One who did so spectacularly was Senior Prophet Jeremiah Omoto Fufeyin, of Mercyland Deliverance Ministry, in Warri, Delta state. He invited his social media followers to participate in what he called "prophetic cash giveaways" by supplying their bank account numbers. These boons, he said, would be given regardless of their faith persuasion.

In those giveaway sessions, the church would start a live broadcast and promise to give people money if they would leave their bank account numbers and their names.[71] They only requested people to "like" or "follow" the pastors' pages, share their videos, and subscribe to their channels. By dishing money out on social media and the boons "magically" appearing in people's bank accounts, as evidenced by the SMS alert people instantly received from their respective banks, belief in the enchantment of the world, occult economies, irruptive miracles, and technological wonders coincided. Fufeyin interspersed his church livestream with video clips of his church location, which he invited people to come see whenever they could. In one of the livestreams, he sat on a swivel chair in a studio. His backdrop displayed images of his churches, Mercy City, in night scenes with lit cityscapes glowing with lights. Occasionally, waterfalls simulated the church's physical environment for viewers. The stage where he sat was surrounded with virtual images, including the floor, where flickering light emanated from below his feet. A few times they paused showing the pastor and showed images of the sprawling buildings in his Mercy City. These were not regular church sessions of prayer and worship meetings; they were other means of congregating and building a church community when it was impossible to do so during the pandemic.

As the service livestreamed, some people called in and thousands of commenters went to Mercyland's Facebook page with their names and their bank account numbers, pleading to be considered for the cash giveaways. The prophet would take a phone call in which the caller would say their name, location, and then share their bank account number. The voice, brimming with excitement, would virtually be screaming over the speakers installed in the church: "Hello, sir! This is my account number, sir!" As the prophet was speaking with the person, taking their details, the video would cut to the screen where those names and bank account details were being filled into a bank transfer form by some of the prophet's associates. Thus, sums of money would be given away with a click of the computer, and the callers' account would be promptly credited with amounts ranging from N10,000 to N50,000.[72] The receiver would squeal in joy, "Thank you, sir!!!!" Throughout these sessions, the prophet gave on a whim; there did not seem to be any method to how he awarded the cash. Sometimes the camera recording from the studio would pan to the Facebook comments section to show the people on the church's page participating in the service and filling the comments sections with their bank account numbers and solicitations for help. They would also display the names of those who had been given money. Thus, the giveaway bonuses by the church seemed miraculous, and the fact that it was facilitated by internet communication made the virtual space seem like a land of signs and wonders.

The giveaways brought traffic to the prophet's social media pages where they announced the church and their services, apparently in anticipation of when the lockdown would be over.[73] Such a crowd might never quite classify as "parishioners," but they nevertheless demonstrated the growing scope of the man of God's influence. Fufeyin had several prophetic cash giveaway sessions in April 2020, and his social media followership count rose. There were thousands of comments, many of them filled with the bank account numbers of people who wanted to be handed doles, a few sending in other prayer solicitations amid all the appeals for financial help.[74] I followed the livestreams and noticed that those drawn to the cash giveaways sessions were not only Nigerians. People mentioned they lived in other African countries and that they needed such benevolence too. Those miracles, conterminous with the modes of relationship on social media, would be the ground on which he—as against fellow pastors standing their physical church grounds—established the grounds of a church-nation that also transcended time and space limits.

Distance Is Not a Barrier: Technology of Miracles and Social Media

In addition to the spectacular miracle of doling out money were the healing miracles performed by Joshua of SCOAN, the same pastor whose reenactment of God's battle axe chopping down a tree on his church's altar opens chapter 2.[75] Already renowned for his miracle performances, Joshua is also a controversial prophet.[76] His methods could be unconventional.[77] His church is domiciled in Ikotun Egbe, Lagos, Nigeria, but it attracts visitors worldwide. In fact, SCOAN is reputed to be almost uniquely responsible for a significant percentage of what constitutes religious tourism to Nigeria.[78] His church has attracted presidents, football stars, actors, and other famous figures from around the world, from various races, ethnicities, and nations.[79] He is quite famous for praying for people's healing, routinely casting out demons, and also getting people to engage in an extended narration of their personal troubles as they would on Jerry

Springer's TV show. His deeds have been controversial in the past, and while other pastors have distanced themselves from him because they see what he practices as occultic, his church has thrived (partly due to patronage by non-Nigerian nationals).[80] His Facebook page, T. B. Joshua Ministries, has more than 5 million followers, and that is about the widest church social media following in Africa. The YouTube page of the SCOAN television network, Emmanuel TV, has 1.81 million subscribers.[81]

A well-traveled preacher, Joshua has held crusades in various countries such as Mexico, Indonesia, Peru, Singapore, Colombia, Australia, Korea, and Paraguay. Unlike most Nigerian preachers who travel abroad to preach to an audience composed mostly of fellow Nigerians in the diaspora, the massive crowds at Joshua's crusades are mostly natives of the countries hosting his crusades.[82] When part of his church building collapsed in 2014, over ninety South Africans died in the incident, also marking how "international" his church is. In 2019, Joshua held a rare crusade in Israel, which, though it was controversial at first, still took place. According to him, "I am the only minister of God that has organised a crusade in Israel, and I also went to Nazareth where Jesus was born and organised a revival there. I am the first man of God to do that and it was carried in newspapers all over the world, Time Magazine and the rest. CNN aired it. After the crusade, a certificate was given to me by the State of Israel. That is the greatest joy for any minister of God."[83] In the early days of the pandemic, he prophesied that the virus would "disappear" on March 27, 2020. The date came, but the prophesy did not come to pass.[84]

During the lockdown, his church at first focused on sharing their old videos and a documentary of their humble beginnings with their extensive social network. On April 26, 2020, he surfaced online when his church's social media page announced that for those who had been curious where the man of God had been, they had an answer. It came in the form of a video they posted. In the video, Joshua, in a vast open land where the rocks jutting out of the earth were covered with lush green foliage, wore a long gown that mimics the prophet dress that Jesus Christ typically wears in artistic depictions of him in the wilderness where he had gone to pray or when he was ministering to crowds.[85] In the images and video shared of Joshua, he was alone (with an invisible team, of course). The photos of him showed him standing on a rock, lying on a rock with a Bible on his chest, or pressing his nose against a standing rock while he prayed against COVID-19, the evil forces besieging the world with sickness, and for victory for medical personnel battling the disease globally. In one of the photos, he stood on elevated ground with his head bowed in prayer. However, from the lower angle where the camera seemingly looked up at him, his photo reminded one of the pictures of Jesus Christ as he stood at a similar godlike height to bless people during his Sermon on the Mount. On the SCOAN Facebook page and the news blogs that reposted the images and video to generate traffic, some people mocked the modern-day prophet who went to seek the face of the Lord in a supposed wilderness while being attended by a camera crew that—judging by the quality of the videography as the camera made sweeping wide-angle shots over the landscape—was quite a professional one. While they insinuated that he must have had other comforts while out there only to come online and act as though he had had an actual wilderness experience, their commentary and their consistent sharing of the images helped to make his video a social experience.

The following month, his church started announcing their forthcoming broadcast church services they called *Distance Is Not a Barrier*. A regular feature of his television network, Emmanuel TV, *Distance Is Not a Barrier* typically shows miracles of healing performed by Joshua in his church and broadcast on its various media platforms. In June 2020, when the studio format of the program was unveiled, it had been upscaled and made more interactive. The healing services moved into the studio they had recently commissioned. Called Emmanuel TV studio, it was an expansive space designed in a proscenium theater format. The stage where the pastors cum anchors stood to face the viewing audience was backgrounded with life-sized virtual interactive screens. The stage occasionally had movable furniture that was set up when needed. On the imposing screens were intermittent images of the church auditorium and other buildings that surrounded it, as well as the street on which they were located. Just like Prophet Fufeyin, simulating the church's physical environment on the screen helped both to create an in-person experience and also to sustain memories of the physical church while people were away. There were also images of green plants that were covered with a text that said, "Distance Is Not a Barrier." It was on this huge screen that Joshua's church associates started healing people from all over the world. While some Nigerian pastors, like Oyedepo and Oyakhilome, deemed online meetings "unscriptural" and construed the lockdown of their churches as a satanic attack, SCOAN made the perspicacious move to create an affective experience for the e-church by focusing on an aspect of miracle performance that is as spectacular, universal, and sensory online as it is in person: healing.

These healing sessions could last as long as three hours. Even though they were prerecorded broadcasts, they had the quality of liveness to them because the audience joining on their individual digital devices and making comments gave the impression that the miracles were happening in real time.[86] The sessions are formulaic—they start with some preaching tailored toward repentance, holiness, and a relationship with God before proceeding to the segment where miracles happen. Unlike typical in-person church services where people make confessional statements about giving their lives to Christ, these sessions do not feature stories of radical ruptures in personal history. The people who appear on the screens come in search of bodily healing, and they are attended to by pastoral associates who point at the large screens to pray for them. Many of those miracles take place in people's personal spaces—their living rooms or bedrooms—where the afflicted (sometimes in the company of a family member) sit before a camera and narrate their circumstances. They are from various regions of the world, as indicated by their names, hyphenated nationalities, phenotypical features, and the names of their countries written on the screen. They could be an American, a South African, a Canadian, an Indian living in New Zealand, a Congolese living in Australia, a South Asian living in East Asia, a West African in France, a Venezuelan living in another part of South America, and so on.

These people who come together to form the utopian world where the people of God transcend all barriers also speak diverse languages. Their faces, diverse human visages that represent different nations and cultures, are arrayed in a grid-like arrangement before the camera.[87] At the same time fellow denominational leaders were construing church lockdown as an anti-church agenda and invoking an authority figure of Christian internationalism like Trump to challenge the satanic agenda of their local authorities as they had so inferred, Joshua's church transcended sociological, spatial, and temporal barriers through modern technology to combat the demonic forces responsible for afflicting people. He used the opportunity to demonstrate the grounds for the possibility of virtual churches, although the boons he used to draw people were healing miracles, not cash.

One of the associates of Joshua, who are also typically of diverse races, nations, languages, and ethnicities, would remind the viewers of the many countries the faces on their screens represent as they stand in front of the camera and pray for those people who had just listed their afflictions. Those people too would be praying at the other end, waiting for the power of God to come upon them. When it did, they would writhe in their homes as the demons left their bodies. Some would vomit "poisonous substances" on the floor of their rooms, stumble under the anointing, or the deadened parts of their body would begin to move in response to the prayers. The screen to the right side of the minister would highlight these cases so that the viewer could better see their demonstration of God's power at a much closer range. Since the screen was huge and the people in them sometimes towered above the person praying, the minister could lay hands on their body parts through the screen to pray for them. After the prayers, the people would share their testimonies: the person who could finally take off their oxygen tube, the footballer with a broken leg who was now dribbling a ball in his living room, the person who tested positive for COVID-19 would display their medical result to the camera and then declare they no longer experienced any symptoms. And that woman in the wheelchair? She is now running around her room. Even the church's subsequent narration of the testimonies we just watched often took this regular format:

LIFTED FROM THE BED OF SICKNESS!

Ivan Lomelí, an administrative analyst from Mexico had been bedridden for four years due to a severe ankle, knee and hip problem that had defied medical solution. Dependent on crutches and the assistance of his mother and his wife to be able to do anything, Ivan worked from his computer on his bed. At the command of Jesus on the lips of Prophetess Yinka, the strange debilitating sickness left his body and miraculously he stood up from his bed unaided and began to walk! Amazed at her son's healing, his mother excitedly followed him walking around the house holding crutches that he had previously used above her head! Describing the divine experience of the interactive prayer, Ivan said, "I felt heat on my feet and the desire to cry."[88]

These looped healing sessions could play for hours on end, and the format was consistent. After the testimonies of some had been concluded, a new set of people would appear on the screen telling everyone their names, the country they were living in (and a number of the people noted they originated from a different country), and the diseases from which they wanted to be healed.

The continuous staging of miracles stimulates the senses of the viewer who also needs a miracle, and participation in this virtual assembly transforms viewers into the subjects of a Christian nation not connected to the conventional politics of nationhood. As political theorist Ruth Marshall noted in her study of Nigerian Pentecostalism, miracles could be an orientation that is cultivated through certain disciplinary ethics rather than momentary irruptions in the norm. As such, miracles are "a prophetic sign that can function as the ground for a new normative order."[89] What happens in the Emmanuel TV studio combines thaumaturgy and dramaturgy to produce a transnational community where humans of all races, united by brokenness and promises of restoration, could constitute church during the lockdown without physically meeting. For Pentecostals, "the production of the real, the experience of its significance, occurs through the ongoing process of personal witness, the development of a receptivity to divine interpellation in everyday life."[90] In this studio space, however, the production of the real was also intertwined with technological processes. The hypermediation of the bodies—seen through the screens of those seeking healing through to the mega-screens that cover the walls of the studio to the screens of participants everywhere—was spectacular, compelling us to gaze at the diverse array of humans seeking and providing providential assistance.

Pentecostals have always been perspicacious enough to structure new forms of sociality that do away with existing relationship structures and inaugurate a kinship based on conversion, faith practices, and fashioning new subjectivities. This vision of a collective of Christians that is not restricted by nationality or differences in language, where there would be neither "Jew nor gentile," was carried further by Joshua's church during the pandemic. SCOAN used miracles to stroke congregants' senses and facilitate a shared Christian identity. Faith practices might be inextricable from the physical spaces and bodies that inhabit them, as Oyedepo argued, but the affects that define the physicality of space and bodies were also simulated through the high sensation of witnessing a miracle and fervently praying for one. The healing sessions posed stories of immediate supernatural transformation and established a new charismatic nation where the notion of subjectivity and identity is denominated by the miracle of transformation of one's sickness-afflicted body. With these miraculous acts, those who have gathered are not just an imagined community—à la Benedict Anderson—but have become an imaginable one, bound together by the commonality of triumph over bodily afflictions.

For the diverse audience logging in from different parts of the world and speaking different languages, the miracles became a mode of creating cultural uniformity. Rather than a spiritual identity tied to the physical grounds of their church, they produced a session informed by our relationship to space and time. This new nation of people being brought together from their different nations through technology still stayed in their respective nations. Their various human messes, vomited out of their orifices, were behind the same screens that brought their visages to the world. Thus "screened out," those messes were ultimately retained within their individual spaces where they expelled them, not messing up the antiseptic cleanliness of the studio space where Joshua and his associates operated.

By summoning many nations under one roof through this brightly lit space where the floodlights rigged in different part of the studio set dispelled all shadows and specters, Joshua modified space and time to shift the grounds of his church to the virtual space. These categories of miracles, one recalls, are carried out in a studio setting where no one sees an "outside," no physical space or landmarks. What we see is the image of the church and the green blossoming foliage that adorns its projection, all in digital images on the magnificent screens through which the miracles were being carried out. He suspended not just the need for one to be grounded in a physical place to receive miracles, but also skewed the temporality that operates in this virtual space to be *the time before* when their healing took place. It is also interesting that the only kind of miracle that was featured in this gathering was that of body healing. It is understandable; this form of miracle is telegenic—it fits snugly into the visual character of an audio-visual medium like an internet broadcast. It was also easy to tell in the most reductive language possible—the devil afflicted me; Jesus healed me.

In her study of written online testimonies to explore how they impress on the psyche and also facilitate a personal relationship with God, Suzanne van Geuns identifies their power to motivate and witness to other believers in the emotions they evoke and the meanings they subsequently generate.[91] On Emmanuel TV, testimonies are not written to be read so much as to be watched, to be consumed through the gaze of othered bodies in the various processes of supplicating before God. Pentecostalism premises visuality; appearances are a crucial part of how spiritual warriors wage war and assert their dominance. It is why, in the age of technology, spiritual warriors actively seek to go viral and be seen by a widest possible audience. Being seen to be doing spiritual warfare generates new modes of visual literacies that galvanize the goals of spiritual warfare. Spiritual warrior Stella Immanuel, as discussed in chapter 3, not only opened multiple social media accounts where she not only broadcast her sermons and her partisan politics, but also livestreamed herself praying in tongues several times.

The otherness of the bodies Joshua and his associates bring up on the huge screens is preemptively inscribed upon them, which almost always makes the listing of their names and their countries on the screen seem overstated. As David Mason indicated in his study of religion and theater, the symbolic display of the body during a performance does not begin on the stage—or in the moment the people are highlighted on the screen in the studio either. Instead, "the body—*every* body—has always been confiscated and colonized by symbolic *ostention*."[92] Thus, their bodies are not just coming on the screen to enact miracles; they are also referencing all categories of difference—race, gender, nationality, social class (at least judging by the modesty of their private spaces), age—and the potential to transcend the otherness of race and nationalism through the transformative power of miracles. Their bodies, though signifying otherness and a strangeness at first, enter into our private spaces through the screens of our devices. Through a system of feelings and emotional impact aroused by the thought that we (the viewer praying on the comment page of Facebook and the person seeking miracles) are all seeking the same thing—that is, to be mended by God—the church begins to familiarize itself with us.

Part of the efficacy of the prayers and healings on *Distance Is Not a Barrier* is the entertainment of watching others talk about the pain of their debility and quickly moving on to watch the dramatization of their triumphs. It is the quintessential tale of Jesus's triumph over Satan, but this time with "real" people telling "real" stories and inducing a desire for similar triumphs. Thousands of viewers interacting with the ongoing miracles through the comments section of the social media page by praying for their own miracles ultimately bond with the others displaying their once-broken and now-mended bodies. The ones who receive their miracles become a virtual point of contact for those still seeking to receive theirs. Joshua's method evoked a sense of community among people who shared common narratives of satanic afflictions and triumphs, and who also shared in a global pandemic.[93] The joint identity is cemented through the dramatization of what makes this assembly of many nations human: corporeal vulnerability to affliction and the possibility of overcoming. In the Emmanuel TV studio where thousands of people from different parts of the world watch each other, engage by posting comments, responses, and "amens," or even publicly post their prayer requests, participants are simultaneously performers, spectators, and even the spectacle. By personally overcoming or witnessing the triumph of others who are like us, we are gradually transformed into joint citizens of one nation under God and on the same page—on social media!

Conclusion

As much as the two categories of church leaders and their church members that I have discussed here represent two opposing sides of how churches should and could operate in the period of the pandemic, it is important not to merely construe both sides in terms of their degree of openness to modern gadgets or ideological conservatism. The contestations that took on the coloration of spiritual warfare were born out of what spiritual warriors saw as threats to the survival of the church during a momentous period of history when churches should be burnishing their bona fides as places of refuge in a time of crisis. The pastors who insisted on standing on their church grounds and worshipping during the pandemic were using the historical event to fight for their autonomy and institute their self-redefinition. They seized on the disruption in the normative order to push for their churches to be independent of the state, to define their status as "essential" and exercise the power to control how and when churches should operate. The idea of a spectrum of political power that was friendly to churches was established in the minds of these Christians, in both the United States and Nigeria, and they called it up in various ways for their cause. That was evident in the actions of pastors in the United States who lobbied Trump and Nigerian pastors who kept alluding to Trump as well.

When the Nigerian government announced that church services could resume starting August 7, 2020, Oyedepo's sermon was on how Satan had deceived the whole world but spiritual warriors had won eventually. He also threatened that the next time anyone tried to shut down the church, "fire would fall."[94] This class of pastors were the ones who reopened their churches immediately after the end of lockdown and announced their triumph over Satan. In a sermon a couple of weeks after churches had reopened, Pastor Oyakhilome maintained his conspiracy theories about the pandemic, even mapping with it some millenarianism, the triumphs of U.S. foreign policy on behalf of Israel, and spiritual warriors' imminent rapture to conclude on a victorious note: "They said those gatherings would never come back and already we are back. They miscalculated!"[95] The pandemic was no longer just about a viral disease, but the scheming of a conspiratorial "they" against the church.

However, the pandemic and the lockdown were not all about seeing demonic forces that negated one's potential. They were also about perceiving opportunities, and another set did this much. In his work on the structuring of the ethics that will denominate life in an increasingly cosmopolitan and networked world, Nimi Wariboko explored the notion of a charismatic city. This charismatic city is a utopian vision of a global city that intersects with religion. He explored the design of a city that factors in the ethics of social unity, connects to nature, enhances spirituality, and ultimately promotes human flourishing.[96] While he does not claim that this charismatic city would be based online, I also see what Joshua achieved as a precursor to such a city where the intense human–divine encounter ignites fresh possibilities. The simulation of that city that took place in the Emmanuel TV studio was a foretaste of how human interactions could happen through miracles and other processes that could facilitate these connections outside the organic ways that cities typically develop.

This is not to ascribe endless sociopolitical possibilities to what is still in formation. This international community is largely ad hoc, and its lack of grounding within a spatiality means it is transient. When spectators show up to those healing sessions, they go straight to the denouement where the miracles happen. The basis of their existence is largely premised on the staging of miracles. As soon as they happen, we hear spiritual warriors' testimonies, they leave the screen, and a new batch starts to stream. God's transforming presence features as an aura that preemptively glides through the technology that connects thousands of humans together. As those on the screen are healed, some of the viewers post their prayers, typing "amen" and "thank you Jesus" in the comments section. Between the pastoral associates in the studio, the humans on the life-size screen, the humans in the comment page, and those who only watch, we have a virtual church auditorium that is never empty. Although this virtual arrangement cannot yet be mapped for its political efficacy, the creativity during the pandemic is remarkable.

Conclusion

....

Jesus Has Won

A lot of times when you are in service to fame, money, manpower, you start to feel like Satan is the most powerful. And you start to feel like if you service God that in life it means you will not prosper. And the only way to prosper is in service to fame. You know it's like the devil stole all the good producers, the devil stole all the good musicians, all the good artists, all the good designers, all the good business people and said you got to come over and work for me. And now the trend, the shift is going to change. Jesus has won the victory. Because now, now I told you about my arrogance and cockiness already, now the greatest artist that God has ever created is now working for Him.
—Kanye West

In early November 2019, I had a dialogue with a Pentecostal, a Nigerian friend living in Nigeria who knew an aspect of my work was about Nigerian Christians and their support for Donald Trump. As we talked, she said that she knew I did not really like "my president," but if I could look at him more objectively,

I would find that he was doing a lot of good for his country. None of that surprised me, knowing how much Christians love Trump, be they Evangelicals, Pentecostals, or spiritual warriors generally. She mentioned how good he was for the Christian soul of America, how he was going to stop abortion and even roll back gains the LGBTQ community made under liberal Barack Obama, and so on. She does not hate gays, she quickly added. She just does not believe in gay marriage because it is antithetical to her faith, and the United States is supposed to be the beacon of Christian values to the rest of the world. She told me that if Trump won reelection, it would be good for the United States and Christians everywhere. As proof that God had sent Trump to redeem the soul of America, she asked me to consider the conversion of the famous singer, Kanye West, who was now born again. She noted,

> Kanye West has given his life to Christ, and he now goes to churches. All over America, people are now searching for Jesus on Google. Did you read the report that "Jesus" started trending after Kanye released his album? That is what I am saying. It is the Trump effect. He has brought the right aura to the United States. A sinner like Kanye West giving his life to Jesus is good publicity for the church. Just imagine what will happen by the time Trump spends eight years in office. Jesus will be back into the USA. Imagine famous people like Beyoncé and Jay-Z lifting holy hands to worship the Lord.

The way she saw Kanye's conversion as Jesus's victory amused me at the time, but it would later cause me to think about another aspect of spiritual warriors as powerful devices: their shrewd ability to look at virtually any issue, no matter how mundane or seemingly far from even religion, and see a perspective that supports their conviction as signs of their conquest and disestablishment of prevailing order. It explains their consistency and tenacity in the face of political setbacks.

Devices renders things visible, and spiritual warriors illustrate the perspicacity to perceive what underlies all human machinations. They easily reconcile all spheres from science to politics to health to popular culture, and approach them with the end goal of disestablishing the reigning authorities and usurping their place. The possibilities that emerge from their retrospective imposition of divine pattern on random events is virtually limitless, and they can map any coordinates of human affairs to affirm a biased outlook. At that time, I had been viewing the whole affair of Kanye West's born-again conversion—and his attendant politics that excited U.S. conservatives—with some skepticism, partly seeing the move as another in a series of contrarian habits for which he has been famous all his public life. I did not think much of it, but this spiritual warrior thought it was a victory for Jesus. Really, what could be more radical, more spectacular, than for a rap artist who has courted notoriety all through his career to give his life to Jesus Christ and even attend church?[1]

After talking with my friend and seeing how Kanye West's conversion seemed to her a portent of an emerging new America bathed in a Christian ethos, I became more significantly interested in the singer's newfound religion. Truly, Kanye West's freshly released album, *Jesus Is King*, spiked internet searches for biblical references and Christian beliefs.[2] The American Bible Society said they gave out thousands of Bibles to those who inquired after *Jesus Is King* launched with its biblical references.[3] It all checked out, and I could see why someone imagined that the whole affair of an album launch by this new convert was the onset of a revival, driven by the power of God and the capitalistic force of American pop culture. To her, Satan had lost a star artiste, but God had gained one, and it was the beginning of a new order in the United States, and probably the world. For people looking to establish the ethos of righteousness in society, Kanye's conversion was understandably a big deal.

When Kanye West himself went to Lakewood Church, a megachurch in Houston, Texas, run by the famous televangelist Joel Osteen, he spoke in the same vein as someone who had found the truth and was ready to work for God. He declared of his being born again—and in the typical Kanye West manner—that Jesus has won because "now the greatest artist that God has ever created is now working for him."[4] From the many media accounts of West's visit to Lakewood, the service that featured West was a spectacular combination of Hollywood glitz and megachurch glamour. When West talked about his spiritual awakening and how his personal choice to follow Jesus demonstrates a victory over satanic forces, I saw why his testimony was appealing to a spiritual warrior. His consigning fellow artists—who mostly subscribe to liberal ideologies anyway—to the side of the devil and declaring his separation from them as a victory for Jesus worked with her instincts to see an existing social order break down and one she approves of taking its place.

Throughout this book, I have explored how spiritual warriors' performances demonstrate their fixation on disestablishing confederacies they see as structuring the world as it is presently shaped, how its structures impact them as believers. The "Jesus has won" angle affirms that such triumphalist tendencies do not seek to merely eradicate what exists but to establish righteousness in its stead. "Jesus has won" is a conquest they can claim because it usurps the worldly structures of fame that made Kanye West and reorients them toward Jesus Christ. Such shrewdness in their politics of disestablishment—and their ability to pinpoint and moralize the public acts of iconic global figures—also accounts for why they find a viable political formation across national and cultural divides, as shown in chapters 3 and 4 of this book. Beyond disestablishing orders is also the drive to supplant with the righteousness, a mode of public contestations that is fueled by drawing energies on spiritual resources and therefore fuels polarisms. Every sphere, from political to popular culture, and even institutions based on science/technology, is a potential battle site.

In chapter 1, where I began by describing the milieu that spiritual warriors inhabit and how they make apocalyptic devices out of prayer, I noted that time control is central to their activities as time is the unit measurement of one's entire life. For spiritual warriors caught in temporalities where time seems to have slowed down, and bureaucratized political power no longer guarantees social reforms because its processes have been corrupted by self-serving human activities, controlling time is an imperative in disestablishing oppressive formation. Some of these activities, of course, becomes enmeshed with the forces of market and neoliberal capitalism that professionalizes the moral intent behind the disestablishment politics. Chapter 2 also shows that their instinct to disestablish calls for a self-reformation into an enhanced being whose destructive abilities link to God's mythic character, and it is therefore only natural to them to act in certain ways because they have been engrafted with divine attributes. This self-reformation is a crucial factor in the galvanization of a hero complex and a fantasy of the self as a purposeful destroyer that shapes political participation of spiritual warriors. A typical spiritual warrior defines their identity around their confrontational attitude.

The COVID-19 pandemic brought the chance to test the disestablishing impulse of the spiritual warriors on a grand global scale, and chapter 3 shows how this played out in their contentions with science-based and global political institutions. The driving agenda of righteousness overlooked historical complexities and nuances of nationalisms as it pursued the goal of implanting righteousness in the spaces where reigning authorities have been or are being disestablished. For people whose spiritual leaders have included people with advanced degrees and for whom the blend of science/technology into faith has been about a performance of power, challenging scientists on their expertise turf became further means of demonstrating their moral superiority and claiming victories. In chapter 4, I also showed how the contest of will played out by religious leaders who insisted that prayer was an essential service. The pragmatism of church leaders in the wake of the pandemic manifested both through their construal of church lockdown as either an opportunity for spiritual warfare against the secular government that underrated the crucial nature of church in social life or to explore other creative means of churching.

Existing social precarities—and this was covered in chapters 1 and 2—that result in the transcendent flights of fantasy and seeing demonic devices leads them to confront science-based institutions, especially those with global reputation or visibility. For those in the developing countries, the fear of holders of scientific knowledge (and the concomitant human arrogance of the hierarchical arrangement such asymmetry leads to) is exacerbated by past histories of malevolence on the part of imperial powers. During the pandemic, there was a more heightened impulse to disrupt the orders that have either been established by science or were illustrated in spiritual warriors' pushback against what they termed "fake science" and through avidly sharing conspiracy theories. The novelty of the event created an ecosystem of hysteria and subsequent conspiracy theorizing that fed and enlarged the moral panic, inducing the heroism of the conspiritualists who satiated appetites that demanded to understand extant happenings beyond official accountings. These conspiritualists charted how discrete developments aligned to shape a narrative of willful malevolence.

Overall, this unflinching desire to see the end of otherwise viable establishments they consider oppressive and malicious connects spiritual warriors everywhere and anywhere, underwrite their religious rituals, political engagements, and their identity formation processes. The self-conditioning towards fighting and disestablishing orders generated through processes of spiritual self-reformation shapes an idea of the self as a public moral guardian; the brave one who dares the uncertainty and promises of the frontier by redrawing its lines; the one with a prophetic unction to awaken the sleeping sheep to the dangers of the snare of the prowler. The attitude informs inventiveness; an impulse to rewrite the ethos of the world that necessitates all kinds of confrontations. The fantasy that underlies this disestablishment politics is also indeterminate, and I have shown how all logic and actions—spiritual and social—are mobilized toward either ending the establishments and the sociocultural order already considered hegemonic or stopping in their tracks the ones still building up. The near-infinite potential of what is discernible through stringing the fictive with reality shows why, for spiritual warriors, social contentions are not a simple matter of their ability to logically "reason" or their "reasonableness." Finally, by considering spiritual warfare as a form of performance activism throughout this book, I wanted spiritual warriors to be seen as radical changers in the same way leftists and progressives are typically viewed. Throughout this book, I demonstrated how the various pushbacks against larger political forces that have defined the assertions of the freedom human spirit have also featured through spiritual warfare prayers of a people who wield a significant dominant cultural power. My hope is that future scholars of performance activism will consider spiritual warfare, in all its colorfulness, as part of the radical art performances artists and activists deploy as means of galvanizing social change, and what such ambivalence might mean in various contexts.

Acknowledgments

My deep gratitude to everyone who helped me in the production of this book. Thanks to the pastors of the Mountain of Fire and Miracles from the general overseer himself, Dr. Daniel K. Olukoya, to his consortium of pastors, especially Pastor Segun Obatunsin and Pastor Femi Ajila. Thanks for the all the time you devoted to me. Thanks to "Aunty Itoro" at the MFM bookstore at the headquarters for all her patience and generous assistance through the time I was there. Also thanks to Dr. Stella Immanuel of Katy, Texas, for agreeing to talk to me. I am equally grateful to my "destiny helpers," Nimi Wariboko and Amy Guenther, who served as conversation partners during the writing process. They plied me with many questions about my writings as they read the drafts, and those inquiries helped me to better formulate my thoughts. I am also grateful to Pastors Prayer Madueke, Daniel Okpara, and Tella Olayeri for all the time they committed to describing and explaining their spiritual labor to me. I cannot forget to thank Tony Araguz, the Black studies financial manager, for all the bother when I needed to finance my trips and fieldwork. I appreciate your efforts. My gratitude extends to the University of Texas at Austin for the generous grants of summer research assignments and a Humanities Research Award that helped me pursue this research. Thank you, everyone! Finally, I thank my family for all the sacrifices they made while I was writing this book. I asked a lot of you, and you gave even more. Thank you and thank you so much!

Notes

Introduction

1   The Shepherd's House, a.k.a. Agape Power Assembly, was established in 1997. The video I describe was posted on Facebook by a certain Kě'ài Awonaike-Kelly on January 27, 2015, and expressed shock at the spectacle. The video is not dated and contains no contextual information about where it took place, when, or what the larger sermon was about. Awonaike-Kelly is also not the creator of the video. However, at the time of updating this manuscript, May 4, 2021, the video had garnered approximately 1.2 million views, attesting to the reach of this particular clip even if it was published by an alternative source. Even at the moment of updating this portion of the manuscript, people are still reacting to the video in the comments section. Awonaike-Kelly, "Unbelievable!"

2   See, for instance, Butticci, "Crazy World, Crazy Faith!"

3   Matthew 11:2.

4   Manseau, "Some Capitol Rioters Believed They Answered God's Call."

5   Grantham-Philips, "Pastor Paula White Calls on Angels."

6   Henry, "Donald Trump Supporters Rock Back and Forth."

7   Ikeji, "Viral Video of Nigerian Christians Praying."

8   See, for instance, Dolan, *Utopia in Performance*; Madison, *Acts of Activism*; Taylor, *Disappearing Acts*.

9   Fletcher, *Preaching to Convert*.

10 Grobe, "The Artist Is President."

11 Wariboko, *Nigerian Pentecostalism*; see also Benyah, "'Apparatus of Belief'"; Igboin and Adedibu, "'Power Must Change Hands.'"

12 Wariboko, *Nigerian Pentecostalism*, 388.

13 McAlister, "Race, Gender, and Christian Diaspora."

14 Garrard, "Hidden in Plain Sight"; O'Donnell, "The Deliverance of the Administrative State."

15 O'Donnell, *Passing Orders*.

16 Marshall, "Destroying Arguments and Captivating Thoughts."

17 Fletcher, *Preaching to Convert*.

18 Coleman, "Spiritual Warfare in Pentecostalism."

McAlister, "The Militarization of Prayer in America."
20 Marshall, *Political Spiritualities*.
21 Adelakun, *Performing Power in Nigeria*.
22 Holvast, *Spiritual Mapping*.
23 Meyer, *Sensational Movies*.
24 See, for instance, Richman, "Machine Gun Prayer."
25 Wariboko, *Nigerian Pentecostalism*.
26 Sofer, *Dark Matter*.
27 Parsitau, "Religion in the Age of Coronavirus"; Pype, "Branhamist *Kindoki*."
28 This separation comes from Theodore Brown's *Imperfect Oracle*, in which he clearly stipulates that technology comes through scientific knowledge, of course, and that it is through "technology, in the form of material changes, that science affects society" (8–9). Though the two cannot be separated, moral authority to speak on a subject comes from science.
29 Robbins, "On Enchanting Science and Disenchanting Nature."
30 Wariboko, "Kalabari: A Study in Synthetic Ideal-Type."
31 Awonaike-Kelly, "Unbelievable!"
32 As James Bridle observed, "That which was intended to enlighten the world in practice darkens it. The abundance of information and the plurality of worldviews now accessible to us through the internet are not producing a coherent consensus reality, but one riven by fundamentalist insistence on simplistic narratives, conspiracy theories, and post-factual politics." Bridle, *New Dark Age*, 15.
33 Spivak, "Religion, Politics, Theology."
34 Brown, *Imperfect Oracle*, 6.
35 Brown, *Imperfect Oracle*.
36 Allen, *Master Mechanics and Wicked Wizards*, 8.
37 If knowledge is truly enlightenment, the person imbued with certain forms of it thus becomes the regulator of light and darkness, the piercer of the darkness of ignorance. With the power to turn on and off the vision that guides a society and "manage uncertainty and risks associated with public issues," such a person and the institutions they build generate the ethos that defines the operations of the society and furthers their claims to authority, which soon transcends the rational to the moral. See O'Brien, "Scientific Authority in Policy Contexts."
38 Olukoya has a wide repertoire of work on the theology of spiritual warfare even while conducting scientific research. If one types his name into Google Scholar, the results show his work both as a scientist and as a spiritualist.

Chapter 1 Aborting Satanic Pregnancies

Epigraph: Law, "Trump Spiritual Advisor Calls for Miscarriage of 'Satanic Pregnancies.'"

1 Perrett, "Paula White."
2 Olokor, "Trump's Spiritual Adviser Adopts MFM Prayers." In the Kindle version of *The Mysteries of Life*, the reference can be found in "Location 392."
3 For some spiritual warrior Twitter commentators, if the powerful political elites in Washington. DC, could resort to literal demon-mongering, extending the limits of their creative imaginations beyond what the varnished surfaces of disenchanting Western modernity grants, then what these spiritual warriors had

always believed—and for which they have been ridiculed at times—was
vindicated.

4 I shared the point of Paula White appropriating Dr. Olukoya's techniques with
one of his U.S.-based pastors while interviewing him. While he conceded that it
was possible Paula White reads Dr. Olukoya's books, he urged me not to think of
her supposed use of it as "appropriation" since this was a spiritual matter. When it
comes to the things of God, he reminded me, everyone draws from the same
wellspring of the Holy Spirit. The same God that speaks to one speaks to the
other, and you cannot claim ownership of spiritual inspiration.

5 Rayner, "Keeping Time," 32.

6 Falola, *A Mouth Sweeter Than Salt: An African Memoir*, 3.

7 Dixon, "Theatre, Technology, and Time," 16.

8 Pellegrini, "Signaling through the Flames."

9 Dark, *Everyday Apocalypse*.

10 McQueen, *Political Realism in Apocalyptic Times*.

11 Pitetti, "Uses of the End of the World."

12 Cascio, "The Apocalypse."

13 Wariboko, *Transcripts of the Sacred in Africa: Beautiful, Monstrous, Ridiculous*.

14 Wariboko, *Ethics and Society in Nigeria*, 84.

15 Wariboko, *Ethics and Time*.

16 Burgess, *Freedom from the Past*.

17 Ebenezer Obadare noted in *Pentecostal Republic* (145) that Olukoya might have
been less scrutinized than his other Pentecostal counterparts, but he is the perfect
embodiment of the Pentecostal zeitgeist.

18 Butticci, "Crazy World, Crazy Faith!"

19 Ukah's observation in "Sacred Surplus and Pentecostal Too-Muchness" (331) is
that megachurches' leaders create the "goods and services of salvation that appeals
to a large number of people . . . these goods have a reputational function for the
producer; they create a market niche for each producer and cultivate a clientele
over time."

20 Wariboko, "African Pentecostal Political Philosophy."

21 Adogame, "Dealing with Local Satanic Technology," 95.

22 Obadare, "'Raising Righteous Billionaires.'"

23 Wariboko, *The Split God*, 113.

24 Eriksen, Llera Blanes, and MacCarthy, *Going to Pentecost*.

25 Kotsko, *Neoliberalism's Demons*.

26 McCloud, *American Possessions*, 108.

27 As an example, in a thesis submitted in partial fulfillment of the requirements
of the MFM School of Prayer, Institute of Spiritual Warfare, in the Ota Study
Centre in Ogun state, Stella Amara Aririguzoh wrote a dedication to Dr. Olukoya.
She noted that he and his ministry are "God's renowned vessel for intelligent
spiritual warfare prayers," and then said, "Thank you for your deep and uncompro-
mising teachings in not retreating from the enemy; but in giving him heartache.
My life took a better turn forever when I listened to your teachings and read your
eye-opening books" (italics mine). Aririguzoh, "The Power of Love."

28 Fantasies of the apocalypse give a glimpse of a better reality that might exist
beyond the curtains of the present one, and the visions induct the socially
unprivileged into the concealed glories of the future possibilities of a newer and
different existence. The conscious processes that produce social flourishing within

a society that have long been sublimated within the pacifying norms and that keep people from exploring what else there is to existence thus yield to a lucid dream of what else could be. The apocalypse not only breaks down the order of reality, but even the vested interests who would have wanted to sustain the normative way of life find themselves relieved of their moral and legal authority. The apocalyptic juncture is "the place where the future pushes into the present. It's the breaking in of another dimension, a new wine for which our old wineskins are unprepared. That which apocalyptic proclaims cannot fit into existing ways of thinking." Because the period also includes a breakdown of meaning, the crisis brings a liminality, the in-between moments where transformation becomes possible. Dark, *Everyday Apocalypse*, 12.

29 Dr. Olukoya, meanwhile, kept publishing jointly written research papers even as the general overseer of a megachurch. Some of his church members that I interviewed gleefully pointed this detail out to me.

30 Part of his scientific achievements included enhancing pap, a local food staple, with nutritional qualities that also help to control diarrhea.

31 After the first time we talked and he agreed to be interviewed, he sent me the video link of the event. I thought it was an important occasion for him in many ways, and he wanted me to factor that into our sessions. https://www.youtube .com/watch?v=wtooBhceFCw.

32 Gifford, "Unity and Diversity within African Pentecostalism."

33 This account came from literary critic and newspaper columnist Biodun Jeyifo's retelling of this story. Jeyifo, "The Religion and Science, Faith and Reason Controversy."

34 Olugbamina, "New Lab, A Miracle, Says Olukoya."

35 This generosity includes giving out a lot of free copies of their books. Each time I interviewed a church bookstore administrator, I left with a gift of books. When I asked my assistant, Kalu Chibuike Daniel, to do some interviews for me, he left with book gifts as well.

36 Abram, *The Spell of the Sensuous*, 33.

37 Personal interview. See articles on Fagunwa, Tutuola, and Soyinka in Irele, "Tradition and the Yoruba Writer"; Lindfors, "Amos Tutuola and D. O. Fagunwa."

38 On prophet Obadare, see Obadare, "1930–2013 Christ Apostolic Church (Aladura) Nigeria," 24.

39 You can read about Aladura churches in Adogame, "Engaging the Rhetoric of Spiritual Warfare"; Ray, "Aladura Christianity."

40 Personal interview.

41 Some of Olukoya's books, such as *Violent Prayers to Disgrace Stubborn Problems*, are dedicated to the famous Aladura preacher Apostle Joseph Ayo Babalola, who "understood the power of prayer." The dedication page notes that "He was a man, mightily used by God to ignite the fire of the first Christian revival in the country in the nineteen thirties. Brother J. A. Babalola and his team of aggressive prayer warriors entered forbidden forests, silenced demons that demanded worship, paralysed deeply-rooted, anti-gospel activities. Sometime, beginning from the highest places, they emptied hospitals by the healing power of the Lord Jesus Christ, rendered witchdoctors jobless, and started the first indigenous Holy-Ghost filled church in Nigeria. So far, and we stand to be corrected—none has equaled, let alone surpassed this humble Brother in the field of aggressive evangelism in this country."

42 Ondo state was the same place in southwestern Nigeria where the famous Yoruba pioneer writer and fantasist Daniel Fagunwa was born and lived. As a Yoruba man socialized in the same cultural spheres that birthed great writers like Daniel Fagunwa and Amos Tutuola, who also extracted a world of magical fantasies from the raw resources of African storytelling traditions, Olukoya's enchanted imagination correlates with such narrative continuities even though his accounts used Judeo-Christian tropes. When I asked if he considered himself as working in the same traditions that birthed Fagunwa, Tutuola, and Wole Soyinka, he firmly rejected the idea. He said he had read their books, and while he respects them as artists, he is not fictionalizing. He might sermonize about an animated world where snakes crawl through walls into high-rise offices and where disembodied spirit forces walk through market squares in broad daylight (visible only to those imbued with spiritual vision), but he is not telling tales. He believes he is expressing reality. As he said to me in one of our interview sessions, "People have said we are merely being superstitious. As matter of fact, I wish it was all superstition. I wish it was not real. Then everyone would be happy. But unfortunately, it is not. There is real warfare going on."

43 Kalu, *African Pentecostalism*, 69.

44 Olofinjana, *20 Pentecostal Pioneers in Nigeria*.

45 In our private discussions, when I raised the point some scholars had made about how the cultural environment shapes his demonic thinking, Olukoya vehemently rejected insinuations that his African background has any connection to what he does. He says his understanding of the supernatural is purely inspired, and the vision that drives him is a global one. See, for instance, Hackett, "Is Satan Local or Global?"

46 Personal interviews.

47 Adogame, "The Anthropology of Evil," 433.

48 Wariboko, *Nigerian Pentecostalism*, xiii.

49 He narrated the story of a pastor whose church invitation he had honored. That pastor met him in a public place afterward and attacked him. He said since the day Olukoya came to his church to minister, he had lost half of his church members.

50 MFM, Los Angeles, 2017, http://mfmlosangeles.com/?page_id=3907.

51 MFM, Finland, 2017, http://www.mfmfinland.org/mfm-prayer-points/.

52 MFM, North America Women's Fellowship, 2017, http://mfmnawomenfoundation .org/wp/2016-august-power-must-change-hands/.

53 Personal interview.

54 As I will show in chapter 3, this belief in seeing the connection between seemingly unconnected events enhances their ideas of conspiracism—that is, "the belief that powerful, hidden, evil forces control human destinies"—and their entire outlook on life becomes that of warfare. Barkun, *A Culture of Conspiracy*, 2.

55 The cover designs of the books are done by his wife, Sade, who also writes now and then. Many of these books are pamphlet-sized and repetitive and are just his sermons transcribed into book form. One of the bookstore managers told me they raised the point of the books' repetitive contents with Olukoya, but he told them that they needed to consider the underprivileged people who cannot get many of his books. The overlap in the contents means they are exposed to various topics and ideas in a single book.

56 The sales of some books, I was told by their bookstore associates, are also seasonal. Some books sell all year round while some sell around special program periods.

The manager said some other books sell because someone shares a testimony about the book and others rush in to buy a copy.

57 Olukoya, *MFM at 30*.

58 Olukoya, *MFM at 30*, 3

59 For the prayers to be effective, one must be spiritually purified. The MFM church insists holiness is a form of "spiritual germicide" and their church must be willing to adhere to the doctrine of purity. For instance, they have strict dress codes and certain prohibitions—even preconversion polygamous marriage, for instance, is not tolerated. They insist that such strict purity is important for their members to maintain "fire in their bones," and they explicitly forbid premarital sex. Adelakun, "Re-Reading 1 Corinthians 6: 12–20."

60 Personal interview.

61 Wariboko, *Nigerian Pentecostalism*, 17–18.

62 All of these figures are gleaned from my interviews with bookshop administrators. I cannot confirm them independently, but one of my recorded interview sessions with a key administrator whose office was located close to the bookshop finance room was punctuated with the unending buzz of several cash-counting machines running at the same time.

63 Personal interview.

64 According to Afe Adogame's description of the MFM prayer city, "Inscribed on an imposing billboard at the major entrance to the camp and, mounted conspicuously in a way that captures the glance of passersby and motorists, is a self-revealing advertorial: 'Prayer City—Where Fervent Prayers Goes on 24 Hours Daily.' This encased ritual space is thus the venue for crusades, open night vigils, church conferences, festivals, and other wide-ranging rituals that draw the patronage of members and non-members alike." Adogame, "Dealing with Local Satanic Technology."

65 Janson and Akinleye, "The Spiritual Highway."

66 The church says this cycle of prayer is necessary because they rely on the "supernatural power of prayer to confront and solve all kinds of human problems," and it is "no wonder the MFM is known to many people around the world as the church that prays militant and violent prayers." They consider prayer as humans' greatest privilege because "through violent prayers, they can access the amazing and inexhaustible blessings that heaven has for all believers." Olukoya, *MFM at 30*.

67 I should note that there is a similar phenomenon in the United States, where some local pastors attempt to transform the city through such rains of prayer. They also believe that the network of ceaseless prayers can, in time, transform a society. Kent and Bowman, *City of Prayer*.

68 Wariboko, *Ethics and Time*, 91.

69 Crary, *24/7: Late Capitalism*.

70 Olukoya, *MFM at 30*.

71 Pentecostal studies scholar Asonzeh Ukah's "The Miracle City" noted that the decision to have these locations is strategic because they are an "entrepreneur space that make the industrial production of religion possible."

72 Adogame, "The Anthropology of Evil," 433.

73 Not all of them are written by Olukoya, but these are some of the titles: *Atomic Decree That Opens Great Doors: Powerful Prayers in the War Room*; *Breaking Evil Yokes: Breaking Bloodline Curses and Redeeming Your Bloodline in 2021*; *War*

Lords in the War Room of Fire: Powerful Prayer Planner; Bombs and Bullets of Prayer and Praises That Silence Witchcraft Powers; Monitoring Spirits: Hidden Mysteries, Dangerous Prayer Points and Declarations to Disarm and Expose Monitoring Spirits; Double Fire, Double Thunder Prayer Book: Why Prayer Is Powerful; Prayer Warfare against 70 Mad Spirits; Dancers at the Gate of Death; Deliverance from Spirit Husband and Spirit Wife; The Lord Is a Man of War; Deliverance of the Brain; Victory over Satanic Dreams; Overpowering Witchcraft; Disgracing Water Spirits; How to Pray When You Are under Attack; Possessing the Tongue of Fire; Spiritual Hospital: The Power in the Blood of Jesus; O Lord Change My Story by Fire: A Volcanic Prayer Book That Changes Destiny; Strange Women! Leave My Husband Alone: The Secret to Love and Marriage That Lasts; 105 Decrees the Roar of Lion of Judah; Prayer of Power Breakers.

74 Another testimony to the popularity of the books is the problem of piracy that the church has encountered. Olukoya says that a lot of what is sold on Amazon are either copies bought in bulk from their bookstores in Nigeria at a low cost (given the exchange rate) and resold at a higher cost in the United States, or they are simply plagiarized copies. The church had been informed that the copies they got when they ordered from Amazon were printed in the United States, and they confirmed as much when they ordered copies themselves. The neoliberal economy that squeezes demons out of the imagination also created and expanded the circuits through which those diabolical forces would be exorcised.

75 Even though a lot of the imagination that underwrote MFM's notions of spiritual warfare is owing to the Yoruba world, they still had to translate their deliverance manuals into Yoruba. It was not until 2012 that "the first Yoruba deliverance" was carried out. It did not take long for deliverance carried out in indigenous languages to become popular, and their lists of those to be delivered and the ministers that would deliver them grew so quickly they had to seek bigger venues and eventually other locations. From Monday to Friday, from 7 A.M. to 10 A.M., they have programs where people are delivered. They also have church for indigenous Egun people, a subethnic group in southwest Nigeria. In 2016, after they had trained Igbo and Efik evangelists, they set up churches that cater to audiences in those languages. The move to establish churches to cater to an audience that wants to be delivered in their local language is significant for how its propagation of demonic encounters continues to slip beyond the cultural bounds of southwestern Nigeria and find connection points with other cultures. One of my interviewees from Calabar, in southern Nigeria, told me that initially some of the ideas Olukoya preached were strange to her. She thought those demonic operations were just a Yoruba thing, but after years of praying those prayers, she has since found convergences with her own indigenous culture.

76 Personal interviews.

77 Personal interviews.

78 César, "From Babel to Pentecost."

79 Here, I refer to Olivier Roy's statement that secularization and globalization have made religion shed the specificity of cultures so it can appear universal. Roy, *Holy Ignorance*, 2–6.

80 "Dr. D.K. Olukoya," *Amazon.com*, https://www.amazon.com/Dr.-D.-K.-Olukoya /e/B00E878VFM?ref_=dbs_p_pbk_r00_abau_000000.

81 Okpara pulled me back from referring to what they do on Amazon.com as "selling" prayer books. He urged me to think of it as promoting the gospel of

Christ to the world through the means that God inspired. He said he would give his merch out entirely free to whoever, but Amazon.com's rules of operating a seller account would not allow it. Thus, while they evangelize, they also sell their prayer literature to overcome the impediments to reaching people.

82 This is a five-star rating by Dixiecup, on September 9, 2020. Italics added.

83 Personal interview at their Lagos headquarters bookstore.

84 Another five-star review by Edith Young.

85 This concept is from the famous book by Alvin Toffler, who described the sense of overwhelming dizziness people undergoing multiple social changes within a short time tend to experience. Toffler, *Future Shock*.

86 Marshall, *Political Spiritualities*.

87 Wariboko, "African Pentecostal Political Philosophy," 396.

88 Wariboko, "African Pentecostal Political Philosophy," 397.

89 Wariboko further states of the time gaps in temporality that there is always a new temporality in the flux of the past, present, and future through which human beings (prayerful and spirit-filled believers) can insert themselves between the infinite past and the infinite future, thereby exercising their uniquely and supremely human capacity to begin something new and display the distinctiveness of each individual and their destiny. See Wariboko, "African Pentecostal Political Philosophy," 389, 390.

90 Evil has been defeated at the cross, true, yet triumph has to be reenacted when "the salvific event of the past, apparently disproved by the necessity of salvation in the present, is in fact verified in the here and now." See Cristofori, "Promises in the Present Tense."

91 These discourses of demonization supply the metaphoric lens "of an exotic, yet culturally meaningful, underworld/underwater imaginary with which to interpret and debate social and political problems," and also "a theory of supernatural agency which can plausibly account for deviance and misfortune in the lives of individuals, families, communities, nations, nay even the global community." Hackett, "Discourses of Demonization in Africa and Beyond."

92 Gifford, *Christianity, Development and Modernity in Africa*.

93 Warner, "Publics and Counterpublics," 11.

94 Abati, "The Spiritual Side of Aso Villa."

95 Olowookere, "The Unspiritual Side of Aso Villa."

Chapter 2   Rehearsing Authority

Epigraph: The sermon is archived at https://www.youtube.com/watch?v=h2TtcTyBzn8.

1 Schechner, *Performance Studies*, 29.

2 Sociologist Afe Adogame, in *The African Christian Diaspora* (85), states that African modes of theology are not deliberated as abstract debates or books, but are "in their heads, thoughts, utterances, and day-to-day actions and live modes and also expressed in daily life." Such a level of pragmatism underscores why Pastor Joshua had to go to the length of providing a tree prop to enact the scene of an ax cutting down a tree.

3 Colbert, Jones, and Vogel, "Introduction."

4 Phelan, *Unmarked*.

5 Brown, *Imperfect Oracle*.
6 As Daniel Olukoya of the Mountain of Fire and Miracles Ministries stated several times, "There is a battle ongoing. There is always one. Even if you don't think you are fighting a battle, you are in a battle anyway and the law of the battle is very straightforward: you either fight or you perish."
7 García-Reidy, "Theatrical Voyeurism."
8 Jeremiah 51:20.
9 FitzGerald, *Spiritual Modalities*; Luhrmann, *When God Talks Back*.
10 Olukoya, *101 Weapons of Spiritual Warfare*, 222.
11 The sermon is archived at https://www.youtube.com/watch?v=qF4_OvSYpf4.
12 McAlister, "The Militarization of Prayer in America."
13 Marshall, "Destroying Arguments and Captivating Thoughts."
14 This elaboration of spiritual warfare as global political praxis comes after her earlier work, *Political Spiritualities*, where she elaborately expounded on the subjectification techniques of the Pentecostal. This study of the militant dimensions of Pentecostal subjectification outlines how the inundation of the social sphere with an all-pervasive presence of the demonic that must be subjected to God's reforming truth generates an economy of discerning good and evil, and militant attitudes.
15 Jones, *Theatrical Jazz*.
16 The following examples from both Ghana and Kenya show that when aspects of modern life break down, Pentecostals still construe prayer as the answer: Asamoah-Gyadu, ""Christ Is the Answer": What Is the Question?""; Maseno, "Prayer for Rain."
17 Personal interview.
18 Olukoya, "The Weapon of the Finger of God."
19 Wariboko, *The Split God*, xii.
20 Wariboko, *The Split God*, xv.
21 Tupamahu and Ramirez, "The Split God."
22 Ukah, "Sacred Surplus and the Split God."
23 Harrison, "Adam Smith and the History of the Invisible Hand"; Hayden, "The Hand of God"; Genschow, Rigoni, and Brass, "The Hand of God or the Hand of Maradona?"
24 However, as this pastor's example of using a tree stump on the altar to demonstrate how an axe works, the virtuosity that people display in worship through various acts of microtheologizing is also acquired by a strategic staging of actions that teach them how to perform those prayers.
25 Blackson, "Apostle Suleman Narrates."
26 Bridle, *New Dark Age*, 41.
27 Ato Quayson describes the airport as a chronotope of disaggregation, a space in which people are not encouraged to remain but that is designed for them to pass through and be redistributed elsewhere according to certain rules and regulations. Within chronotopes, time is materialized and space is temporalized, and time passes according to how we travel through spaces.
28 I should also note how his status as a missionary is used to override moral questions around his undocumented status.
29 Wariboko, "African Pentecostal Political Philosophy," 395.
30 Olukoya, *101 Weapons of Spiritual Warfare*, 124–125.
31 Wariboko, "African Pentecostal Political Philosophy," 388–389.

32 Hebrews 12:29.
33 God as a pillar of fire also played a protective role for his children in the book of Exodus. A compendium of those Bible verses is at https://bible.knowing-jesus.com /topics/Burning-Sacrifices.
34 1 Kings 18:20–40.
35 Jeremiah 5:14.
36 Okpara, Daniel. *21 Days of Intensive Word Immersion*, 76.
37 Asaju, "Noise, Fire and Flame," 96–97.
38 Goddard, Halligan, and Hegarty, *Reverberations*, 2.
39 Wariboko, "African Pentecostalism," 21.
40 The sermon is archived at https://www.youtube.com/watch?v=qF4_OvSYpf4.
41 Thompson, *Beyond Unwanted Sound*, 5.
42 Kendrick and Roesner, *Theatre Noise*.
43 Voegelin, *Listening to Noise and Silence*, xv.
44 As they sound out their vengeance against these forces through extremely loud shouting, they also collectively desensitize to the symbolic violence they promote when they ask things and forces to die. In the shouts of "Die! Die! Die!" as they ring out across the auditorium or arena, all that can be felt is the bodily sensation of the immersive experience and not the pangs of conscience.
45 Meyer, "Aesthetics of Persuasion," 756.
46 Biggin, *Immersive Theatre and Audience Experience*, 5. See also Nield, "The Rise of the Character Named Spectator."
47 Luhrmann, *When God Talks Back*.
48 Richman, "Machine Gun Prayer."
49 In "The Demons as Guests," Wariboko shows that this distinction is not really helpful because people move between both agencies.
50 Caroline Jeannerat is another scholar who construes the body as a conduit. See Jeannerat, "Of Lizards, Misfortune and Deliverance."
51 Olayeri, *Fire for Fire, Part 2*, 15.
52 In traditional African society, where life is homogenous and social transitional phases are more drawn out, people who try to build explanatory models for social causality find their answers in structures of family and social relations. In a modern globalized world, where "the impersonal is the preferred locus of order and regularity," the stories of demonic attack from intimate relationships are one of the ways deliverance ministers shrink the world and undo the defamiliarization of the expansion of the world. As the African world has expanded into national and global scopes, and the economic horizons of former village dwellers have been annexed to global capital systems such that they are opened to a wider universe of possibilities along with shifts in money and morality, the moral influence of God and deities also weakened, and over time, people have opted for more globalized gods of monotheism whose influence has a global scope. See Wariboko, "Management in Postcolonial Africa."
53 Olukoya, *Victory over Satanic Dreams*, 5–6.
54 Robin Shoaps notes how the repetition of scripted prayer can take away individual expressivity. This could have been true for the contents of prayer literature given that it can be formulaic, but the different exotic tales that these accounts include also invite the reader to supply their individual stories to the archetypal structures provided. See Shoaps, "'Pray Earnestly.'"
55 Olukoya, *The Mystery of Water Cure*, 99–100.

56 Olukoya, *Too Hot to Handle*, 30.
57 Not all are stories are accounts of overcoming. In *Igniting Your Inner Fire*, for instance, Olukoya also tells the story of a sister who lacked the spiritual fire and yet went to preach in a man's house. The man offered her a drink, and when she rejected it, he turned on reggae music for her instead. She tapped her feet to the song as it played. She also sang along to another song, underscoring her familiarity with worldliness and its artifacts. When she started to preach, the man stopped her and showed her his wardrobe, which contained different parts of a human body that had been arranged and labeled. The woman wanted to start praying but she was overwhelmed by the power of the occult the man had over her. She was entirely powerless. The man opened another wardrobe, from which a snake crawled out and squeezed her. She managed to break free, but it took a while for her to recover from the experience. According to the story, "she could not talk, she rushed to her pastor and asked him to pray for her. The pastor prayed and it took several days to get her out of the trouble" (23).
58 As an example of these fighting instincts, this list of book titles written by Tella Olayeri, a self-described "spiritual warlord," demonstrate this cultivated sense of embattlement: *War Lords in the War Room of Fire: Powerful Prayer Planner*; *Double Fire, Double Thunder Prayer Book: Why Prayer Is Powerful*; *Prayer to Break the Head of the Dragon: It Is War!*; *Declare Your Enemies Defeated and Destroy Them: Tongue of Fire and Warfare Deliverance*; *Thunder Prayer That Provokes Angelic Violence against Works of Darkness*; *Prayer That Makes Enemies Surrender and Flee*; *I Decree Fire to Consume and Destroy Witchcraft Powers*; *Dangerous Prayer That Makes Satan Flee and Surrender Your Possession*; *Fury Fire Fury Thunder That Gives Instant Solution to Challenges of Life*.
59 Maggi, "Christian Demonology in Contemporary American Popular Culture."
60 Personal interviews, October 2020.
61 One can also argue they desensitize one to the violence that the process of ensuring victory entails, just as soldiers are trained, and they have mastered the techniques through self-simulation and demonstrating God's destructive attributes; they are ambivalent about destruction.
62 O'Donnell, "Islamophobic Conspiracism and Neoliberal Subjectivity."
63 Olukoya, *101 Weapons of Spiritual Warfare*, 222.

Chapter 3 The Noisome Pestilence

Epigraph: "Oyedepo Backs Stella Immanuel."

1 According to the organizers on their website, "American life has fallen casualty to a massive disinformation campaign. We can speculate on how this has happened, and why it has continued, but the purpose of the inaugural White Coat Summit is to empower Americans to stop living in fear. If Americans continue to let so-called experts and media personalities make their decisions, the great American experiment of a Constitutional Republic with Representative Democracy, will cease." See https://www.getinvolvedwi.com/americas-front-line-doctors/.
2 On the church website, their definition of "firepower"—lifted from Wikipedia, actually—describes modern warfare. In summary, firepower, as they apply it, is a combatant force and the weapons directed at enemy forces to destroy or repress them in war operations. See http://drstella.org.

3 In one of the video clips that circulated in the media, she was at the altar and talking about "astral sex" as one of the topics of spiritual warfare. In the background was written the name of the church, "Firepower Ministries," and on the right corner of the screen it was noted that the videos were pulled "From You-Tube." Immanuel stood behind a pulpit adorned with a cover that carried the name and the insignia of the Mountain of Fire and Miracles Church. The U.S. mainstream news anchors obviously did not pick up on the significance of this church as a foremost spiritual warfare ministry where apocalyptic insights into another order of reality-making is an everyday affair.

4 Qiu, "Trump's Inaccurate Claims on Hydroxychloroquine."

5 While some church members circulated her video on their social media accounts, some played it in worship services—which they now have to broadcast on social media—as "proof" that they were right all along about the diabolical intention behind the pandemic.

6 His church is one of the biggest in Nigeria. The present auditorium reputedly has a seating capacity of 50,000 and they are currently building another one that will hold a congregation of 100,000.

7 "Bishop Oyedepo Reacts to African-American Doctor Virus Cure Claim."

8 Oyedepo's characterization of the pandemic as the "noisome pestilence" (Psalms 91:3) while preaching about its politics raised doubts as to the validity of official reports of the disease by couching it in biblical terms that are quite familiar to his audience. He wedded conspiracy theory to spiritual warfare and thrust himself forward as a privileged possessor of the ability to discern the mischievous intent of global agencies purportedly behind the pandemic. His interjection is another instance of how spiritual warfare and conspiracy theories align beyond the predisposition to an instinct to be paranoid or vigilant in dealing with the complexity of the world. Spiritual warfare particularly tries to bring the villains it identifies to judgment, because it is no longer about what some other people do secretly, but what spiritual warriors consider themselves permitted to do as God's battle axe in a *War* with an outcome that will determine the course of history. Also, by reminding his congregation that scientific authorities in Western societies have a history of predicting that certain diseases would ravage Africa—such as the case of Ebola around 2014 to 2016—only to have the arithmetical projections of fatalities made with epidemiological models turn out to be mere hype, he weaponizes recent history to stir feelings of self-defense in the congregation, who will consider those Western epidemiologists malevolent enemies of Africans. When they are directed to pray by the bishop, they will do so from the politicized angle of their African identity. In all of this, he is the central figure of authority directing them to see the truth and react to it.

9 Sommer, "Trump's New COVID Doctor Says Sex with Demons Makes You Sick."

10 Coleman, "Spiritual Warfare in Pentecostalism."

11 Marshall, "Destroying Arguments and Captivating Thoughts."

12 https://twitter.com/stella_immanuel/status/1284195400547803137?lang=en.

13 Farkas and Schou, "Fake News as a Floating Signifier."

14 Farkas and Schou, "Fake News as a Floating Signifier."

15 See, for instance, Cosentino, *Social Media and the Post-Truth World Order.*

16 Personal interview.

17 Private interview on October 24, 2020.

18 Andrews, "Madonna Keeps Making Controversial Covid-19 Claims."

19 Oliver and Wood, "Conspiracy Theories and the Paranoid Style(s) of Mass Opinion."
20 Hofstadter, *The Paranoid Style in American Politics*.
21 Ward and Voas, "The Emergence of Conspirituality." David Robertson is one example of someone who considered conspiracy theories in the context of organized religion. For the most part, however, the focus has been on the New Age spiritualties. See Robertson, "The Hidden Hand."
22 Ward and Voas, "The Emergence of Conspirituality."
23 Vonk and Visser. "An Exploration of Spiritual Superiority."
24 To buttress the unease of Christians with New Age spirituality, I should point out that Frank Peretti, the famous Christian writer who significantly impacted the Christian spiritual imagination with his dramatization of spiritual warfare, railed consistently against New Age spirituality. He considered it a political agenda antithetical to Christianity. Peretti's thrillers did not merely portray the spiritual warfare he engaged in as mere fantasy for Christians to indulge as entertainment. His books were political statements against New Age spirituality. As Andrew Connolly noted, Peretti's works were shot through with political conservatism, as the regular villains always involved in conspiracy against Christians never failed to include "progressive politicians, liberal education, psychology, pro-choice activities, the media . . . [and] the New Age Movement," whose motivating actions are instigated by demons. Connolly, "Masculinity, Political Action, and Spiritual Warfare."
25 Here are examples of articles that show a convergence of the beliefs of both Icke and Immanuel: loxley.6, "David Icke: Love and Lizard People"; Ahmed, "Aliens and 'Reptilians.'"
26 Asprem and Dyrendal, "Conspirituality Reconsidered."
27 Locke, "Conspiracy Culture, Blame Culture, and Rationalisation"; Sunstein and Vermeule, "Conspiracy Theories," 205; Uscinski and Parent, *American Conspiracy Theories*.
28 This came from one of the videos of her sermon she referred me to: Immanuel, "Revival—PUSH Day 7."
29 Immanuel, "Revival—PUSH Day 7."
30 Private interview on October 24, 2020. In this interview, she also related how much prayer meant to her and how she prays endlessly. According to her, she was born again in Louisiana in 2002 in a White church, but their Christianity never felt right. She thought there was more to the world than what was seen, and what the church practiced was too watered down. One day, while visiting her cousin in Houston, she came across Daniel Olukoya's book *Prayer Rain* (see chapter 1), and after reading only a few pages, her eyes were immediately opened and she began to pray "like crazy." (There was a bookshelf beside her, and it would have been empty but for the two copies of *Prayer Rain* on it.) Reading the book, she said, changed her life. She said, "Within the first seven days, I slept for the first time in years. I used to have insomnia. I used to have migraine headaches and I started praying and those migraines left. I had had an accident the year before. I would get on the highway and get a panic attack. My chest would close. Within that same year, I went down the street. I traveled to Houston within that same week of prayer. I was able to drive on the highway. I said this is it! This is it! I was in Louisiana and I would probably drive three to four hours to Houston two to three times a month to attend MFM. They did not have a church in Louisiana."

31 Marshall, "Destroying Arguments and Captivating Thoughts."

32 Private interview on October 24, 2020.

33 She even posted the article from the *Daily Beast* on her Twitter page and stated, "The Daily Beast did a great job summarizing our deliverance ministry and exposing incubus and succubus. Thank you Daily Beast. If you need deliverance from these spirits. Contact us." To the journalist who wrote the piece she also tweeted and tagged, "Awesome job exposing these demons. Do you want to do a piece on witchcraft. And while we are at it I could cast some demons out of you. It will help you a great deal."

34 Her road as a minister of an independent church was a challenging one, and she astutely recognized how going viral helped to shorten the road to fame. She mentioned a meeting she organized in Houston (before she went viral) as a minister that did not go well. She said in the sermon, "We put it in the papers, we rented to places. I fasted, three days dry fast, we prayed, we drove around the city praying, because God has said we take over Houston. You won't believe in that conference only three people showed up. Three people! I had spent almost 10,000 dollars. I went back to the hotel that night and I cried myself to sleep!" Immanuel, "Revival—PUSH Day 7."

35 Titlestad, "The Ongoing End," 1, 2.

36 Aupers, "'Trust No One.'"

37 Brotherton, *Suspicious Minds*.

38 Barkun, *A Culture of Conspiracy*.

39 "Epistemic anxiety" and "epistemic instability" came from Adam Ashforth and Jaron Harambam, respectively. Ashforth, *Witchcraft, Violence, and Democracy*; Harambam, *Contemporary Conspiracy Culture*.

40 Wasserman, "Bill Gates Warned the Coronavirus Could Hit Africa Worse Than China."

41 According to Jean-Paul Mira, head of intensive care at Cochin Hospital in Paris, "If I can be provocative, shouldn't we be doing this study in Africa, where there are no masks, no treatments, no resuscitation? A bit like as it is done elsewhere for some studies on AIDS. In prostitutes, we try things because we know that they are highly exposed and that they do not protect themselves." See "Coronavirus: France Racism Row over Doctors' Africa Testing Comments."

42 See "Melinda Gates: Covid-19 Will Be Horrible in the Developing World."

43 See Bavier, "At Least 300,000 Africans Expected to Die in Pandemic."

44 WHO stated clearly that this prediction was based on modeling, but that did not alleviate the fear among people. "New WHO Estimates: Up to 190 000 People Could Die."

45 Worsening the crisis of trust in existing institutions, the corruption of the Nigerian government officials as they disbursed relief funds during the pandemic left some people believing that the whole affair was nothing more than a scheme to use mass deaths to distract from their siphoning public funds into private pockets. See Adepegba, "N2.67bn School Feeding Funds Found in Private Accounts."

46 Baker and Chadwick, "Corrupted Infrastructures of Meaning"; Cosentino, *Social Media and the Post-Truth World Order*; Harambam, *Contemporary Conspiracy Culture*; O'Donnell, "The Deliverance of the Administrative State."

47 As a modern folklore of sorts, conspiracy theories typically emerge in times of great social stress and uncertainty; the accounts are never quite original and are

typically woven from the shared sensibilities of cultural groups and existing narratives. Shahsavari et al., "Conspiracy in the Time of Corona."

48 Belief in conspiracy theories drove many of the people who should have adhered to precautionary measures such as social distancing to willfully ignore them, including in Nigeria, in defiance of the instructions of scientists. See Bierwiaczonek, Kunst, and Pich, "Belief in COVID-19 Conspiracy Theories Reduces Social Distancing over Time."

49 The news of Nigeria's test of 5G technology occurred months earlier and had petered out, only to reappear at the time of the pandemic. As some researchers demonstrated in their tracking of the obscure origins of the conspiracy theory linking COVID-19 to 5G, the link between the two had existed in spots on the internet as far back as January 2020 and only began to gain traction in February 2020, when it spread globally. The rumors and calls became so intense that Nigerian lawmakers urged the government to suspend its plans for the technology. See Bruns, Harrington, and Hurcombe, "Covid19? 'Corona? 5G? or Both?'" Also see "Suspend 5G Network Deployment, Lawmakers Tell Nigerian Government."

50 "Future shock" is from Alvin Toffler's book of the same name. The book describes the sense of disorientation that comes from rapid social, political, and technological change.

51 Miller, "Psychological, Political, and Situational Factors Combine."

52 Elwood and Leszczynski, in "New Spatial Media, New Knowledge Politics," noted that WhatsApp can significantly "enable, extend, or enhance our ability to interact with or create geographic information online."

53 Studies on WhatsApp in Nigeria and Africa include exploring social empowerment and the changes in the structures of civic and political participation. See, for instance, Abubakar, Hafiz, and Dasuki, "Empowerment in Their Hands"; Cheeseman et al., "Social Media Disruption."

54 Depoux et al., "The Pandemic of Social Media Panic Travels Faster Than the COVID-19 Outbreak."

55 Waterson, "Revealed."

56 This article gives some broad context to the accusations: Blythe, "Bill Gates' Comments on Covid-19 Vaccine."

57 This preoccupation with retailing the "truth" that one privately possesses also reflects the ethos of late capitalism that urges each one of us to perform the best of ourselves to potentially attract neoliberal rewards (also discussed in chapter 1). The ascendance of the prosperity gospel is an index of how much capitalism has subjugated Pentecostalism—its teachings driving people to work even more to attain the ever-elusive goals of forces of late capitalism—and imposes "the pseudo urgency to *act now* . . . the urgency to act is often coming from a body and its desires that have been invaded by capitalism and its forces." This imperative of urgent action is even more reflected in the disestablishment practices of spiritual warfare that first open the eyes to otherworldly realities and impending doom, and then subject one to self-enhancing spiritual training in a bid to establish an antidote to establishment power. During the pandemic, people were self-directed to social spheres like the one Okechukwu created to promulgate the truth of what others do not see, and also sought a share of the ideologically polarized audience, whose numbers potentially cut through worldwide. Wariboko, *The Split God*, 116. Also see the video of his Trump campaign launch: "Nollywood Actor, Joseph Okechukwu Launches Africans for Trump Campaign."

58 Meanwhile, some of those who circulated conspiracy theories about 5G and COVID-19 also sold products that helped to protect against the electromagnetic field. Others who also made videos would even throw around terms already familiar to Christians and apocalyptists such as "end time," "mark of the beast," along with the demonization of "socialism" and "liberalism." Ahmed et al., "COVID-19 and the 5G Conspiracy Theory."

59 Aupers, "'Trust No One.'"

60 Miller, Saunders, and Farhart, "Conspiracy Endorsement as Motivated Reasoning."

61 Miller, "Do COVID-19 Conspiracy Theory Beliefs Form a Monological Belief System?"

62 Grobe, "The Artist Is President."

63 Schechner, "Donald John Trump, President?"

64 Solomon, "My Epistemological Crisis."

65 Perucci, "The Trump Is Present."

66 Obadare, "Goodluck the Performer."

67 Boletsi, "Crisis, Terrorism, and Post-Truth."

68 Silverman, "Is There a Deep State, and If So What Is It?"

69 Marvin and Ingle, *Blood Sacrifice and the Nation*.

70 This self-lowering for the sake of the common man, the "real" American includes not maintaining the distance between occupants of the high echelons of public offices and the "people." For instance, the fact that his supporters could tag him in their comments and videos on Twitter, and he could—if he wished or considered them controversial enough—retweet them and give them some visibility, makes them connect to him as an adulatory figure. For a president who has the equivalent of the population of entire countries as his Twitter followers, retweeting them was an affirmation of their visibility. With the president's retweet, one could go from being one of the millions of anonymous handles on social media to instantly becoming seen within the Twitter universe. He not only "sees" them, the real Americans—alongside, if not even above—the hyped-up figures of the powerful and famous people, but also grants access to the corridors of power by relating directly with them. In a world where social media networks have democratized communication, but where we still rely on powerful influencers to give us a voice, such gestures are seen as generous.

71 Grobe, "The Artist Is President"; Poniewozik, *Audience of One*; Reid, "Trump as Capitalist Folk Hero."

72 Reid, "Trump as Capitalist Folk Hero," 93.

73 Reid, "Trump as Capitalist Folk Hero," 94.

74 McCloud, *American Possessions*; O'Donnell, "The Deliverance of the Administrative State."

75 Kotsko, *Neoliberalism's Demons*.

76 Just as Immanuel was celebrated, when another "scientist" broke ranks and made the documentary *Plandemic*, it was eagerly accepted as positive apostasy by conspiritualists. The video, produced by Mikki Willis, a conspiracy theorist, and Dr. Judy Mikovits, a researcher whose work had been discredited by her peers, was eagerly circulated by those who needed to believe they were not wrong in their belief.

77 One of many stories that circulated on WhatsApp stated:

Call your friends in the US or forward this message to them. What is going on is an occultic arrow. Please beloved in Christ let us intercede for the US and Donald Trump. Ask yourself one question; Who are the people that will truly rejoice if Donald Trump loose [*sic*] the election at the long run? Let us watch and Pray. Ephesians 6:10–18. US has great influence and impact on Christianity all over the world. Most European nations are on a fast lane to Islam but the headache of the Muslims is the US and this President Donald Trump. Another tenure in office will cost them 50 to 70 years set back so they are out. We must not be ignorant of the devices of the devil lest Satan have an advantage of us 2Cor 2:11.

78 President Rajoelina had touted an herbal potion that he claimed could cure COVID-19. While his announcement set off waves of pride in many Africans who were quite excited to see that an African could provide a solution that would redeem a world beleaguered by a disease, the WHO voiced concerns about the efficacy of the medicine before it had passed through clinical trials. President Rajoelina was resolute about what they had achieved. He told some journalists that the WHO was being condescending by subjecting him to rigorous questioning on the drug. He told journalists, "If it wasn't Madagascar, and if it was a European country that had actually discovered this remedy, would there be so much doubt? I don't think so." "Madagascar Virus Potion Scorned Because It's from Africa."

79 Here are some of the articles: "China: Covid-19 Discrimination against Africans"; Hsiao-Hung Pai, "The Coronavirus Crisis Has Exposed China's Long History of Racism"; Marsh, "China Says It Has a 'Zero-Tolerance Policy' for Racism."

80 There was also a viral video of a Nigerian official quarrelling with Chinese officials said to be seizing the passports of Africans and forcing them into extended quarantine. The Nigerian official became an instant hero, and his action caused the Nigerian lawmakers to summon the Chinese ambassador to Nigeria for a discussion on Chinese racism.

81 In one instance, a Chinese person opened a restaurant in Lagos, Nigeria's largest and most cosmopolitan city. Then people started reporting on social media that the place did not admit Blacks/Africans. Nigerians got quite upset about it, and some people started mobilizing to stage a protest at the place. The government quickly shut the place down, and hopefully prevented a catastrophe. Awal, "Nigeria Shuts Chinese Eatery."

82 In prayers led by a pastor of megachurches, he divined that COVID-19 was a satanic attack, and one leading pastor urged his congregation to pray against the "dragon from the East." Within the context of the conspiracy theory of China being a global center of mischief through their purported globalized technology and a disease that originated from there, he gave the Chinese totem of a dragon a new meaning employable by those who saw nations embroiled in a war between good and evil. This priming to see China as a malevolent neoimperialist power driven by uncontrolled ambition and that would stop at nothing to achieve global dominance is juxtaposed against the only other world power that could stop them: the United States. With Trump also posturing as Christian, the choice is between the "Christian" United States and its president against "godless" China. Sorting countries using such ethical valuations feeds into other sensibilities. For instance, these issues are not just metaphoric for those concerned. Some genuinely

dislike the Chinese because they see them as exploiters and racists. The fact that China could be ahead of the United States in a world-changing technology like 5G was unsettling, because it meant being at the mercy of a world leader who did not represent the truth they possess. The recrudescence of the Cold War in the 5G technology contest is also striking, and it underwrote how these interpretations exacerbated the urgency that drove prayers within the period. See Stephens, "A Geospatial Infodemic."

83 See the video of Pastor Paul Enenche, a trained medical doctor and pastor of Dunamis International leading a prayer against Bill Gates here: https://www .youtube.com/watch?v=oaoCAJNfSQo.

84 This figure was last updated in January 2022.

85 Here are the articles that document these instances: Muhindo, "BBC Africa Retracts 'Offensive' Headline"; Winning, "Puzzled Scientists Seek Reasons behind Africa's Low Fatality Rates"; Nordling, "The Pandemic Appears to Have Spared Africa so Far."

Chapter 4 Churches Going Virtual

Epigraph: Wahab, "COVID-19: Oyakhilome Says Pastors That Are Yet to Reopen Churches Are Not Believers."

1 In places where the risk of infection was lower, people could gather to worship if they did not exceed a certain number. In May, twenty-one out of thirty-six states in Nigeria were allowed eventually to fully reopen. The remaining fifteen states where the risks were higher had to maintain the lockdown. Ugbodaga, "Coronavirus."

2 Yesufu, "How John MacArthur Inspired a Church Gathering in Ibadan."

3 Grace community Church is a megachurch with a membership that varies from 7,000 to 10,000 depending on which medium is reporting their numbers.

4 This is an allusion to Mark 12:17, where Jesus says, "Render unto Caesar the things that are Caesar's, and unto God the things that are God's" to settle the question of loyalty to either God or the state.

5 See Asad's *Formations of the Secular*.

6 Superior Court of the State of California, August 17, 2020. https://beta .documentcloud.org/documents/20399011-county-worker-declaration#document /p2.

7 Cosgrove, "L.A. Megachurch Pastor Mocks Pandemic Health Orders."

8 One of Nigeria's foremost Pentecostal denomination, Christ Embassy, has a network of branches in Nigeria, the United States, Canada, the UK, South Africa, and so on.

9 Diokpa, "Pastor Chris Trends on Twitter."

10 The statement is archived on the YouTube page. While it was uploaded on April 30, 2020, there is no formal record of when the sermon was actually preached. WatchPastorChris, "Pastor Chris: COVID 19 Compliant Churches???"

11 Abellanosa, "The Church as a Sacrament in a Time of Pandemic."

12 One pastor who also happened to be a former Nigerian presidential candidate said in a message titled "The Covid-19 Mystery" that holding church online was "unscriptural." He claimed the viral disease was a scheme by Bill Gates and the WHO to consolidate their agenda of making humans covenant with Lucifer by consuming GMO products and taking a vaccine that would make them seek

blood for sustenance and eventually turn into vampires. Okogba, "Chris Okotie Says It's Unscriptural to Hold Services Online."

13 Mohr, "Faith Tabernacle Congregation."

14 Sim, "Compliant Singaporean Christians?"

15 Wariboko, *Nigerian Pentecostalism*.

16 Conejo, "Revolution and Revolt."

17 Jennings, *The Christian Imagination*.

18 As someone told me of their resistance to state regulations, "Not meeting in church means we cannot take the bread and blood of Jesus as he commanded us."

19 Korede, "Online Service Cannot Be Compared to Physical Church Gathering."

20 Asamoah-Gyadu, "'We Are on the Internet'"; Hackett, "The New Virtual Interface of African Pentecostalism."

21 Asamoah-Gyadu, "'"Get on the Internet!" says the Lord.'"

22 See, for instance, Henrietta Nyamnjoh, who studies the phenomenon of social media and churches. Nyamnjoh, "'When Are You Going to Change Those Stones to Phones?'"

23 Asamoah-Gyadu, "'"Get on the Internet!" says the Lord.'"

24 As a couple of church leaders told me, one way they managed this shortfall was to expand their broadcasting operations on local television stations.

25 Omojuwa, "Nigeria Shakes the World!" This post by a Nigerian political and social commentator archives the pastor's claim.

26 Adogame, "Engaging the Rhetoric of Spiritual Warfare."

27 Also see similar examples from other regions during the pandemic: Chow and Kurlberg, "Two or Three Gathered Online"; Wong, "Longing for Home."

28 Auslander, *Liveness*; Schneider, *Performing Remains*.

29 Personal interview.

30 Nigeria, by the way, identified its first COVID patient, an Italian, on February 27, 2020. Kazeem, "Africa's Largest City Is Trying to Shut Down to Beat Coronavirus."

31 Ogundipe, "Coronavirus."

32 Onyeji, "Coronavirus."

33 These three areas have a population of about 30 million people, and they are major business districts. They are also the places that house some of the largest and richest churches in the country.

34 Ajayi, "Lockdown Violation."

35 Ajayi, "COVID-19 Restriction."

36 Chukwuorji and Iorfa, "Commentary on the Coronavirus Pandemic."

37 During a sermon in June 2020, Oyedepo also claimed that there was nothing to COVID-19, as their church had recorded only 114 COVID-19 healing testimonies so far. In one of his sermons, he stated, "Can you imagine anyone bringing a coronavirus patient to me and I won't lay hands on him? Will I wear gloves to lay hands on them? I will lay hands on them; breathe into them; embrace them. What you carry is eternal life, it's not human life. You should know that. You'll now wear everything like a doctor, you have never been to a theatre in your life. You will be moving like somebody is under some attack. Someday, they will know that they have been deceived. . . . It's all the devil trying to dehumanise humanity." Augoye, "I'll Lay My Bare Hands on COVID-19 Patient."

38 This was on June 17, 2020. In that same sermon, he talked about how life must go on even if people die. He gave an example of how his classmate died when they

were in primary school and the rest of the class still went to school the next day. He said, "If someone dies in your family today, won't you go to work tomorrow?"

39 "Bishop Oyedepo Questions Lockdown Order."

40 In times of great uncertainty such as the pandemic, the boredom and paranoia that people experience also drives them to hold on to conspiracy theories which, at least, produces some excitement as it purports to explain what they were experiencing. See, for instance, Brotherton and Eser, "Bored to Fears."

41 WatchPastorChris, "Pastor Chris:: 5G is LOVELY but . . ."

42 See, for instance, Aluko, "Covid-19 Pandemic in Nigeria"; Amanambu, "Critical Reflections on the Impacts of Covid-19 Pandemic on Nigerian Religiosity"; Pontianus, "Covid-19 Pandemic, Conspiracy Theory and the Nigerian Experience"; Ukwuru and Nwankwo. "Social Media and Fake News on Corona Virus."

43 Thomas and Zhang, "ID2020, Bill Gates and the Mark of the Beast."

44 On the aspect of Oyakhilome as a miracle healer, see Ekenna, "Oyakhilome's Miracles"; Magbadelo, "Pentecostalism in Nigeria"; Ukah, "Banishing Miracles."

45 As Deji Yesufu, the blogger cited earlier, noted, modern-day Christians have enjoyed stretches of peace and liberal freedoms during which the sense of trauma and persecution by higher authorities that forged the identity of early Christians has been lost. The symbols and myths of Christianity that gained deep meaning through the experiences of early Christians who were tortured due to their faith needed to be deepened through a contest with secular authority. Castelli (*Martyrdom and Memory*) noted that Christianity itself was founded upon "an archetype of religio-political persecution, the execution of Jesus by the Romans." The times of persecution of religious adherents are thus crucial ones; their resolve of faith is steeled when a sense of insecurity and fear of being killed drives them to pray and get closer to God. Gathering in defiance of regulations by health officials and pushing narratives of conspiracies was thus an opportunity to play the martyr in a bid to retrieve something that had been lost through time.

46 As Shelly Matthews (*Perfect Martyr*) pointed out, martyrdom is not an event in itself but a discourse that "attempts to wrest meaning out of violence through inverting categories of strength and weakness, victory and loss, life and death."

47 Matthews, *Perfect Martyr*, 4.

48 Nation Scoops, "Pastor Chris Has Kicked Off Again."

49 Personal interview; also, Pastor Bakare repeated the statement to the public. Ramon, "I Can't Open Church, Endanger People's Lives."

50 Just to note, in California some pastors stated that they were bewildered that shops selling "donuts, clothes, and cannabis" were marked "essential services" and allowed to open while churches were lumped into the same category as beauty shops, entertainment centers, and gyms, and their opening was moved to the third phase of reopening. To the church leaders, this kind of classification was demeaning. Coming at a time when the world was seeing uncertainty—job loss, unemployment, depression, isolation, suicide—because of the COVID-19 pandemic, not treating the churches as "essential services" was seen as a ploy to make them irrelevant through institutional processes. Mahbubani, "'The Governor Is a Servant of the State.'"

51 I should note that similar grievances played out in the United States for people who were disappointed that grocery stores, abortion clinics, and liquor stores could open but not churches. To establish how essential the service of faith was, some people started taking the risk of meeting in Walmarts or casinos to challenge

the rules against physical meetings. Since the pandemic also happened in an election year, the battle of defining the church's status played along political lines. Lubold and Lucey, "Trump Says Places of Worship Are Essential Services."

52 Personal interview.

53 For instance, a pastor arrested for breaching COVID-19 regulations in Akwa Ibom state in southern Nigeria instituted a legal action against the COVID-19 task force for breaching his rights by arresting and detaining him. Emmanuel, "Christ Embassy Sues Akwa Ibom Govt over Arrest."

54 Phillips, "Deviance, Persecution and the Roman Creation of Christianity."

55 Baker, "Firing a Salvo in Culture Wars."

56 The faith his supporters demonstrated in him as a politician overruled their confidence in the recommendation of the scientists, and that worsened the disease crisis because they were less likely to comply with directives such as social distancing. Graham et al., "Faith in Trump, Moral Foundations, and Social Distancing Defiance during the Coronavirus Pandemic."

57 Ugbodaga, "Coronavirus."

58 "Trump Orders Opening of Churches in 'the Month of Opening.'"

59 The Baker article cited above noted, "Churches, synagogues and mosques already are allowed to operate in more than half of the states, although many remain under social distancing instructions, and individual institutions have opted to remain closed for safety." In May 2020, Trump called on state governors to "allow our churches and places of worship to open immediately." Although legal scholars noted that he had no power to overrule the states on churches reopening, he still threatened to do so. Trump said, "The governors need to do the right thing and allow these very important, essential places of faith to open right now for this weekend. If they don't do it, I will override the governors. In America, we need more prayer, not less." Baker, "Firing a Salvo in Culture Wars."

60 Months later, Oyakhilome preached a sermon, stating that "they" hate Trump not because of what he had done wrong, but they hate the Christians on whose behalf he was fighting. His comment was not circulated only in Nigeria; it also appeared on social media and some Americans expressed their appreciation that a Nigerian pastor understood what was at stake for the world if Trump won reelection in November. In that respect, he was "better" than even Americans who did not see any good in Trump. "Video: They Hate Trump for Supporting Christians."

61 When Senior Pastor Jack Hibbs of Calvary Chapel in Chino Hills, California, asked Trump's Attorney General William Barr during a "pastor call" with administration officials whether the Justice Department would support California churches in their self-determination quest, the AG reportedly answered, "Absolutely." Supporters thought that proved the shutdown showed unnecessary hostility against their faith. When Trump joined the "pastor call," he reportedly told those pastors, "Some of these Democrat governors, they'd be happy if you never opened again." Gjelten, "President Trump Sides with Churches Asserting a Right to Open."

62 MacArthur, "Open Your Church."

63 Toulouse, *God in Public*, 75.

64 Marvin and Ingle, *Blood Sacrifice and the Nation*, 4.

65 Such interactive features included interactions, e-ushers, and asking for prayer requests.

66 Garner, "Praying with Machines."

67 In the Bible, of course, this means stone tablets. "'Tablets' in the Bible."
68 Personal interview.
69 Noble, *The Religion of Technology*, 5.
70 Stolow, "Religion and/as Media," 126.
71 I should note that before the pandemic, "cash giveaways" were a thing with social media influencers seeking to build a large following.
72 At the time, the exchange rate would put the figures at about $30–$150.
73 Compared to their videos before and after the cash giveaways during the months of the lockdown, the giving sessions were watched thousands of times, and they have not replicated that success since then.
74 In one of the miracle sessions he claimed God already shown him that the COVID-19 pandemic would happen as far back as 2014. He stated that he could not fight against the virus when God showed him because the event of the pandemic was too big for one prophet of God to single-handedly cancel. Besides, if it did not happen, people would not have drawn so close to God. As he spoke, the eye of the camera would run all over his body to show his designer outfits. The people on the thread mostly did not respond to the prophecy as much as they posted to his page with their account numbers and prayer requests. Fufeyin, "Prophetic Cash Give Away Day 14 Live"; Christ Mercyland, "Prophetic Cash Give Away Day."
75 According to the church blog, Joshua was born June 12, 1963, in Ondo state, Nigeria, to a "poverty-stricken" family. From humble beginnings, he has become "a mentor to presidents yet a friend to the widows and less privileged, a role model to his generation yet a humble and hardworking man, toiling tirelessly for the advancement of God's kingdom." "Prophet TB Joshua."
76 At the inception of his ministry, he was embroiled in various controversies, and it did not help that his origin as a prophet—his religious fathers and training for the ministry—was shrouded in mystery. His mode of performing miracles on television was so unconventional that it created unease within government agencies. In 2004, the Nigerian Broadcasting Commission (NBC) banned miracle performances from being broadcast on television. However, SCOAN circumvented this ban by using satellite broadcast and internet technology to both broadcast their miracle healing sessions and expand their reach. Ukah, "Banishing Miracles."
77 Other pastors, especially his fellow Pentecostals, viewed him with suspicion of his possessing occult powers and gave him a wide berth. For instance, his efforts to join the league of fellow pastors in the Pentecostal Fellowship of Nigeria failed as his various applications for membership were turned down. This article explores the context of the many controversies about the prophet: Amanze, "The Role of Prophecy."
78 He is famous for his prophesies, some of which are only shared with the public after they have come to pass—like plane crashes, events involving political figures, and even the death of music legend Michael Jackson. Joshua is one Nigerian preacher and pastor whose ethos of internationalism that churches typically append to their names is more than aspirational. Izuekwe, "How T.B. Joshua Leads Nigeria's Religious Tourism Drive." Also see Tazanu, "Practices and Narratives of Breakthrough."
79 Masoga, "Chasing the Wind amidst Roaring Lions!"
80 In 2014, when Ebola was reported in West Africa and officials of the Lagos State Ministry of Health and the federal government needed to put in precautionary

measures for the country, they asked him to appeal to Africans who might be coming from their various countries to seek miracles in his church. Joshua cooperated with them. Ezeamalu, "T.B. Joshua Asks Ebola Victims to Stay in Their Countries."

81 These figures were last updated on December 29, 2020.

82 I reviewed photos from those crusades to arrive at this conclusion.

83 I could not independently confirm his claims that CNN aired his crusade and that *Time* magazine featured it in the interview with *This Day*. However, local news reports in Israel attested to the events, and the fact that many people attended from various countries around the world. He was crowned "Ambassador of Tourism" by the mayor of Nazareth. "A Day at the Synagogue"; Shpigel, "Famed Exorcist's Festival Draws Thousands."

84 He also prophesied that a woman would win the 2016 U.S. presidential election. When the prophecy failed, he deleted the claim from his social media page. In 2020, his prophecy about who would win the U.S. presidency was worded ambiguously. See "Nigerian Preacher TB Joshua Deletes Prophecy of Clinton Win."

85 Iranzi, "TB Joshua on Four-Day Visit to 'Prayer Mountain' over COVID-19."

86 These sessions are modeled on earlier forms of healing and anointing people through their screens, except these sessions are more interactive, cut across several screens at the same time, and combine multiple simultaneous actions to the point that one cannot pinpoint where the acting and the spectatorship lie. As the broadcast played on our screen and we responded with our eyes and our fingers, we all became parts of the process of meaning-making and the immediacy of this act. When it is recalled from the archived social media page, the video still plays with the comments streaming, and more comments can be added even many years after its initial broadcast date. The modes of communication are also far more enhanced through the imposing screens, and unlike what can be obtained at healing revivals, this one makes a show of its ability to attract people from many countries. As Phillip Auslander has shown, television appropriated theater's ontological liveness in its earliest stages to structure its format, and in that sense this format was not new. However, these miracle healing sessions collapsed the same qualities of theater and the ways we have been trained to fixate on TV, plus one more quality: the immediacy of response that cuts across time and space. Auslander, *Liveness*.

87 However, there is usually an interpreter who translates their stories and the prayers made on their behalf. There is minimal preaching in much of these broadcasts, but extended time can be spent in listening to stories of how the callers became afflicted. Some of the stories of their broken bodies were accompanied by photos of their "presickness" life where they were involved in activities such as playing football or rugby.

88 See TB Joshua Ministries, "Lifted from the Bed of Sickness!"

89 Marshall, "The Sovereignty of Miracles."

90 Marshall, "The Sovereignty of Miracles," 210.

91 Van Geuns, "Reading, Feeling, Believing."

92 Mason, *The Performative Ground of Religion and Theatre.*

93 The reference to flock and shepherd is, of course, from John 10:16 in the Bible.

94 "Fire Will Fall if Churches Are Shut Down Again—Bishop Oyedepo."

95 Church Gist, "They Said Our Large Gatherings Will Never Come Back but We Already Are Back."

96 Wariboko, *The Charismatic City.*

Conclusion

Epigraph: Lemon, "Kanye West Tells Joel Osteen's Church That 'Jesus Has Won the Victory.'"

1   Just days before, I had followed the charge by Tony Rapu, senior pastor of the House of Freedom, to Christians who were debating the conversion of Kanye West mostly because the discussion popped up on my social media timelines several times. "Pastor Tony Rapu Shares His Opinion about Kanye West Becoming a Christian (Video)."
2   Goins-Phillips, "Massive Spike in Faith-Based Google Searches."
3   Rogers, "American Bible Society Gives 8,800 Free Bibles to Kanye West Fans."
4   Lemon, "Kanye West Tells Joel Osteen's Church That 'Jesus Has Won the Victory.'"

Bibliography

Abati, Reuben. "The Spiritual Side of Aso Villa." *The Guardian*, October 14, 2016. https://guardian.ng/opinion/the-spiritual-side-of-aso-villa/.

Abellanosa, Rhoderick John Suarez. "The Church as a Sacrament in a Time of Pandemic: The Philippine Experience." *Studies in World Christianity* 26, no. 3 (2020): 261–280.

Abram, David. *The Spell of the Sensuous: Perception and Language in a More-Than-Human World*. New York: Vintage, 2012.

Abubakar, Naima Hafiz, and Salihu Ibrahim Dasuki. "Empowerment in Their Hands: Use of WhatsApp by Women in Nigeria." *Gender, Technology and Development* 22, no. 2 (2018): 164–183.

Adebulu, Taiwo. "Exposed: UK Pastor behind Viral 5G Conspiracy Video." *The Cable*, April 24, 2020. www.thecable.ng/exposed-uk-pastor-behind-viral-5g-conspiracy-video.

Adelakun, Abimbola Adunni. *Performing Power in Nigeria: Identity, Politics, and Pentecostalism*. New York: Cambridge University Press, 2021.

Adelakun, Adewale J. "Re-Reading 1 Corinthians 6: 12–20 in the Context of Nigerian Pentecostals' Theology of Sex." *Verbum et Ecclesia* 37, no. 1 (2016): 1–8.

Adepegba, Adelani, "N2.67bn School Feeding Funds Found in Private Accounts—ICPC." *Punch*, September 28, 2020. https://punchng.com/n2-67bn-school-feeding-funds-found-in-private-accounts-icpc/.

Adogame, Afe. *The African Christian Diaspora: New Currents and Emerging Trends in World Christianity*. New York: A&C Black, 2013.

———. "The Anthropology of Evil." In *Christianity in Sub-Saharan Africa*, edited by Kenneth R. Ross, J. Kwabena Asamoah-Gyanu, and Todd M. Johnson, 433–444. Edinburgh: Edinburgh University Press, 2017.

———. "Dealing with Local Satanic Technology: Deliverance Rhetoric in the Mountain of Fire and Miracles Ministries." *Journal of World Christianity* 5, no. 1 (2012): 75–101.

———. "Engaging the Rhetoric of Spiritual Warfare: The Public Face of Aladura in Diaspora." *Journal of Religion in Africa* 34, no. 4 (2004): 493–522.

Ahmed, Issam. "Aliens and 'Reptilians': US Viral Video Doctor's Odd Beliefs." *Yahoo! Entertainment*, July 28, 2020. https://www.yahoo.com/entertainment/aliens-reptilians-us-viral-video-doctors-odd-beliefs-205417662.html.

Ahmed, Wasim, Josep Vidal-Alaball, Joseph Downing, and Francesc López Seguí. "COVID-19 and the 5G Conspiracy Theory: Social Network Analysis of Twitter Data." *Journal of Medical Internet Research* 22, no. 5 (2020): e19458.

Ajayi, Omeiza. "COVID-19 Restriction: Pastors Deny Ministry, Members to Evade Arrest." *Vanguard*, May 17, 2020. https://www.vanguardngr.com/2020/05/covid-19 -restriction-pastors-deny-ministry-members-to-evade-arrest/.

———. "Lockdown Violation: Abuja Pastor, Deacons, Ushers Scale Fence to Evade Arrest." *Vanguard*, May 3, 2020. https://www.vanguardngr.com/2020/05 /lockdown-violation-abuja-pastor-deacons-ushers-scale-fence-to-evade-arrest/.

Akor, Ojoma, Olayemi John-Mensah, and Risikat Ramoni. "Nigeria: Covid-19—One Year after Nigeria's Index Case." *AllAfrica.com*, March 5, 2021. https://www .allafrica.com/stories/202103050235.html.

Allen, Glenn Scott. *Master Mechanics and Wicked Wizards: Images of the American Scientist as Hero and Villain from Colonial Times to the Present*. Amherst: University of Massachusetts Press, 2009.

Aluko, Oluwasegun Peter. "Covid-19 Pandemic in Nigeria: The Response of the Christian Church." *African Journal of Biology and Medical Research* 3, no. 2 (2020): 111–125.

Amanambu, Uchenna Ebony. "Critical Reflections on the Impacts of Covid-19 Pandemic on Nigerian Religiosity." *Journal of African Studies and Sustainable Development* 3, no. 4 (2020): 39–62.

———. "The Unwanted Metonymy of the 1804 Usman Dan Fodio's Jihad to the Contemporary Nigerian State." *International Journal Online of Humanities* 3, no. 3 (2017). https://doi:10.24113/ijohmn.v3i3.28.

Amanze, James N. "The Role of Prophecy in the Growth and Expansion of the Synagogue Church of All Nations." *Scriptura: Journal for Contextual Hermeneutics in Southern Africa* 112, no. 1 (2013): 1–14.

"American Bible Society Gives 8,800 Free Bibles to Kanye West Fans." *My Christian Daily*, November 13, 2019. https://www.mychristiandaily.com/american-bible -society-gives-8800-free-bibles-to-kanye-west-fans/.

Andrews, Travis. "Madonna Keeps Making Controversial Covid-19 Claims, Calling a Misinformation-Spreading Doctor Her 'Hero.'" *Washington Post*, July 29, 2020. https://www.washingtonpost.com/technology/2020/07/29/madonna-instagram -covid-coronavirus-stella-immanuel-bathtub/.

Aririguzoh, Stella Amara. "The Power of Love." Thesis, Covenant University, Ota Ogun, Nigeria, 2015. https://www.researchgate.net/profile/Stella_Aririguzoh /publication/280530407_The_Power_of_Love/links/55b7a34108aec0e5f438 3025.pdf.

Asad, Talal. *Formations of the Secular: Christianity, Islam, Modernity*. Stanford, CA: Stanford University Press.

Asaju, Dapo F. "Noise, Fire and Flame: Anointing and Breakthrough Phenomena among the Evangelicals." In *Creativity and Change in Nigerian Christianity*, edited by David Ogungbile and Akintunde Akinade, 95–108. Lagos: Malthouse Press, 2010.

Asamoah-Gyadu, J. Kwabena. "'Christ Is the Answer': What Is the Question?' A Ghana Airways Prayer Vigil and Its Implications for Religion, Evil and Public Space." *Journal of Religion in Africa* 35, no. 1 (2005): 93–117.

———. "'Get on the Internet!' Says the Lord': Religion, Cyberspace and Christianity in Contemporary Africa." *Studies in World Christianity* 13 (2007): 225–242.

———. "'We Are on the Internet': Contemporary Pentecostalism in Africa and the New Culture of Online Religion." In *New Media and Religious Transformations in Africa*, edited by Rosalind Hackett and Benjamin Soares, 157–170. Bloomington: Indiana University Press, 2015.

Ashforth, Adam. *Witchcraft, Violence, and Democracy in South Africa*. Chicago: University of Chicago Press, 2005.

Asiedu, Kwasi Gyamfi, and Yomi Kazeem. "Chinese Workers Are Facing a Backlash across Africa over the Guangzhou Racism Incidents." *Quartz Africa*, May 22, 2020. https://qz.com/africa/1860045/china-faces-african-backlash-of-guangzou-racism -incidents/.

Asprem, Egil, and Asbjørn Dyrendal. "Conspirituality Reconsidered: How Surprising and How New Is the Confluence of Spirituality and Conspiracy Theory?" *Journal of Contemporary Religion* 30, no. 3 (2015): 367–382.

Augoye, Jayne. "I'll Lay My Bare Hands on COVID-19 Patient, Breathe into Them— Oyedepo." *Premium Times Nigeria*, August 30, 2020. https://www .premiumtimesng.com/entertainment/naija-fashion/411625-ill-lay-my-bare-hands -on-covid-19-patient-breathe-into-them-oyedepo.html.

Aupers, Stef. "'Trust No One': Modernization, Paranoia and Conspiracy Culture." *European Journal of Communication* 27, no. 1 (2012): 22–34.

Auslander, Philip. *Liveness: Performance in a Mediatized Culture*. London: Routledge, 2019.

Awal, Mohammed. "Nigeria Shuts Chinese Eatery for Refusing to Serve Nigerians." *Face2Face Africa*, March 16, 2020. https://www.face2faceafrica.com/article/nigeria -shuts-chinese-eatery-for-refusing-to-serve-nigerians.

Awonaike-Kelly, Kě'ài. "Unbelieveable!" *Facebook Watch*, January 27, 2015. www .facebook.com/kemisola.awonaikekelly/videos/10205840847677934/.

Baker, Catherine R., and Andrew Chadwick. "Corrupted Infrastructures of Meaning: Post-Truth Identities Online." In *The Routledge Companion to Media Misinformation and Populism*, edited by Howard Tumber and Silvio Waisbord. Abingdon, UK: Routledge, 2021.

Baker, Peter. "Firing a Salvo in Culture Wars, Trump Pushes for Churches to Reopen." *New York Times*, May 22, 2020. https://www.nytimes.com/2020/05/22/us/politics /trump-churches-coronavirus.html.

Barkun, Michael. *A Culture of Conspiracy: Apocalyptic Visions in Contemporary America*. Berkeley: University of California Press, 2013.

Bavier, Joe. "At Least 300,000 Africans Expected to Die in Pandemic: U.N. Agency." *Reuters*, April 17, 2020. https://www.reuters.com/article/us-health-coronavirus -africa-un/at-least-300000-africans-expected-to-die-in-pandemic-u-n-agency -idUSKBN21Z1LW.

Benyah, Francis. "'Apparatus of Belief': Prayer, Material Objects/Media and Spiritual Warfare in African Pentecostalism." *Material Religion* 16, no. 5 (2020): 614–638.

Bierwiaczonek, Kinga, Jonas R. Kunst, and Olivia Pich. "Belief in COVID-19 Conspiracy Theories Reduces Social Distancing over Time." *Applied Psychology: Health and Well-Being* 12, no. 4 (2020): 1270–1285.

Biggin, Rose. *Immersive Theatre and Audience Experience*. Basingstoke, UK: Palgrave Macmillan, 2017.

"Bishop Oyedepo Questions Lockdown Order: Why Should Market Open for 6 Hours and Churches Can't Open." *YouTube*, May 6, 2020. https://www.youtube .com/watch?v=EMZxI1ExPfc.

"Bishop Oyedepo Reacts to African-American Doctor Virus Cure Claim." *Nation Scoops*, August 3, 2020. https://www.nationscoops.com/bishop-oyedepo-reacts-to-african-american-doctor-virus-cure-claim-nation-scoops/.

Blackson, Neil. "Apostle Suleman Narrates How His Member Teleported to France from Germany Spiritually without Flying in a Plane." *OccupyGH.com*, November 13, 2020. https://occupygh.com/apostle-suleman-narrates-how-his-member-teleported-to-france-from-germany-spiritually-without-flying-in-a-plane-video.

Blythe, Christopher James. "Bill Gates' Comments on Covid-19 Vaccine Enflame 'Mark of the Beast' Worries in Some Christian Circles." *Religion Dispatches*, December 17, 2020. https://www.religiondispatches.org/bill-gates-comments-on-covid-19-vaccine-enflame-mark-of-the-beast-worries-in-some-christian-circles/.

Boletsi, Maria. "Crisis, Terrorism, and Post-Truth: Processes of Othering and Self-Definition in the Culturalization of Politics." In *Subjects Barbarian, Monstrous, and Wild*, edited by Maria Boletsi and Tyler Sage, 17–50. Amsterdam: Brill Rodopi, 2017.

Bridle, James. *New Dark Age*. London: Verso Books, 2018.

Brotherton, Rob. *Suspicious Minds: Why We Believe Conspiracy Theories*. New York: Bloomsbury, 2015.

Brotherton, Robert, and Silan Eser. "Bored to Fears: Boredom Proneness, Paranoia, and Conspiracy Theories." *Personality and Individual Differences* 80 (2015): 1–5. https://doi:10.1016/j.paid.2015.02.011.

Brown, Theodore L. *Imperfect Oracle: The Epistemic and Moral Authority of Science*. State College: Penn State University Press, 2009.

Bruns, Axel, Stephen Harrington, and Edward Hurcombe. "Covid19? 'Corona? 5G? Or Both?' The Dynamics of COVID-19/5G Conspiracy Theories on Facebook." *Media International Australia* 177, no. 1 (2020): 12–29.

Burgess, R. "Freedom from the Past and Faith for the Future: Nigerian Pentecostal Theology in Global Perspective." *PentecoStudies* 7, no 2, (2008): 29–63.

Butticci, Annalisa. "Crazy World, Crazy Faith! Prayer, Power and Transformation in a Nigerian Prayer City." *Annual Review of the Sociology of Religion* 4, no. 2 (2013): 243–261.

Cascio, Jamais. "The Apocalypse: It's Not the End of the World." *Bulletin of the Atomic Scientists* 75, no. 6 (2019): 269–272.

Castelli, Elizabeth A. *Martyrdom and Memory: Early Christian Culture Making*. New York: Columbia University Press, 2004.

César, Waldo. "From Babel to Pentecost: A Social-Historical-Theological Study of the Growth of Pentecostalism." In *Between Babel and Pentecost: Transnational Pentecostalism in Africa and Latin America*, edited by Andre Corten and Ruth Marshall, 22–40. Bloomington: Indiana University Press, 2001.

Cheeseman, Nic, Jonathan Fisher, Idayat Hassan, and Jamie Hitchen. "Social Media Disruption: Nigeria's WhatsApp Politics." *Journal of Democracy* 31, no. 3 (2020): 145–159.

"China: Covid-19 Discrimination against Africans." *Human Rights Watch*, October 28, 2020. https://www.hrw.org/news/2020/05/05/china-covid-19-discrimination-against-africans.

Chow, Alexander, and Jonas Kurlberg. "Two or Three Gathered Online: Asian and European Responses to COVID-19 and the Digital Church." *Studies in World Christianity* 26, no. 3 (2020): 298–318.

Christ Mercyland. "Prophetic Cash Give Away Day 16 Live with Snr. Prophet Jeremiah Omoto Fufeyin 16/04/2020." *YouTube*, April 16, 2020. https://www

.youtube.com/watch?v=LK9igoRrg_Q&feature=youtu.be&fbclid=IwAR3UQGw
Y8bjLJ6QK1lVpaRMn73TkHzV1ABspwnTq8FLeIOXjVAhqexk7cQI.

Chukwuorji, JohnBosco Chika, and Steven Kator Iorfa. "Commentary on the
Coronavirus Pandemic: Nigeria." *Psychological Trauma: Theory, Research, Practice,
and Policy* 12, no. S1 (2020): S188–S190.

Church Gist. "Pastor Paul Enenche Blows Hot on Bill Gates Vaccine." *YouTube*,
May 18, 2020. https://www.youtube.com/watch?v=oaoCAJNfSQo.

———. "They Said Our Large Gatherings Will Never Come Back but We Already Are
Back." *Facebook*, August 23, 2020. https://www.facebook.com/Churchgist.org
/posts/they-said-our-large-gatherings-will-never-come-back-but-already-we-are
-backrever/2157135471096979/.

Colbert, Soyica Diggs, Douglas A. Jones Jr., and Shane Vogel, eds. "Introduction." In
Race and Performance after Repetition. Durham, NC: Duke University Press, 2020.

Coleman, Simon. "Spiritual Warfare in Pentecostalism: Metaphors and Materialities."
In *The Wiley Blackwell Companion to Religion and Materiality*, edited by Vasudha
Narayanan, 171–186. Hoboken, NJ: John Wiley & Sons, 2020.

Conejo, Juan Manuel Ávila. "Revolution and Revolt: Identitarian Space, Magic, and
the Land in Decolonial Latin American and African Writing." In *Art, Creativity,
and Politics in Africa and the Diaspora*, edited by Abimbola Adelakun and Toyin
Falola, 47–67. Cham, Switzerland: Palgrave Macmillan, 2018.

Connolly, Andrew. "Masculinity, Political Action, and Spiritual Warfare in the
Fictional Ministry of Frank E. Peretti." *Christianity & Literature* 69, no. 1 (2020):
53–72.

"Coronavirus: France Racism Row over Doctors' Africa Testing Comments." *BBC
News*, April 3, 2020. www.bbc.com/news/world-europe-52151722.

"Coronavirus: Oyedepo Reacts to Move to Re-Open Churches." *P.M. News*, May 23,
2020. https://www.pmnewsnigeria.com/2020/05/23/coronavirus-oyedepo-reacts
-to-move-to-re-open-churches.

Cosentino, Gabriele. *Social Media and the Post-Truth World Order*. London: Palgrave
Pivot, 2020.

Cosgrove, Jaclyn. "L.A. Megachurch Pastor Mocks Pandemic Health Orders, Even as
Church Members Fall Ill." *Los Angeles Times*, November 9, 2020. https://www
.latimes.com/california/story/2020-11-08/la-pastor-mocks-covid-19-rules-church
-members-ill.

Crary, Jonathan. *24/7: Late Capitalism and the Ends of Sleep*. New York: Verso Books,
2013.

Cristofori, S. "Promises in the Present Tense: Ritual Work on the Bible in Pentecostal
Spiritual Warfare." *L'Uomo* 9, no. 1 (2019): 145–170.

Dark, David. *Everyday Apocalypse: The Sacred Revealed in Radiohead, the Simpsons,
and Other Pop Culture Icons*. Grand Rapids, MI: Brazos Press, 2002.

"A Day at the Synagogue." *This Day*, October 28, 2020. https://www.thisdaylive.com
/index.php/2020/10/28/a-day-at-the-synagogue/.

"De-Emphasize Money, Focus More on Prayers, Lagos PFN Tells Pastors as Churches
Plan to Reopen." *Church Times Nigeria*, August 1, 2020. https://www.churchtimesnigeria
.net/lagos-churches-money-pfn/.

Deleuze, Gilles. *Difference and Repetition*. New York: Columbia University Press,
1994.

Depoux, Anneliese, Sam Martin, Emilie Karafillakis, Raman Preet, Annelies
Wilder-Smith, and Heidi Larson. "The Pandemic of Social Media Panic Travels

Faster Than the COVID-19 Outbreak." *Journal of Travel Medicine* 27, no 3 (2020): taaa031. https://doi.org/10.1093/jtm/taaa031.

Diokpa, Nwa. "Pastor Chris Trends on Twitter over Sermon on Regulation of Churches amid COVID-19." *African Examiner*, August 2, 2020. https://www .africanexaminer.com/pastor-chris-trends-on-twitter-over-sermon-on-regulation -of-churches-amid-covid-19/.

Dixon, Steve. "Theatre, Technology, and Time." *International Journal of Performance Arts and Digital Media* 1, no. 1 (2005): 11–30.

Dolan, Jill. *Utopia in Performance: Finding Hope at the Theater*. Ann Arbor: University of Michigan Press, 2010.

Ekenna, Geoffrey. "Oyakhilome's Miracles: Real or Fake?" *Newswatch*, April 15, 2002.

Elwood, Sarah, and Agnieszka Leszczynski. "New Spatial Media, New Knowledge Politics." *Transactions of the Institute of British Geographers* 38, no. 4 (2013): 544–559.

Emmanuel, Haris. "Christ Embassy Sues Akwa Ibom Govt over Arrest, Detention of Pastor." *Vanguard*, June 23, 2020. https://www.vanguardngr.com/2020/06/christ -embassy-sues-akwa-ibom-govt-over-arrest-detention-of-pastor/.

Eriksen, Annelin, Ruy Llera Blanes, and Michelle MacCarthy. *Going to Pentecost: An Experimental Approach to Studies in Pentecostalism*. New York: Berghahn Books, 2019.

Ezeamalu, Ben. "T.B. Joshua Asks Ebola Victims to Stay in Their Countries." *Premium Times Nigeria*, August 4, 2014. https://www.premiumtimesng.com /news/166051-t-b-joshua-asks-ebola-victims-to-stay-in-their-countries.html.

Falola, Toyin. "Contextualising Nimi Wariboko: Nigerian Pentecostalism and Its Critics." *Premium Times Opinion*, November 26, 2020. https://www.opinion .premiumtimesng.com/2020/11/26/contextualising-nimi-wariboko-nigerian -pentecostalism-and-its-critics-by-toyin-falola/.

———. *A Mouth Sweeter Than Salt: An African Memoir*. Ann Arbor: University of Michigan Press, 2004.

Farkas, Johan, and Jannick Schou. "Fake News as a Floating Signifier: Hegemony, Antagonism and the Politics of Falsehood." *Javnost—The Public* 25, no. 3 (2018): 298–314.

"Fire Will Fall if Churches Are Shut Down Again—Bishop Oyedepo." *GhanaWeb*, August 2, 2020. https://www.ghanaweb.com/GhanaHomePage/africa/Fire-will -fall-if-Churches-are-shut-down-again-Bishop-Oyedepo-1023853.

FitzGerald, William. *Spiritual Modalities: Prayer as Rhetoric and Performance*. State College: Penn State University Press, 2012.

Fletcher, John. *Preaching to Convert: Evangelical Outreach and Performance Activism in a Secular Age*. Ann Arbor: University of Michigan Press, 2013.

Fufeyin, Jeremiah Omoto. "Prophetic Cash Give Away Day 14 Live with Snr. Prophet Jeremiah Omoto Fufeyin." *Facebook Watch*, April 14, 2020. https://www.facebook .com/prophetjeremiahministries/videos/2718306495067208.

García-Reidy, Alejandro. "Theatrical Voyeurism: Performing Rehearsal in the Spanish Comedia Nueva." *Modern Language Notes* 131, no. 2 (2016): 356–377.

Garner, Stephen. "Praying with Machines: Religious Dreaming in Cyberspace." *Stimulus: The New Zealand Journal of Christian Thought and Practice* 12 (2004): 16–22.

Garrard, Virginia. "Hidden in Plain Sight: Dominion Theology, Spiritual Warfare, and Violence in Latin America." *Religions* 11, no. 12 (2020): 1–14.

Genschow, Oliver, Davide Rigoni, and Marcel Brass. "The Hand of God or the Hand of Maradona? Believing in Free Will Increases Perceived Intentionality of Others' Behavior." *Consciousness and Cognition* 70 (2019): 80–87.

Gifford, Paul. *Christianity, Development and Modernity in Africa*. London: Hurst, 2015.

———. "Unity and Diversity within African Pentecostalism: Comparison of the Christianities of Daniel Olukoya and David Oyedepo." In *Pentecostalism in Africa: Presence and Impact of Pneumatic Christianity in Postcolonial Societies*, edited by Martin Lindhard. Leiden: Brill, 2014.

Gjelten, Tom. "President Trump Sides with Churches Asserting a Right to Open." *National Public Radio*, May 23, 2020. https://www.npr.org/sections/coronavirus -live-updates/2020/05/23/861386816/president-trump-sides-with-churches -asserting-a-right-to-reopen.

Goddard, Michael, Benjamin Halligan, and Paul Hegarty, eds. *Reverberations: The Philosophy, Aesthetics and Politics of Noise*. New York: Bloomsbury, 2012.

Goins-Phillips, Tré. "Massive Spike in Faith-Based Google Searches after Kanye's 'Jesus Is King.'" *CBN News*, November 1, 2019. https://www1.cbn.com/cbnnews /entertainment/2019/november/massive-spike-in-faith-based-google-searches-after -lsquo-jesus-is-king-rsquo.

Graham, Amanda, Frank Cullen, Justin Pickett, Cheryl Jonson, Murat Haner, and Melissa Sloan. "Faith in Trump, Moral Foundations, and Social Distancing Defiance during the Coronavirus Pandemic." *Social Science Research Network*, April 22, 2020. https://doi:10.2139/ssrn.3586626.

Grantham-Philips, Wyatte. "Pastor Paula White Calls on Angels from Africa and South America to Bring Trump Victory." *USA Today*, November 5, 2020. https:// www.usatoday.com/story/news/nation/2020/11/05/paula-white-trumps-spiritual -adviser-african-south-american-angels/6173576002.

Grobe, Christopher. "The Artist Is President: Performance Art and Other Keywords in the Age of Donald Trump." *Critical Inquiry* 46, no. 4 (2020).

Hackett, Rosalind I. J. "Discourses of Demonization in Africa and Beyond." *Diogenes* 50, no. 3 (2003): 61–75.

———. "The New Virtual Interface of African Pentecostalism." *Global Perspectives on Pentecostalism* 46 (2009): 496–503.

———. "Is Satan Local or Global? Reflections on a Nigerian Deliverance Movement." In *Who Is Afraid of the Holy Ghost? Pentecostalism and Globalization in Africa and Beyond*, edited by Afe Adogame, 111–131. Trenton, NJ: Africa World Press, 2011.

Harambam, Jaron. *Contemporary Conspiracy Culture: Truth and Knowledge in an Era of Epistemic Instability*. Abingdon, UK: Routledge, 2020.

Harrison, Peter. "Adam Smith and the History of the Invisible Hand." *Journal of the History of Ideas* 72, no. 1 (2011): 29–49.

Hayden, Bridget. "The Hand of God: Capitalism, Inequality, and Moral Geographies in Mississippi after Hurricane Katrina." *Anthropological Quarterly* 83, no. 1 (2010): 177–203.

Henry, Jacob. "Donald Trump Supporters Rock Back and Forth While Praying for His Win." *Metro*, November 6, 2020. https://www.metro.co.uk/2020/11/06 /donald-trump-supporters-rock-back-and-forth-while-praying-for-his-win-13551150/.

Hofstadter, Richard. *The Paranoid Style in American Politics*. New York: Vintage, 2012.

Holvast, René. *Spiritual Mapping in the United States and Argentina, 1989–2005: A Geography of Fear*. Leiden: Brill, 2008.

Hsiao-Hung Pai. "The Coronavirus Crisis Has Exposed China's Long History of Racism." *The Guardian*, April 25, 2020. https://www.theguardian.com /commentisfree/2020/apr/25/coronavirus-exposed-china-history-racism-africans -guangzhou.

Ibrahim, Oluwasegun Micheal, and Damilola Daniel Ekundayo. "COVID-19 Pandemic in Nigeria: Misconception among Individuals, Impact on Animal and the Role of Mathematical Epidemiologists." *Preprints* 2020. https://doi:10.20944 /preprints202004.0492.v1.

Igboin, Benson O., and Babatunde Adedibu. "'Power Must Change Hands': Militarisation of Prayer and the Quest for Better Life among Nigerian Pentecostals." *Cyberjournal for Pentecostal-Charismatic Research* 26 (2019). http://www.pctii.org /cyberj/cyberj26/Igboin_Adedibu1.html.

Ikeji, Linda. "Viral Video of Nigerian Christians Praying for Joe Biden's Votes to Be Upturned in Donald Trump's Favour." *Linda Ikeji's Blog*, November 20, 2020. www.lindaikejisblog.com/2020/11/viral-video-of-nigerian-christians-praying-for -joe-bidens-votes-to-be-upturned-in-donald-trumps-favour.html.

Immanuel, Stella. "Revival—PUSH Day 7. Non Humans Exposed." *YouTube*, August 15, 2020. https://www.youtube.com/watch?v=bGD0z5I3N3w.

Iranzi, Fabrice. "TB Joshua on Four-Day Visit to 'Prayer Mountain' over COVID-19." *RegionWeek*, April 27, 2020. https://www.regionweek.com/tb-joshua-on-four-day -vist-to-prayer-mountain-over-covid-19/.

Irele, Abiola. "Tradition and the Yoruba Writer: D.O. Fagunwa, Amos Tutuola and Wole Soyinka." *Odù: Journal of Yoruba and Related Studies* 11 (1975): 75–100.

Izuekwe, Cyriacus. "How T.B. Joshua Leads Nigeria's Religious Tourism Drive." *P.M. Express*, September 1, 2018. https://pmexpressng.com/t-b-joshua-leads-nigerias -religious-tourism-drive/.

Janson, Marloes, and Akintunde Akinleye. "The Spiritual Highway: Religious World Making in Megacity Lagos (Nigeria)." *Material Religion* 11, no. 4 (2015): 550–562.

Jeannerat, Caroline. "Of Lizards, Misfortune and Deliverance: Pentecostal Soteriology in the Life of a Migrant." *African Studies* 68, no. 2 (2009): 251–271.

Jennings, Willie James. *The Christian Imagination: Theology and the Origins of Race.* New Haven, CT: Yale University Press, 2010.

Jeyifo, Biodun. "The Religion and Science, Faith and Reason Controversy—Again (2)." *The Nation*, October 11, 2014. https://www.thenationonlineng.net/the -religion-and-science-faith-and-reason-controversy-again-2/.

Jones, Omi Osun Joni L. *Theatrical Jazz: Performance, Àṣẹ, and the Power of the Present Moment.* Columbus: Ohio State University Press, 2015.

Kalu, Ogbu. *African Pentecostalism: An Introduction.* New York: Oxford University Press, 2008.

Kazeem, Yomi. "Africa's Largest City Is Trying to Shut Down to Beat Coronavirus— That's Easier Said Than Done." *Quartz Africa*, March 19, 2020. https://qz.com /africa/1821361/coronavirus-lagos-nigeria-shuts-schools-ban-public-gatherings/.

Kendrick, Lynne, and David Roesner, eds. *Theatre Noise: The Sound of Performance.* Newcastle, UK: Cambridge Scholars, 2012.

Kent, Trey, and Kie Bowman. *City of Prayer: Transform Your Community through Praying Churches.* Terre Haute, IN: PrayerShop Publishing, 2019.

Korede, Tunde. "Online Service Cannot Be Compared to Physical Church Gathering—David Oyedepo." *Opera News*, n.d. https://ng.opera.news/ng/en /religion/c04a24f4cffcb9e1f16a1d0005c61798.

Kotsko, Adam. *Neoliberalism's Demons*. Stanford, CA: Stanford University Press, 2018.

———. *The Prince of This World*. Stanford, CA: Stanford University Press, 2016.

Law, Tara. "Trump Advisor Calls for Miscarriage of 'Satanic Pregnancies.'" *Time*, January 26, 2020. https://www.time.com/5771920/trump-paula-white-miscarriage -satanic-pregnancies/.

Lemon, Jason. "Kanye West Tells Joel Osteen's Church That 'Jesus Has Won the Victory' Because He's Working for God Now." *Newsweek*, November 17, 2019. https://www.newsweek.com/kanye-west-joel-osteen-working-god-now-1472272.

Lindfors, Bernth. "Amos Tutuola and D. O. Fagunwa." *Journal of Commonwealth Literature* 5, no. 1 (1970): 57–65.

Locke, Simon. "Conspiracy Culture, Blame Culture, and Rationalisation." *Sociological Review* 57, no. 4 (2009): 567–585.

loxley.6. "David Icke: Love and Lizard People." *Psychology of Extraordinary Beliefs*, April 3, 2019. https://u.osu.edu/vanzandt/2019/02/11/david-icke-love-and-lizard -people/.

Lubold, Gordon, and Catherine Lucey. "Trump Says Places of Worship Are Essential Services." *Wall Street Journal*, May 22, 2020. www.wsj.com/articles/trump-calls -places-of-worship-essential-11590172336.

Luhrmann, Tanya M. *When God Talks Back: Understanding the American Evangelical Relationship with God*. New York: Knopf, 2012.

MacArthur, John. "Open Your Church." *Facebook Watch*, May 14, 2021. . https://www .facebook.com/JohnMacArthurGTY/videos/1649268771909715/?__so__=channel _tab&__rv__=all_videos_card.

MacCarthy, Michelle, and Knut Rio, eds. *Pentecostalism and Witchcraft: Spiritual Warfare in Africa and Melanesia*. Cham, Switzerland: Springer Nature, 2017.

"Madagascar Virus Potion Scorned Because It's from Africa: President." *France 24*, May 11, 2020. https://www.france24.com/en/20200511-madagascar-virus-potion -scorned-because-it-s-from-africa-president.

Madison, D. Soyini. *Acts of Activism: Human Rights as Radical Performance*. New York: Cambridge University Press, 2010.

Magbadelo, John O. "Pentecostalism in Nigeria: Exploiting or Edifying the Masses?" *African Sociological Review/Revue Africaine de Sociologie* 8, no. 2 (2004): 15–29.

Maggi, Armando. "Christian Demonology in Contemporary American Popular Culture." *Social Research* 81, no. 4 (2014): 769–793.

Mahbubani, Rhea. "'The Governor Is a Servant of the State. I Am a Servant of God': 3 Pastors Defend Why They're Leading the Charge to Reopen Churches." *Business Insider*, May 24, 2020. . https://www.images.markets.businessinsider.com/pastors -leading-charge-reopen-churches-coronavirus-first-amendment-2020-5.

Manseau, Peter. "Some Capitol Rioters Believed They Answered God's Call, Not Just Trump's." *Washington Post*, February 11, 2021. . https://www.washingtonpost.com /outlook/2021/02/11/christian-religion-insurrection-capitol-trump/.

Marsh, Jenni. "China Says It Has a 'Zero-Tolerance Policy' for Racism, but Discrimi- nation Goes Back Decades." *CNN*, March 18, 2021. . https://www.cnn.com/2020 /05/25/asia/china-anti-african-attacks-history-hnk-intl/index.html.

Marshall, Ruth. "Destroying Arguments and Captivating Thoughts: Spiritual Warfare Prayer as Global Praxis." *Journal of Religious and Political Practice* 2, no. 1 (2016): 92–113.

———. *Political Spiritualities: The Pentecostal Revolution in Nigeria*. Chicago: University of Chicago Press, 2009.

———. "The Sovereignty of Miracles: Pentecostal Political Theology in Nigeria." *Constellations* 17, no. 2 (2010): 214.

Marvin, Carolyn, and David W. Ingle. *Blood Sacrifice and the Nation: Totem Rituals and the American Flag.* Cambridge: Cambridge University Press, 1999.

Maseno, Loreen. "Prayer for Rain: A Pentecostal Perspective from Kenya." *Ecumenical Review* 69, no. 3 (2017): 336–347.

Masoga, M. A. "Chasing the Wind amidst Roaring Lions! Problematisation of Religiosity in the Current South African Socio-Political and Economic Landscape." *Theologia Viatorum* 40, no. 1 (2016): 68–89.

Mason, David V. *The Performative Ground of Religion and Theatre.* London: Routledge, 2018.

Matthews, Shelly. *Perfect Martyr: The Stoning of Stephen and the Construction of Christian Identity.* New York: Oxford University Press, 2012.

McAlister, Elizabeth. "The Militarization of Prayer in America: White and Native American Spiritual Warfare." *Journal of Religious and Political Practice* 2, no. 1 (2016): 114–130.

———. "Race, Gender, and Christian Diaspora." In *Spirit on the Move: Black Women and Pentecostalism in Africa and the Diaspora,* edited by Judith Casselberry and Elizabeth A. Pritchard, 44–46. Durham, NC: Duke University Press, 2019.

McCloud, Sean. *American Possessions: Fighting Demons in the Contemporary United States.* New York: Oxford University Press, 2015.

McQueen, Alison. *Political Realism in Apocalyptic Times.* Cambridge: Cambridge University Press, 2017.

"Melinda Gates: Covid-19 Will Be Horrible in the Developing World." *CNN,* April 10, 2020.. https://www.cnn.com/videos/business/2020/04/10/melinda-gates -coronavirus.cnn-business.

Meyer, Birgit. "Aesthetics of Persuasion: Global Christianity and Pentecostalism's Sensational Forms." *South Atlantic Quarterly* 109, no. 4 (2010): 741–763.

———. *Sensational Movies: Video, Vision, and Christianity in Ghana.* Oakland: University of California Press, 2015.

Miller, Joanne M. "Do COVID-19 Conspiracy Theory Beliefs Form a Monological Belief System?" *Canadian Journal of Political Science/Revue Canadienne de Science Politique* 53, no. 2 (2020): 319–326.

———. "Psychological, Political, and Situational Factors Combine to Boost COVID-19 Conspiracy Theory Beliefs." *Canadian Journal of Political Science/Revue Canadienne de Science Politique* 53, no. 2 (2020): 327–334.

Miller, Joanne M., Kyle L. Saunders, and Christina E. Farhart. "Conspiracy Endorsement as Motivated Reasoning: The Moderating Roles of Political Knowledge and Trust." *American Journal of Political Science* 60, no. 4 (2016): 824–844.

Mohr, Adam. "Faith Tabernacle Congregation, the 1918–19 Influenza Pandemic and Classical Pentecostalism in Colonial West Africa." *Studies in World Christianity* 26, no. 3 (2020): 219–238.

Muhindo, Clare. "BBC Africa Retracts 'Offensive' Headline Following Social Media Criticism." *African Centre for Media Excellence,* September 4, 2020. https://acme -ug.org/2020/09/04/bbc-africa-retracts-offensive-headline-following-social-media -criticism/.

Nation Scoops. "Pastor Chris Has Kicked Off Again This Time the COVID-19 Church Inspectors." *Facebook Watch,* July 9, 2020. https://www.facebook.com /nationscoops/videos/275708647091799.

"New WHO Estimates: Up to 190 000 People Could Die of COVID-19 in Africa if Not Controlled." *World Health Organization*, May 7, 2020. https://www.afro.who .int/news/new-who-estimates-190-000-people-could-die-covid-19-africa-if-not -controlled.

Nield, Sophie. "The Rise of the Character Named Spectator." *Contemporary Theatre Review* 18, no. 4 (2008): 531–544.

"Nigerian Preacher TB Joshua Deletes Prophecy of Clinton Win." *BBC News,* November 9, 2016. https://www.bbc.com/news/world-africa-37924086.

Noble, David F. *The Religion of Technology: The Divinity of Man and the Spirit of Invention*. New York: Knopf, 2013.

"Nollywood Actor, Joseph Okechukwu Launches Africans for Trump Campaign." *Nation Scoops*, August 29, 2020. nationscoops.com/2020/08/29/nollywood-actor -joseph-okechukwu-launches-africans-for-trump-campaign/.

Nordling, Linda. "The Pandemic Appears to Have Spared Africa so Far. Scientists Are Struggling to Explain Why." *Science*, August 12, 2020. https://www.sciencemag.org /news/2020/08/pandemic-appears-have-spared-africa-so-far-scientists-are -struggling-explain-why.

Nwachukwu, John Owen. "Coronavirus: Pastor Chris Makes Fearful Revelations about COVID-19, New Vaccine, 5G, Antichrist [VIDEO]." *Daily Post,* May 12, 2020. https://dailypost.ng/2020/04/05/coronavirus-pastor-chris-makes-fearful -revelations-about-covd-19-new-vaccine-5g-antichrist-video/.

Nyamnjoh, Henrietta M. "'When Are You Going to Change Those Stones to Phones?' Social Media Appropriation by Pentecostal Churches in Cape Town." *Journal for the Study of the Religions of Africa and Its Diaspora* 5 (2019): 122–142.

Obadare, Ebenezer. "Goodluck the Performer." *Performance Matters* 3, no. 1 (2017): 103–111.

———. *Pentecostal Republic: Religion and the Struggle for State Power in Nigeria*. London: Zed Books, 2018.

———. "'Raising Righteous Billionaires': The Prosperity Gospel Reconsidered." *HTS Theological Studies* 72, no. 4 (2016): 1–8.

Obadare, Timothy Oluwole. "1930–2013 Christ Apostolic Church (Aladura) Nigeria." *Journal of African Christian Biography* 3, no. 4 (2018): 24–25.

O'Brien, Timothy L. "Scientific Authority in Policy Contexts: Public Attitudes about Environmental Scientists, Medical Researchers, and Economists." *Public Understanding of Science* 22, no. 7 (2013): 799–816.

O'Donnell, S. Jonathon. "The Deliverance of the Administrative State: Deep State Conspiracism, Charismatic Demonology, and the Post-Truth Politics of American Christian Nationalism." *Religion* 50, no. 4 (2020): 696–719.

———. "Islamophobic Conspiracism and Neoliberal Subjectivity: The Inassimilable Society." *Patterns of Prejudice* 52, no. 1 (2018): 1–23.

———. *Passing Orders: Demonology and Sovereignty in American Spiritual Warfare*. New York: Fordham University Press, 2020.

Ogundipe, Samuel. "Coronavirus: Oyedepo Holds Service, Vows to Keep Winners Chapel Open." *Premium Times Nigeria*, March 23, 2020. https://www.premium timesng.com/news/headlines/383340-coronavirus-oyedepo-holds-service-vows-to -keep-winners-chapel-open.html.

Okogba, Emmanuel. "Chris Okotie Says It's Unscriptural to Hold Church Services Online." *Vanguard*, July 14, 2020. https://www.vanguardngr.com/2020/07/chris -okotie-says-its-unscriptural-to-hold-church-services-online/.

Okpara, Daniel. *21 Days of Intensive Word Immersion, and Fire Prayers for Total Healing, Deliverance, Breakthrough, and Divine Intervention*. Lagos: Better Life Media, 2018.

Olaitan, Jide A. "Jide." *Facebook Watch*, January 3, 2021. https://www.facebook.com /arthur.j.olaitan/videos/10216448001745791/.

Olayeri, Tella. *Fire for Fire, Part 2: Double Thunder, Double Fire*. Lagos: CreateSpace Independent Publishing Platform, 2018.

Oliver, J. Eric, and Thomas J. Wood. "Conspiracy Theories and the Paranoid Style(s) of Mass Opinion." *American Journal of Political Science* 58, no. 4 (2014): 952–966.

Olofinjana, Israel O. *20 Pentecostal Pioneers in Nigeria: Their Lives, Their Legacies*. Bloomington, IN: Xlibris Corporation, 2011.

Olokor, Friday. "Trump's Spiritual Adviser Adopts MFM Prayers." *Punch*, January 31, 2020. https://punchng.com/trumps-spiritual-adviser-adopts-mfm-prayers/.

Olowookere, Dipo. "The Unspiritual Side of Aso Villa." *Business Post*, October 23, 2016. https://businesspost.ng/featureoped/unspiritual-side-aso-villa/.

Olugbamina, Adegunle. "New Lab, a Miracle, Says Olukoya." *The Nation*, June 19, 2014. https://thenationonlineng.net/new-lab-miracle-says-olukoya/.

Olukoya, Daniel K. *101 Weapons of Spiritual Warfare*. Lagos: Battle Cry Christian Ministries, 2013.

———. *Igniting Your Inner Fire*. Lagos: Mountain of Fire and Miracles Ministries, 2015.

———. *MFM at 30: Milestones of God's Grace and Fire Exploits*. Lagos: Battle Cry Ministries: 2019.

———. *The Mysteries of Life*. Lagos: Battle Cry Ministries, 2010.

———. *The Mystery of Water Cure*. Lagos: Battle Cry Ministries, 2014.

———. *Too Hot to Handle*. Lagos: Battle Cry Ministries, 2001.

———. *Victory over Satanic Dreams*. Lagos: Battle Cry Ministries, 2014.

———. *Violent Prayers to Disgrace Stubborn Problems* Lagos: Battle Cry Ministries, 2013.

———. "The Weapon of the Finger of God 2018 Message." *AnointedTube*, n.d. https://anointedtube.com/video/81448/the-weapon-of-the-finger-of-god-2018 -message-dr-d-k-olukoya-mp4/.

Omojuwa, J. J. "Nigeria Shakes the World! At 3.25 Billion and 227 Countries, This Broadcast by Pastor Chris Oyakhilome Is Now the Most Watched Live Event in the History of the World and Mankind." *Twitter*, April 13, 2020. twitter.com /omojuwa/status/1249674159145332736?lang=en.

Onyeji, Ebuka. "Coronavirus: Oyedepo Speaks on Sunday Service after Backlash." *Premium Times Nigeria*, April 3, 2020. https://www.premiumtimesng.com/news /more-news/383517-coronavirus-oyedepo-speaks-on-sunday-service-after-backlash .html.

Osinulu, Adedamola. "A Transnational History of Pentecostalism in West Africa." *History Compass* 15, no. 6 (2017): e12386.

"Oyedepo Backs Stella Immanuel, Says Coronavirus Has a Cure." *GhanaWeb*, August 1, 2020. https://www.ghanaweb.com/GhanaHomePage/africa/Oyedepo -backs-Stella-Immanuel-says-coronavirus-has-a-cure-1023037.

Parsitau, Damaris. "Religion in the Age of Coronavirus." *The Elephant*, March 23, 2020. https://www.theelephant.info/features/2020/03/23/religion-in-the-age-of -coronavirus/

"Pastor Tony Rapu Shares His Opinion about Kanye West Becoming a Christian (Video)." *GQBuzz.com*, November 18, 2019. https://www.gqbuzz.com/pastor-tony -rapu-shares-his-opinion-about-kanye-west-becoming-a-christian-video/.

Pellegrini, Ann. "Signaling through the Flames: Hell House Performances and Structures of Religious Feeling." *American Quarterly* 59, no. 3 (2007): 911–935.

Perrett, Connor. "Paula White, a White House Employee and Trump's Spiritual Adviser, Calls for 'Satanic Pregnancies to Miscarry Right Now.'" *Business Insider*, January 26, 2020. https://www.businessinsider.com/paula-white-calls-for-satanic -pregnancies-to-miscarry-right-now-2020-1.

Perucci, Tony. "The Trump Is Present." *Performance Research* 22, no. 3 (2017): 127–135.

Phelan, Peggy. *Unmarked: The Politics of Performance*. London: Routledge, 2003.

Phillips, Gervase. "Deviance, Persecution and the Roman Creation of Christianity." *Journal of Historical Sociology* 29, no. 2 (2016): 250–270.

Pitetti, Connor. "Uses of the End of the World: Apocalypse and Postapocalypse as Narrative Modes." *Science Fiction Studies* 44, no. 3 (2017): 437–454.

Poniewozik, James. *Audience of One: Trump, Television, and the Fracturing of America*. New York: Liveright Publishing, 2019.

Pontianus, Vitalis Jafla. "Covid-19 Pandemic, Conspiracy Theory and the Nigerian Experience: A Critical Discourse." *Igwebuike: African Journal of Arts and Humanities* 6, No. 6 (2020): 34–48.

"Prophet TB Joshua." *SCOAN International*, July 8, 2019. https://www.scoan.org /about/prophet-tb-joshua/.

Pype, Katrien. "Branhamist *Kindoki*: Ethnographic Notes on Connectivity, Technology, and Urban Witchcraft in Contemporary Kinshasa." In *Pentecostalism and Witchcraft: Spiritual Warfare in Africa and Melanesia*, 115–144. Cham, Switzerland: Palgrave Macmillan, 2017.

Qiu, Linda. "Trump's Inaccurate Claims on Hydroxychloroquine." *New York Times*, May 21, 2020. https://www.nytimes.com/2020/05/21/us/politics/trump-fact-check -hydroxychloroquine-coronavirus-.html.

Ramon, Oladimeji. "I Can't Open Church, Endanger People's Lives—Bakare." *Punch*, June 8, 2020. https://punchng.com/i-cant-open-church-endanger-peoples-lives -bakare/.

Ray, Benjamin C. "Aladura Christianity: A Yoruba Religion." *Journal of Religion in Africa* 23, no. 3 (1993): 266–291.

Rayner, Alice. "Keeping Time." *Performance Research* 19, no. 3 (2014): 32–36.

Reid, Roddey. "Trump as Capitalist Folk Hero, or the Rise of the White Entrepreneur as Political Bully." *Black Renaissance* 16, no. 2 (2016).

Richman, Naomi. "Machine Gun Prayer: The Politics of Embodied Desire in Pentecostal Worship." *Journal of Contemporary Religion* 35, no. 3 (2020): 469–483.

Robbins, Joel. "On Enchanting Science and Disenchanting Nature: Spiritual Warfare in North America and Papua New Guinea." In *Nature, Science, and Religion: Intersections Shaping Society and the Environment*, edited by Catherine M. Tucker, 45–64. Santa Fe, NM: School for Advanced Research Press, 2012.

Robertson, David G. "The Hidden Hand: Why Religious Studies Need to Take Conspiracy Theories Seriously." *Religion Compass* 11, nos. 3–4 (2017): e12233.

Rogers, David. "American Bible Society Gives 8,800 Free Bibles to Kanye West Fans." *My Christian Daily*, November 13, 2019. https://mychristiandaily.com/american -bible-society-gives-8800-free-bibles-to-kanye-west-fans/.

Roy, Olivier. *Holy Ignorance: When Religion and Culture Part Ways*. New York: Oxford University Press, 2014.

Schechner, Richard. "Donald John Trump, President?" *Drama Review* 61, no. 2 (2017):

7–10. https://www.direct.mit.edu/dram/article/61/2 (234)/7/42988/
Donald-John-Trump-President.

———. *Performance Studies: An Introduction*. London: Routledge, 2002.

Schneider, Rebecca. *Performing Remains: Art and War in Times of Theatrical Reenact-ment*. New York: Routledge, 2011.

Shahsavari, Shadi, Pavan Holur, Timothy R. Tangherlini, and Vwani Roychowdhury. "Conspiracy in the Time of Corona: Automatic Detection of Covid-19 Conspiracy Theories in Social Media and the News." *Journal of Computational Social Science* 3 (2020): 279–317.

Shoaps, Robin A. "'Pray Earnestly': The Textual Construction of Personal Involve-ment in Pentecostal Prayer and Song." *Journal of Linguistic Anthropology* 12, no. 1 (2002).

Shpigel, Noah. "Famed Exorcist's Festival Draws Thousands from around the World to Nazareth." *Haaretz*, June 24, 2019. https://www.haaretz.com/israel-news/ .premium-famed-nigerian-t-b-joshua-exorcist-s-festival-draws-thousands-from -around-the-world-1.7404430.

Silverman, Jacob. "Is There a Deep State, and If So What Is It?" *New Labor Forum* 27, no. 3 (2018): 26–33.

Sim, Joshua Dao Wei. "Compliant Singaporean Christians? State-Centred Christian Responses to COVID-19 in a Single-Party Dominant State." *Studies in World Christianity* 26, no. 3 (2020): 239–260.

Sofer, Andrew. *Dark Matter: Invisibility in Drama, Theater, and Performance*. Ann Arbor: University of Michigan Press, 2013.

Solomon, Alisa. "My Epistemological Crisis: Arts Criticism in the Times of Trump." *Drama Review* 60, no. 2 (2016): 7–12.

Sommer, Will. "Trump's New COVID Doctor Says Sex with Demons Makes You Sick." *Daily Beast*, July 28, 2020. https://www.thedailybeast.com/stella-immanuel -trumps-new-covid-doctor-believes-in-alien-dna-demon-sperm-and -hydroxychloroquine.

Spivak, Gayatri Chakravorty. "Religion, Politics, Theology: A Conversation with Achille Mbembe." *Boundary 2* 34, no. 2 (2007): 149–170.

Stephens, Monica. "A Geospatial Infodemic: Mapping Twitter Conspiracy Theories of COVID-19." *Dialogues in Human Geography* 10, no. 2 (2020): 276–281.

Stolow, Jeremy. "Religion and/as Media." *Theory, Culture & Society* 22, no. 4 (2005): 119–145.

Sunstein, Cass R., and Adrian Vermeule. "Conspiracy Theories: Causes and Cures." *Journal of Political Philosophy* 17, no. 2 (2009): 202–227.

"Suspend 5G Network Deployment, Lawmakers Tell Nigerian Government." *Sahara Reporters*, May 5, 2020. https://www.saharareporters.com/2020/05/05/suspend-5g -network-deployment-lawmakers-tell-nigerian-government.

"'Tablets' in the Bible." *Knowing Jesus*, n.d. bible.knowing-jesus.com/words/Tablets.

Taylor, Diana. *Disappearing Acts: Spectacles of Gender and Nationalism in Argentina's "Dirty War."* Durham, NC: Duke University Press, 1997.

Tazanu, Primus M. "Practices and Narratives of Breakthrough: Pentecostal Represen-tations, the Quest for Success, and Liberation from Bondage." *Journal of Religion in Africa* 46, no. 1 (2016): 32–66.

TB Joshua Ministries. "Lifted from the Bed of Sickness!" *Facebook Watch*, July 13, 2020. https://www.facebook.com/tbjministries/posts/3364809000306519.

Thomas, Elise, and Albert Zhang. "ID2020, Bill Gates and the Mark of the Beast:

How COVID-19 Catalyses Existing Online Conspiracy Movements." *World Health Organization*, 2020.

Thompson, Marie. *Beyond Unwanted Sound: Noise, Affect and Aesthetic Moralism*. New York: Bloomsbury, 2017.

Titlestad, Michael. "The Ongoing End: On the Limits of Apocalyptic Narrative." *Studia Neophilologica* 88, no. S1 (2016): 1–3.

Toffler, Alvin. *Future Shock*. London: Bantam, 1970.

Toulouse, Mark G. *God in Public: Four Ways American Christianity and Public Life Relate*. Louisville, KY: Presbyterian Publishing, 2006.

"Trump Orders Opening of Churches in 'the Month of Opening.'" *LoveWorld News*, n.d. https://www.loveworldnews.com/posts/trump-orders-opening-of-churches-in -the-month-of-opening.

Tupamahu, Ekaputra, and Erica Ramirez. "The Split God: Wariboko, Deconstruction, and the Carnivalesque Structure." In *The Philosophy of Nimi Wariboko: Social Ethics, Economy, and Religion*, edited by Toyin Falola, 363–387. Durham, NC: Carolina Academic Press, 2020.

Ugbodaga, Kazeem. "Coronavirus: Oyedepo Reacts to Move to Re-Open Churches." *P.M. News*, May 23, 2020. https://www.pmnewsnigeria.com/2020/05/23 /coronavirus-oyedepo-reacts-to-move-to-re-open-churches/.

Ukah, Asonzeh. "Banishing Miracles: Politics and Policies of Religious Broadcasting in Nigeria." *Politics and Religion Journal* 5, no. 1 (2011): 39–60.

———. "The Miracle City: Pentecostal Entrepreneurialism and the Remaking of Lagos." *Nsibidi Institute*, May 15, 2020. https://http://nsibidiinstitute.org/the -miracle-city-pentecostal-entrepreneurialism-and-the-remaking-of-lagos/.

———. "Sacred Surplus and Pentecostal Too-Muchness: The Salvation Economy of African Megachurches." In *Handbook of Megachurches*, edited by Stephen Hunt, 323–344. Leiden: Brill, 2020.

———. "Sacred Surplus and the Split God: The Moral Economy of Salvation and Miracle in African Pentecostalism." In *The Philosophy of Nimi Wariboko: Social Ethics, Economy, and Religion*, edited by Toyin Falola, 209–229. Durham, NC: Carolina Academic Press, 2020.

Ukwuru, Sandra, and Prisca Nwankwo. "Social Media and Fake News on Corona Virus: A Review of Literature." *Nnamdi Azikiwe University Journal of Communication and Media Studies* 1, no. 2 (2020).

Uscinski, Joseph E., and Joseph M. Parent. *American Conspiracy Theories*. New York: Oxford University Press, 2014.

van Geuns, Suzanne. "Reading, Feeling, Believing: Online Testimonies and the Making of Evangelical Emotion." *Journal of Contemporary Religion* 34, no. 1 (2019): 97–115.

"Video: They Hate Trump for Supporting Christians—Pastor Chris." *Vanguard*, November 9, 2020. https://www.vanguardngr.com/2020/11/video-they-hate -trump-for-supporting-christians-pastor-chris/.

Voegelin, Salomé. *Listening to Noise and Silence: Towards a Philosophy of Sound Art*. New York: Bloomsbury, 2010.

Vonk, Roos, and Anouk Visser. "An Exploration of Spiritual Superiority: The Paradox of Self-Enhancement." *European Journal of Social Psychology* 51, no. 1 (2021): 152–165.

Wahab, Bayo. "COVID-19: Oyakhilome Says Pastors That Are Yet to Reopen Churches Are Not Believers." *Pulse.ng*, August 20, 2020. https://www.pulse.ng

/news/local/covid-19-oyakhilome-says-pastors-that-are-yet-to-reopen-churches-are
-not-believers/jffl9y4.

Ward, Charlotte, and David Voas. "The Emergence of Conspirituality." *Journal of
Contemporary Religion* 26, no. 1 (2011): 103–121.

Wariboko, Nimi. "African Pentecostal Political Philosophy: New Directions in the
Study of Pentecostalism and Politics." In *Pentecostalism and Politics in Africa*,
edited by Adeshina Afolayan, Olajumoke Yacob-Haliso, and Toyin Falola, 385–417.
Cham, Switzerland: Palgrave Macmillan, 2018.

———. "African Pentecostalism: A Kinetic Description." In *Na God: Aesthetics of
African Charismatic Power*, edited by Annalisa Buttici, 21–22. Padua: Grafiche
Turato Edizioni, 2013.

———. *The Charismatic City and the Public Resurgence of Religion: A Pentecostal Social
Ethics of Cosmopolitan Urban Life*. New York: Springer, 2014.

———. "The Demons as Guests: Aesthetics of African Traditional Religion and
Pentecostal Hot Prayers in Nigeria." Delivered at Boston University, November 15,
2016.

———. *Ethics and Society in Nigeria: Identity, History, Political Theory*. Rochester,
NY: University of Rochester Press, 2019.

———. *Ethics and Time: Ethos of Temporal Orientation in Politics and Religion of the
Niger Delta*. Lanham, MD: Lexington Books, 2010.

———. "Kalabari: A Study in Synthetic Ideal-Type." *Nordic Journal of African Studies*
8, no. 1 (1999): 80–92.

———. "Management in Postcolonial Africa: Historical and Comparative Perspectives." In *Black Business and Economic Power*, edited by Alusine Jalloh and Toyin
Falola, 279–284. Rochester, NY: University of Rochester Press, 2002.

———. *Nigerian Pentecostalism*. Rochester, NY: University of Rochester Press, 2014.

———. *The Split God: Pentecostalism and Critical Theory*. Albany: State University of
New York Press, 2018.

———. *Transcripts of the Sacred in Africa: Beautiful, Monstrous, Ridiculous*. Bloomington: Indiana University Press, 2022.

Warner, Michael. "Publics and Counterpublics." *Public Culture* 14, no. 1 (2002):
49–90.

Wasserman, Helena. "Bill Gates Warned the Coronavirus Could Hit Africa Worse
Than China." *Business Insider*, February 25, 2020. www.businessinsider.com/bill
-gates-warns-coronavirus-could-hit-africa-with-dire-consequences-2020-2.

Waterson, Jim. "Revealed: 'Former Vodaphone Executive' in 5G Conspiracy Video is
UK Pastor." *The Guardian*, April 24, 2020. https://www.theguardian.com/world
/2020/apr/24/vodafone-exec-5g-coronavirus-conspiracy-theory-video-revealed
-pastor-luton-jonathon-james.

WatchPastorChris. "Pastor Chris: COVID19 Compliant Churches???" *YouTube*,
April 30, 2020. https://www.youtube.com/watch?v=j3BBzFmudXA.

———. "Pastor Chris: 5G is LOVELY but . . ." *YouTube*, April 8, 2020." https://www
.youtube.com/watch?v=lXnLwtAS6Fk.

———. "Pastor Chris Prays against the Corona Virus!" *YouTube*, March 16, 2020.
https://www.youtube.com/watch?v=vEM8wqpro8o.

"Whatever Stop God's People from Worshiping in Church Has Destroy Their
Strength—Bishop Oyedepo." *YouTube*, September 13, 2020. https://www.youtube
.com/watch?v=-Hy7MoA8zmY.

Winning, Alexander. "Puzzled Scientists Seek Reasons behind Africa's Low Fatality Rates from Pandemic." *Reuters*, September 29, 2020. https://www.reuters.com/article/us-health-coronavirus-africa-mortality-i/puzzled-scientists-seek-reasons-behind-africas-low-fatality-rates-from-pandemic-idUSKBN26K0AI.

Wise, Jacqui. "Covid-19: Push to Reopen Schools Risks New Wave of Infections, Says Independent SAGE." *BMJ* (2020): 369:m2161. doi:10.1136/bmj.m2161.

Wong, Briana. "Longing for Home: The Impact of COVID-19 on Cambodian Evangelical Life." *Studies in World Christianity* 26, no 3 (2020): 281–297.

Yesufu, Deji. "How John MacArthur Inspired a Church Gathering in Ibadan." *Text and Publishing*, August 3, 2020. https://www.textandpublishing.com/how-john-macarthur-inspired-a-church-gathering-in-ibadan/.

Index

About the Author

ABIMBOLA A. ADELAKUN is an assistant professor in the Department of African and African Diaspora Studies at the University of Texas at Austin.